The ten essays in this volume explore different aspects of the performance of instrumental works by Beethoven. Each essay discusses performance issues from Beethoven's time to the present whether the objective be to realise a performance in a historically appropriate manner, to elucidate the interpretation of Beethoven's music by conductors and performers, to clarify transcriptions by editors or to reconstruct the experience of the listener in various different periods. Four contributions focus on the piano music (Tibor Szász, Barry Cooper, David Rowland and Martin Hughes) while another group concentrates on Beethoven's music for strings (David Watkin, Clive Brown and Robin Stowell). These chapters are complemented by an examination of Beethoven's exploitation of the developing wind choir (Colin Lawson), an evaluation of early-twentieth-century recording as pointers to early-nineteenth-century performance practice (Robert Philip) and a historical survey of rescorings in Beethoven's symphonies (David Pickett).

CAMBRIDGE STUDIES IN PERFORMANCE PRACTICE 4

Performing Beethoven

CAMBRIDGE STUDIES IN PERFORMANCE PRACTICE 4

Performing Beethoven

Edited by

ROBIN STOWELL

Professor of Music,
University of Wales College of Cardiff

Published by the Press Syndicate of the University of Cambridge
The Pitt Building, Trumpington Street, Cambridge CB2 1RP
40 West 20th Street, New York, NY 10011–4211, USA
10 Stamford Road, Oakleigh, Melbourne 3166, Australia

First published 1994

Printed in Great Britain at the University Press, Cambridge

A catalogue record for this book is available from the British Library

Library of Congress cataloguing in publication data

Performing Beethoven / edited by Robin Stowell.
   p.   cm.   – (Cambridge studies in performance practice ; 4)
Includes bibliographical references and indexes.
ISBN 0 521 41644 2 (hardback)
1. Beethoven, Ludwig van, 1770–1827 – Criticism and interpretation.
2. Performance practice (Music) – 18th century.   3. Performance practice (Music) – 19th century.
I. Stowell, Robin.   II. Series.
ML410.B42P47   1994   780' .92–dc20   93–31379 CIP MN

ISBN 0 521 41644 2 hardback

To the memory of
PETER LE HURAY
(1932–1992)

CONTENTS

FIGURES

GENERAL PREFACE

No doubt the claim, heard frequently today, that 'authentic performance' is a chimera, and that even the idea of an 'authentic edition' cannot be sustained for (most) music before the last century or two, is itself the consequence of too sanguine an expectation raised by performers and scholars alike in the recent past. Both have been understandably concerned to establish that a certain composer 'intended so-and-so' or 'had such-and-such conditions of performance in mind' or 'meant it to sound in this way or that'. Scholars are inclined to rule on problems ('research confirms the following . . .'), performers to make the music a living experience ('artistry or musicianship suggests the following . . .'). Both are there in order to answer certain questions and establish an authority for what they do; both demonstrate and persuade by the rhetoric of their utterance, whether well-documented research on the one hand or convincing artistic performance on the other; and the academic/commercial success of both depends on the effectiveness of that rhetoric. Some musicians even set out to convey authority in both scholarship and performance, recognising that music is conceptual *and* perceptual and thus not gainfully divisible into separate, competitive disciplines. In general, if not always, the scholar appears to aim at the firm, affirmative statement, often seeing questions as something to be answered confidently rather than searchingly re-defined or refined. In general, with some exceptions, performers have to aim at the confident statement, for their very livelihood hangs on an unhesitating decisiveness in front of audience or microphone. In the process, both sometimes have the effect, perhaps even the intention, of killing the dialectic – of thwarting the progress that comes with further questions and a constant 'yes, but' response to what is seen, in the light of changing definitions, as 'scholarly evidence' or 'convincing performance'.

In the belief that the immense activity in prose and sound over the last few decades is now being accompanied by an increasing awareness of the issues arising – a greater knowledge at last enabling the question to be more closely defined – the Cambridge Studies in Performance Practice will attempt to make regular contributions to this area of study, on the basis of several assumptions. Firstly, at its best,

Performance Practice is so difficult a branch of study as to be an almost impossibly elusive ideal. It cannot be merely a practical way of 'combining performance and scholarship', for these two are fundamentally different activities, each able to inform the other only up to a certain point. Secondly, if Performance Practice has moved beyond the questions (now seen to be very dated) that exercised performance groups of the 1950s and 60s, it can widen itself to include any or all music written before the last few years. In this respect, such studies are a musician's equivalent to the cry of literary studies, 'Only contextualise!', and this can serve as a useful starting-point for the historically minded performer or the practically minded scholar. (The Derridaesque paradox that there is no context may have already affected some literary studies, but context is still clearly crucial across the broader field of music, the original Comparative Literature.) Cambridge Studies in Performance Practice will devote volumes to any period in which useful questions can be asked, ranging from at least Gregorian chant to at least Stravinsky.

Thirdly, Performance Practice is not merely about performing, neither 'this is how music was played' nor 'this is how you should play it in a concert or recording today'. (These two statements are as often as not irreconcilable.) In studying all that we can about the practical realisation of a piece of music we are studying not so much how it was played but how it was heard, both literally and on a deeper level. How it was conceived by the composer and how it was perceived by the period's listener are endless questions deserving constant study, for they bring one into intimate contact with the historical art of music as nothing else can. It is the *music* we fail to understand, not its performance as such, if we do not explore these endless questions. As we know, every basic musical element has had to be found, plucked out of thin air – the notes, their tuning, compass, volume, timbre, pace, timing, tone, combining – and they have constantly changed. In attempting to grasp or describe these elements as they belong to a certain piece of music, it could become clear that any modern re-realisation in (public) performance is a quite separate issue. Nevertheless, it is an issue of importance to the wider musical community, as can be seen from the popular success of performers and publications (records, journals, books) concerned with 'authenticity'. In recognising this practical importance, Cambridge Studies in Performance Practice will frequently call upon authoritative performers to join scholars in the common cause, each offering insights to the process of learning to ask and explore the right questions.

PETER WILLIAMS

PREFACE

Although it explores only a few performance issues which relate to a small cross-section of Beethoven's *oeuvre*, it is my sincere hope that the present volume, in keeping with the aims of the 'Cambridge Studies in Performance Practice' series, will inspire scholars and performers to further thought about the various subjects discussed and perhaps even open up some new avenues for more detailed consideration. It includes essays by distinguished musicologists and performers, each exploring a different aspect of Beethoven's instrumental music in performance, whether the objective be to realise a performance in a historically appropriate manner and context or to elucidate how Beethoven's music was interpreted by conductors and performers, transcribed by editors, or heard and perceived by the listener in various periods since its composition.

Four studies focus on the music for pianoforte: David Rowland discusses the various issues involved in pianoforte pedalling; Martin Hughes deals with some of the numerous problems involved in the presentation of selected piano works on the modern instrument; Tibor Szász reviews Beethoven's application of figured bass, focusing in particular on two of the piano concertos; while Barry Cooper explores the composer's more virtuosic, sophisticated and imaginative revisions to his Fourth Piano Concerto.

Another group of essays concentrates on Beethoven's music for strings and demonstrates how playing techniques and approaches to performance and expression have changed over the years. David Watkin surveys the development of the cello and its technique during Beethoven's lifetime, using as principal source materials the treatises of Jean-Louis Duport, J. J. Friedrich Dotzauer, Bernhard Romberg, Jean-Baptiste Bréval and others, which shed significant light on matters of expression such as bowing style, vibrato, fingering and portamento; Clive Brown focuses on Ferdinand David's editions of Beethoven's music and shows how they reveal a style and technique of performance which has a close relationship with practices that were current in the composer's lifetime; while the present writer has cast an eye over the textual history and various editions of one piece, the Violin Concerto Op. 61, and discusses how interpretations have changed in print over the years.

Meanwhile, Robert Philip lends an ear to early-twentieth-century recordings of Beethoven's instrumental music and examines some features of performance practice which are characteristic of the period, arguing that these features should not be dismissed as merely old-fashioned but that they offer clues to nineteenth-century performance of Beethoven, in some cases as far back as the composer's own time. Colin Lawson investigates Beethoven's exploitation of the expanded range of idioms offered by the developing wind choir and assesses its implications for today's performers, whether of modern or historical instruments. Last, but by no means least, David Pickett examines some of the numerous emendations made to Beethoven's original scoring by composers and conductors of the late nineteenth and early twentieth centuries.

Peter le Huray was to have contributed to this volume. Up to a few weeks before his untimely death he was working on an essay on phrasing in Beethoven's keyboard works. It is deeply regrettable that this book has been deprived of a contribution from a scholar and practical musician of such rare excellence, who did so much as a teacher, writer and executant to promote the development in performers of stylistic and historical awareness in their performances. I dedicate this volume to his memory.

Finally, I would like to express my gratitude to a number of individuals who have assisted with the preparation of this volume. I am indebted to my contributors for their co-operative attitude, promptness of response to various problems and queries and for giving readily of their expertise; to my wife and family for their patience and encouragement throughout the duration of this project; to my colleague, Dr Timothy Taylor, for his assistance in computer setting the musical examples; to the Department of Music, University of Wales College of Cardiff for some financial assistance towards expenses involved in the preparation of the project for the press; and to the series editors and Penny Souster and her team at Cambridge University Press for their guidance and professionalism in seeing the volume into print.

ROBIN STOWELL

Pitch registers are indicated by the following letter scheme

Acknowledgement for kind permission to reproduce illustrations is due to the Royal College of Music, London, for Figs. 5.1a, 5.2, 5.3, 5.4 and 5.5.

1/71 refers to the first movement, bar 71

BEETHOVEN'S *BASSO CONTINUO*: NOTATION AND PERFORMANCE

TIBOR SZÁSZ

Malcolm Frager *in memoriam*

It was not long ago that London's musical public was swept into a controversy triggered off by Adolf Aber's strong words that graced the first page of *The Musical Times* of June 1948:

the recent [Adolf] Busch concerts at Kingsway Hall stood out as high-lights of the concert season . . . the chief factor, it cannot be doubted, was the conviction that the music of Bach and Handel was being performed in the only right and proper way . . . many in the audience heard for the first time in their lives how these works ought to sound.

To come straight to the point: the fundamental difference between a Busch performance and a normal 'modern' performance lies in the treatment of that one line, the *basso continuo*. It is lamentable that so many artists in these days have forgotten that this line was written, beyond any doubt, for a keyboard instrument . . .[1]

The pioneering efforts of Busch and Aber have long since been fulfilled, at least in the sense that even among 'modern' performances (to use Aber's term) of the Baroque orchestral and choral repertoire, the presence of keyboard continuo is the rule rather than the exception.

If Aber and Busch returned today to champion the cause of reinstating Beethoven's figured and unfigured bass to its rightful place in musical performance, their task would be much more difficult. First of all, they would not find a modern edition of Beethoven's *Materialien zum Generalbass*,[2] or a modern edition that accurately reflects the thrust of Beethoven's notation with regard to keyboard continuo practices in his piano concertos[3] and masses.[4] Furthermore, if they tried to produce

---

1 Adolf Aber, 'On the Continuo in Bach', *Musical Times*, 89 (1948), pp. 169–71 and 367–8.

2 The *Materialien* – a compilation of rules and examples for the notation and realisation of keyboard harmony and accompaniment – represents the beginning section of *Beethovenautograph* 75 preserved in Vienna's Archiv der Gesellschaft der Musikfreunde.

3 In all modern editions, the continuo and cue notation found in the original editions were ignored. Under Beethoven's supervision, the five piano concertos and the Triple Concerto Op. 56 were published with a figured or unfigured bass engraved with the same size noteheads as the keyboard solos; by contrast, instrumental cues were consistently represented by small-size noteheads.

4 In all modern editions, the figured-bass notation found in the original edition of the Mass in C major

a modern edition incorporating Beethoven's continuo instructions, they would first
have to solve the problem of evaluating the function of Beethoven's figured bass:[5]
does it exclusively represent authentic keyboard continuo, or is it also used to
represent harmonic cues of the orchestral activity?

In a recent article devoted to Beethoven's Piano Concerto No. 5 in E♭ major[6]
(written in 1809 and published first in England and then in Germany),[7] I attempted
to show that the composer's detailed figured bass instructions clearly require the
soloist to realise the continuo in long tuttis while prohibiting the realisation of
figures that occur in very short ones. In other words, the overwhelming majority
of the autograph and printed figures in the 'Emperor' represent genuine keyboard
continuo that must be realised in performances with full orchestra.[8]

Linda Ferguson's evaluation of Beethoven's tutti notation in the 'Emperor' is
correct: 'the soloist would be left to play . . . all of the longer tuttis . . . plus by far
the majority of short tuttis within long solo sections'.[9] Also correct is Ferguson's conclusion that keyboard continuo is required in all of Beethoven's piano concertos
and the Triple Concerto for piano, violin and cello in C major Op. 56.[10] The only
exception is the slow movement of the Piano Concerto in G major Op. 58 where
keyboard continuo is excluded.[11]

But every solution of a problem is a new problem. Now that the need for
continuo in Beethoven's piano concertos does seem to have been established, an
even thornier problem remains: how do we realise the composer's directions in
performance? Because no nineteenth-century realisation of Beethoven's concertos
is known to have survived, the difficulties of solving this new problem are considerable. However, this essay aims to provide some practical guidelines for realising
Beethoven's continuo indications in his five piano concertos and the Triple
Concerto, as well as in his Mass in C major Op. 86 and the *Missa solemnis* Op. 123.

Op. 86 was altered, and the autograph and printed figures for the *Missa solemnis* were suppressed; in both
works, the undocumented addition of the term *Organo* in Breitkopf and Härtel's *Gesamtausgabe* obscures
the meaning of the original notation.

5 Beethoven's figured bass in sketches and cue-staves was never transferred into published scores and lies
   outside the scope of this essay.

6 Tibor Szász, 'Figured Bass in Beethoven's "Emperor" Concerto: Basso Continuo or Orchestral Cues?',
   Early Keyboard Journal, 6–7 (1988–9), pp. 5–71.

7 The English edition (1810) reproduces only the composer's detailed *col Basso* adaptation of the string
   bass to the keyboard idiom; by contrast, the German edition (1811) reproduces the almost full range of
   Beethoven's autograph continuo instructions.

8 Szász, 'Figured Bass in Beethoven's "Emperor" Concerto', pp. 62–3.

9 Linda Faye Ferguson, '*Col Basso* and *Generalbass* in Mozart's Keyboard Concertos: Notation, Performance
   Theory, and Practice' (PhD diss. University of Princeton 1983), p. 271. This author disagrees, however,
   with some of Ferguson's interpretations of where continuo is to be provided.

10 Ferguson, '*Col Basso* and *Generalbass* in Mozart's Keyboard Concertos', pp. 243–71.

11 *ibid.*, pp. 265–8.

BEETHOVEN'S CONTINUO TERMINOLOGY: DEFINITIONS AND
COMMENTS

When evaluating the explicitness of autograph and printed continuo indications, Beethoven's *Materialien zum Generalbass* (1809) provides a convenient dividing line.[12] In works published before the *Materialien*, Beethoven left the realisation of continuo to the ingenuity of the performer, whereas in works published thereafter, he explicitly notated how it is to be realised.

Written probably right after his compilation of the *Materialien*,[13] the unsurpassed clarity of Beethoven's continuo instructions in the full-score autographs of the 'Emperor' is due in part to the presence of one technical term: *tasto solo* (*t.s.*). With it, Beethoven indicated when the soloist must abstain from realising continuo.[14] Whereas Beethoven never used *t.s.* in his earlier work published with figured or unfigured bass, he consistently included it in works published after his compilation of the *Materialien*.

In effect, every technical term used in autograph, manuscript, and printed sources of Beethoven's works finds its definition in the composer's *Materialien*. But since the *Materialien* was never assessed in terms of its relevance for performance practice, Beethoven's definitions need to be quoted, translated, and commented upon. For readers unfamiliar with Beethoven's continuo[15] and cue[16] notation in autograph and printed sources, two tables follow.[17] Table 1.1. is then discussed in detail.

---

12 According to Gustav Nottebohm, at least the first sixteen pages of the *Materialien* were written during the second quarter of 1809 ('Beethovens theoretische Studien', *Allgemeine Musikalische Zeitung*, 41 (1863), pp. 689–90).

13 The date 1809 is inscribed by Beethoven in his full-score autograph of the 'Emperor'.

14 Szász, 'Figured Bass in Beethoven's "Emperor" Concerto', pp. 10–14. In the present essay, the term continuo will consistently and exclusively mean the right hand's activity of providing accompaniment in tuttis. Nevertheless, the absence of continuo activity does not necessarily imply the absence of keyboard sound: it may still be present through the left hand's customary activity of adapting the string bass to the keyboard idiom.

15 For details on Beethoven's continuo notation, see Szász, 'Figured Bass in Beethoven's "Emperor" Concerto', pp. 10–28. Though listed in the category of continuo notation, Beethoven's figured and unfigured bass may exceptionally represent harmonic cues of the orchestral activity (Szász, 'Figured Bass in Beethoven's "Emperor" Concerto', pp. 44–54). In Table 1.1, the term 'idiomatic bass' is used only for works in which the notated bass line contains fragments that represent a purposeful adaptation of the string bass to the keyboard idiom.

16 For details on Beethoven's cue notation, see Szász, 'Figured Bass in Beethoven's "Emperor" Concerto', pp. 8–9. In Table 1.2, the term 'cues' refers to instrumental cues in the right- or left-hand staff. The term *Clavierauszug* means the modern equivalent of a piano reduction. Due to carelessness, some instrumental cues which appear in the original editions of Beethoven's works were engraved in improper large-size notes.

17 In the two tables, autograph sources are reduced to those used as *Kopiaturvorlage* or, when not extant, to a relevant autograph source; printed sources are limited to the last version supervised by Beethoven.

Table 1.1. 'Col basso continuo' *notation in piano concertos and masses*
Beethoven autographs *v* editions (Y = present; N = absent; ? = not known)

Opus numbers		15	19	37	56	58	73	86	123
Figured bass	– autograph	Y	N	N	N	?	Y	?	Y
	– edition	Y	N	N	N	N	Y	Y	Y
Tasto solo	– autograph	N	N	N	N	?	Y	?	Y
	– edition	N	N	N	N	N	Y	Y	Y
All'ottava	– autograph	N	N	N	N	?	Y	?	Y
	– edition	Y	N	N	N	N	Y	N	Y
Unisono	– autograph	N	N	N	N	?	N	?	N
	– edition	Y	N	N	N	N	N	N	N
Telemannbogen	– autograph	N	N	N	N	?	Y	?	Y
	– edition	N	N	N	N	N	N	N	N
Unfigured bass	– autograph	Y	Y	Y	Y	?	Y	?	Y
	– edition	N	Y	Y	Y	Y	Y	Y	Y
Realisation	– autograph	N	N	N	N	?	N	?	N
	– edition	N	N	N	N	N	N	N	Y
Idiomatic bass	– autograph	N	Y	N	N	?	Y	?	Y
	– edition	N	Y	N	N	N	Y	N	Y

Tasto solo (t.s.)

Definition: '*t.s.* signifies that one should depress only the keys notated [in the left-hand staff] without adding any accompaniment [with the right hand], until the figures return [to indicate the resumption of two-handed accompaniment]'.[18]

By its very nature, *t.s.* qualifies the function of figures immediately surrounding it. Because *t.s.* designates a momentary cessation of right-hand accompaniment, its occurrence in a given tutti substantiates the logical inference that the figures that precede and follow its advent represent authentic keyboard continuo.[19] When the

18 Nottebohm, 'Beethovens theoretische Studien', *Allgemeine Musikalische Zeitung*, 41 (1863), p. 688.
   'T.S. zeigt an, daß man nur die vorgeschriebene Taste ohne alle weitere Begleitung anschlagen solle, bis wieder Ziffern kommen.' Beethoven's sentence represents a conscious rewording (i.e. not an absent-minded copy) of Daniel Gottlob Türk's definition in *Kurze Anweisung zum Generalbaßspielen* (Halle and Leipzig 1791), p. 29. Both definitions are identical in effect with those of Johann Albrechtsberger, Friedrich Wilhelm Marpurg, C.P.E. Bach, Johann Michael Bach, Johann Joseph Klein, Georg Simon Löhlein, August Eberhard Müller, Joachim Hoffman and Adolph Bernhard Marx. Beethoven's accompanying musical example is not reproduced, since it is an exact copy of Türk's original.
19 The presence of *t.s.* constitutes an effective way to identify authentic continuo practices. Significantly, the Archduke Rudolph's theoretical figured bass drills do not contain a single occurrence of *t.s.*; see Susan Kagan, *Archduke Rudolph, Beethoven's Patron, Pupil, and Friend: His Life and Music* (Stuyvesant, N.Y., 1988), pp. 58–67.

Table 1.2. *Cue notation in piano concertos and masses*
Beethoven Autographs *v* Editions (Y=present; N=absent; ?=not known)

Opus numbers		15	19	37	56	58	73	86	123
Cues – R.H.	– autograph	N	Y	N	Y	?	Y	?	N
	– edition	N	Y	Y	Y	Y	Y	N	N
Cues – L.H.	– autograph	N	Y	N	Y	?	Y	?	Y
	– edition	N	Y	Y	Y	Y	Y	Y	Y
Clavierauszug	– autograph	N	N	N	N	?	N	?	N
	– edition	N	N	N	N	Y	N	N	N
Separate cue system	– autograph	N	N	N	N	?	N	?	N
	– edition	N	N	N	N	Y	N	N	N

keyboard player is expected to provide uninterrupted right-hand accompaniment in a given tutti, the term *t.s.* must, of course, be absent during that tutti.

The above continuo notation limits the freedom of the performer to the maximum extent by prescribing every detail of accompaniment: right-hand activity (figures) *v* inactivity (*t.s.*), and left-hand activity (the purposeful adaptation of the string bass-line to the keyboard idiom) *v* inactivity (rests or instrumental cues entered in the left-hand staff). Among Beethoven's concertos, only the 'Emperor' contains such detailed continuo instructions.

In the concertos published before the compilation of the *Materialien* (i.e. Nos. 1–4 and the Triple Concerto), Beethoven did not curtail the freedom of the soloist. In these works, the total absence of the term *t.s.* suggests that the soloist is free to determine the specific alternation of the three complementary forms of accompaniment: playing with both hands, with the left hand alone, or with neither. In the original editions of these works, the tutti notation is limited to a constant flow of figures (as in the Piano Concerto in C major Op. 15) or of melodic and harmonic cues (as in the other concertos). Whether figured or unfigured, the *basso continuo* line is engraved with the same size noteheads as the solo passages, whereas cues are distinguished by small-size noteheads. The composer's sparse figured bass notation in the full-score autograph of the Piano Concerto Op. 15 will be discussed later.

All'ottava and unisono

Definition: 'In places marked with *unisono* (*un.*, *all'unisono*, *all'ottava*) the right hand must play along with the left by reproducing the latter's pitches at the higher octave; where the accompanist is to resume playing chords, figures must be recommenced.'[20]

The term *all'ottava* is often mistaken for the term *col ottava bassa*. The two terms should never be interchanged, for one designates the right hand's continuo activity (paralleling the cello line by playing single pitches at the higher octave – *all'ottava*), while the other designates the left hand's idiomatic keyboard adaptation of the string bass (doubling the cello line plus adding the double-bass pitch – *col ottava bassa*). Confusing the two terms is an age-old problem that had already plagued the preparation of both the English and the German editions of the 'Emperor'.[21] Recently, Ferguson has confused the two terms by equating the keyboard player's activity of reproducing 'both cello and double-bass pitches' with the indications *all'ottava* or *all'unisono*.[22] Consequently, her assertion that the 'Emperor's autograph *all'ottava* indications are 'sometimes written simply as "8"' appears to be flawed.[23] What Ferguson is probably referring to is Beethoven's figure '8' placed beneath the bass line, in which case it represents not the right hand's *all'ottava* but the left hand's *col ottava bassa* activity.[24]

Nevertheless, when placed above the bass line, the figure '8' can indeed be used to represent the right hand's *all'ottava* activity.[25] This notational alternative is mentioned in Beethoven's truncated sentence from the *Materialien*: 'Auch vermittelst der Zahl 8 8 8 oder abgekürzt 8–.'[26] According to Beethoven's consistent notational custom, distinction between *all'ottava* and *col ottava bassa* is achieved through the placement of the figure '8' on the music staff. When placed above the bass note, '8' always denotes the doubling of the bass note at the higher octave (i.e. with the right hand); when placed below, '8' always indicates the doubling of the bass note at the lower octave (i.e. with the left hand).

Because Beethoven preferred to reserve the term *all'ottava* as a nearly exclusive notational symbol for doubling a succession of bass notes at the higher octave,[27] his

20 Nottebohm, 'Beethovens theoretische Studien', p. 688. 'Bei den mit unisono (un., all'unisono, all'ottava) bezeichneten Stellen spielt man in der rechten Hand und zwar die nächstliegende höhere Oktave mit; wo der Begleiter wieder ganze Akkorde angeben soll, setzt man wieder Ziffern hin.'

21 Szász, 'Figured Bass in Beethoven's "Emperor" Concerto', p. 16, ns. 22 and 23; p. 21, Fig. 1; and p. 37, paragraphs 1 and 2.

22 Ferguson, '*Col Basso* and *Generalbass* in Mozart's Keyboard Concertos', p. 235.

23 *ibid.*, p. 268

24 Szász, 'Figured Bass in Beethoven's "Emperor" Concerto', p. 52, Ex. 16a.

25 *ibid.*, p. 17, Ex. 3a, 1/71, downbeat.

26 Nottebohm, 'Beethovens theoretische Studien', p. 688. In Türk's original, the sentence is rounded off with these additional words: 'pflegen Einige das *all'unisono* zu bezeichnen'. (*Kurze Anweisung*, p. 29). The completed sentence translates: 'Some [composers] prefer to notate *all'unisono* by means of a chain of 8 8 8 or, in shortened form, 8–' [placed *above* the bass notes in Türk's original example and its reproduction in Beethoven's autograph].

27 *Missa solemnis*, beginning of Gloria.

choice of the numerical alternative ('8' placed above an isolated bass note) must not as a rule be equated with the sound of an empty octave. The full-score autograph of the 'Emperor' and the realisation incorporated in the original edition of the *Missa solemnis* clarify Beethoven's use of the numerical alternative: when placed above an isolated bass note, '8' generally represents a full chord, its treble note doubling the bass pitch.[28]

One of the most difficult interpretational problems in Beethoven's *oeuvre* arises through the presence of *t.s.* coupled with the total absence of *all'ottava* indications in the original edition of the Mass Op. 86. The undocumented *all'ottava* and *Organo* additions in Breitkopf and Härtel's *Gesamtausgabe* of Op. 86 suggest that the editors' interpretations of the original edition are not always reliable.

⌒ Telemannbogen (the arc of Telemann).[29]

Definition: 'By means of an arc certain composers indicate the diminished triad, certain incomplete chords, suspensions, harmonic changes over an unchanged pitch, and other places that must be accompanied in the right hand with a two-voiced texture.'[30]

Beethoven's *Telemannbogen* indications were consistently ignored in printed editions, though they are retained in the subscription copy of the *Missa solemnis* purchased by the King of France.[31] In the 'Emperor', Beethoven's use of the *Telemannbogen* is limited to a single situation: the arc is placed above the figure '5' in order to alert the soloist that the chord to be realised must not contain any pitches in addition to those of the diminished triad.[32] In the *Missa solemnis*, the arc is used in two situations. Most commonly, it is used as in the 'Emperor';[33] less frequently, it indicates incomplete chords (such as two pitches at the interval of a major second and a perfect fourth respectively played above the bass).[34] The above *Telemannbogen* indications found in the manuscript copy of the *Missa solemnis* purchased by the King of France are always correctly realised. This same realisation was incorporated (with minor changes) into the printed edition supervised by

28 'Emperor', 1/62 and *Missa solemnis*, Kyrie, bar 128. In both, '8' marks the resumption of chordal continuo activity.

29 See Wolf Hobohm, 'Der Telemannische Bogen', *Studien zur Aufführungspraxis und Interpretation der Musik des 18. Jahrhunderts*, 32 (1987), pp. 32–5.

30 Nottebohm, 'Beethovens theoretische Studien', p. 688. 'Vermittelst eines ⌒ bezeichnen manche Componisten der verminderten Dreiklang, gewisse unvollständige Akkorde, Vorhalte, durchgehende Harmonien und andere nur zweistimmig zu begleitende Stellen.'

31 Bibliothèque nationale, Paris, catalogued as L. 1121.

32 Szász, 'Figured Bass in Beethoven's "Emperor" Concerto', p. 20, Ex 4 b, bar 251; and p. 22, n. 26.

33 Gloria, bar 115, second beat; Sanctus, bar 41, second beat; and Agnus dei, bar 240, downbeat.

34 Gloria, bar 334, downbeat, notated as a '4–2' capped by a *Telemannbogen*.

Beethoven.[35] Though the origin of the printed realisation is not known, it is obviously the work of an experienced continuo player. That this person may have been Beethoven himself is certainly a possibility: in his early teens, he was employed both as a 'Cembalo player in the orchestra, i.e. one who provides the thoroughbass during symphonies', and as 'Court Organist of the Prince'.[36] Because Beethoven had repeatedly authorised the incorporation of this realisation into manuscript copies and the original edition, it should not be dismissed on the grounds of its unknown origin; in fact, it may be accepted as the last authoritative version of the Mass.[37] Therefore, organists can rely on the printed realisation (excepting obvious misprints or mistakes) rather than attempt to realise the composer's early version of the piece as recorded in the figured bass notation of the full-score autograph.[38]

PARALLELS BETWEEN MOZART'S AND BEETHOVEN'S SHORTHAND CONTINUO NOTATIONS IN FULL-SCORE AUTOGRAPHS

In the Henle edition of the first three piano concertos, Hans-Werner Küthen has played down the continuo implications of the figured and unfigured bass found in the original editions of these works. Citing an alleged absence of autograph continuo indications in the full-score autographs, Küthen has produced an edition that shows the soloist at rest in tuttis.[39] By contrast, Ferguson has reasoned that a full-score autograph can be used as evidence of performance practice only if it has been prepared with the clear purpose of serving as *Kopiaturvorlage* for the printed piano part.[40] Among Beethoven's piano concertos, only the full-score autograph of the 'Emperor' fits this condition: in it, Beethoven has presented posterity with the most detailed performance practice instructions that can be given within the framework of *Generalbass* notation: the right hand's continuo activity (figures or *all'ottavas*) or inactivity (*t.s.*), and the left hand's idiomatic keyboard adaptation of the string bass.

---

35 Aside from a few improvements in the realisation itself, the figured bass notation engraved in the original edition is inferior to that found in the copy purchased by the King of France.

36 *Allgemeine Musikalische Zeitung*, 21 (1827), p. 346. 'Im vierzehnten Jahre ward er Cembalist im Orchester, d.i. der bey Symphonieen den Generalbass begleitete; im 16ten Hoforganist des Kurfürsten.'

37 The term 'authoritative' is used in the sense defined by William S. Newman, 'On the Problem of Determining Beethoven's Most Authoritative Lifetime Editions', in *Beiträge zur Beethoven-Bibliographie* (Munich 1978), p. 128.

38 For example, in Gloria, bars 4, 38, 42, and 184–5, the organist should play *all'ottava* as in the realisation, and not *t.s.* as in the full-score autograph. The undocumented addition of the term *Organo* in Breitkopf and Härtel's *Gesamtausgabe* suggests that the editors did not understand the meaning of Beethoven's term *tasto solo*.

39 L. van Beethoven, '*Neue Ausgabe sämtlicher Werke*', III, Band 2, *Klavierkonzerte I*, ed. H.–W. Küthen (Munich 1984).

40 Ferguson, '*Col Basso* and *Generalbass* in Mozart's Keyboard Concertos', p. 244.

Ferguson's admirable line of reasoning concerning autograph evidence of performance practice seems to be weakened by her parenthetical statement pertaining to shorthand notation in the full-score autograph of the Piano Concerto in C major Op. 15, where Beethoven's habit of extending the keyboard bass 'into the first [bar] or two of tutti' is characterised as 'perhaps absent-minded'.[41] I prefer to characterise it as a deliberate shorthand convention that reflects the persistence of continuo practices in the Classical period. To assess the purport of Beethoven's notational habit (i.e. extending the keyboard bass into the tuttis), one must place it in the larger context of Baroque and Classical notational history.

For the twentieth-century mind, the greatest difficulty with autograph continuo notation lies in grasping the broad implications of time-saving conventions such as incomplete and shorthand notation. Take, for example, one of the most elementary shorthand terms, *col basso*. When applied to the keyboard idiom, this term was used generically; as such, it made no distinction between the left hand's restricted *col Basso* as opposed to the two hands' *col basso continuo* activity. The term was usually condensed to *colB* (as used by Mozart) or *Cb* (as in the full-score autograph of Beethoven's Piano Concerto Op. 15).[42] The purpose of these generically used abbreviations was to spare the composer from having to write a realisation, write a figured bass, or write out separately the keyboard and the string bass. Naturally, composers took full advantage of each and every option, and it is nothing short of miraculous that we possess even a scrap of positive proof for continuo beyond the traditional shorthand.

How keen composers were on saving time can be ascertained from the third option. Though it spared the composer from having to write two sets of bass lines, it still did not eliminate the task of writing out in longhand notation one or the other. Two options were available: to use longhand for the string bass and enter the shorthand *cB* into the keyboard system's left-hand staff; or to use longhand for the keyboard bass and enter the shorthand *col cembalo* into the empty string bass staff. That composers overwhelmingly chose the first option is not surprising: it saved them several letters. Ironically, what saved ink in the eighteenth and nineteenth centuries has caused an inordinate amount of it to be spilled in the ongoing twentieth-century debate on whether *cB* represents *bona fide* keyboard continuo or a mere cue *continuum* of the orchestral activity. As with any widely practised time-saving conventions, the answer is contained only in a few documents created by composers or copyists who took the trouble to walk the extra mile as did Beethoven in the notation of his 'Emperor'.

41 *ibid.*, p. 248.
42 See 1/453 downbeat; in 1/452, Beethoven had entered in longhand the beginning of the soloist's *col basso* activity. Beethoven's notation is an exact replica of Mozart's habitual way of indicating the inception of continuo activity in long tuttis.

By discovering the true ending to Mozart's *Konzert-Rondo* in A major K386, preserved in the British Library, Alan Tyson has unwittingly unearthed the Rosetta stone of this composer's *cB* shorthand. Contrary to his habit of entering cB into the piano system's empty left-hand staff (a habit so ingrained that no exceptions are known either earlier in this piece or in any of his piano concertos), Mozart filled out the keyboard system's left-hand staff with a longhand bass line; thereafter, on two consecutive pages, he entered this shorthand term into the empty string-bass staff: *col cembalo*.[43]

Should anyone suggest that the case of K386 is but an accident, two manuscript copies of instrumental concertos prove that Mozart's 'accident' is not unique in the notational history of the Baroque and the Classical eras. What appears to be accidental in Mozart's autograph is revealed as the premeditated notational principle in Johann Friedrich Agricola's full-score manuscript copy (*c.* 1750) of J. S. Bach's Triple Concerto in A minor BWV 1044,[44] and in a manuscript copy of Joseph Haydn's Concerto for organ (harpsichord) and violin in F major Hob. XVIII:6.[45] In both, the copyist has consistently entered the bass pitches into the keyboard soloist's left-hand staff while marking the empty string-bass staff with the shorthand *col Cembalo*.

The Haydn concerto's manuscript copy offers some revealing insights into the mentality of the copyist who, it seems, had encountered an unexpected problem while copying the first movement's second long tutti: was *col Cembalo* perhaps too ambiguous a term? So at the next turn of the page, our conscientious copyist coined a new term: *col B. del Cemb.* (*col Basso del Cembalo*) – the string basses should reproduce only the pitches produced by the soloist's left hand.[46]

Had eighteenth- and nineteenth-century composers used the shorthand term *col Basso del Cembalo* in lieu of *cB* (*col Basso*), performers today would doubtless no longer be busy debating whether or not to play continuo, but rather how to play it in a style proper for a particular composer. What they would discover is that the term *basso continuo* is a misnomer when applied in an unqualified sense to the piano concertos of Mozart and Beethoven.

The first person to sin against Mozart's concept of keyboard continuo was none other than his father Leopold who, with the best of intentions, 'improved' his son's

---

43 See facsimile in Alan Tyson, *Mozart: Studies of the Autograph Scores* (Cambridge, Mass., 1987), pp. 284–5.
44 See facsimile on p. XI of the *Neue Bach Ausgabe*, VII:3.
45 Page 1 of the manuscript bears the title: *Concerto per il cembalo e violino principale/ con 2 violini, viola e basso./ di/ J. Haydn*; it is catalogued as *Littera W, No. 13.490* in the Brussels Conservatory Library. The *Kopiaturvorlage* for this document was a manuscript now preserved in the Sächsische Landesbibliothek, Dresden, Musica 3356/O/16a. The *cembalo secondo* part that begins at the first solo of the *Violino principale* does not represent a continuo realisation: it is a keyboard adaptation of the violin solo part, to be executed only when a violin soloist is unavailable for performance (i.e. it represents an alternate version for two solo keyboards and orchestra).
46 The term occurs on p. 12 in the Brussels copy.

autograph notation by providing figured or unfigured bass in short tuttis where Wolfgang had prohibited keyboard activity.[47] Beethoven fared no better at the hands of his dedicated copyists and engravers: they, too, 'improved' his notation by ignoring certain autograph indications that were meant to qualify figures in short tuttis as representing orchestral cues.[48]

Through the curtailment of continuo activity in short tuttis, Mozart and Beethoven, perhaps more than other composers, granted the soloist a prominent status as *primus inter pares*.[49]

MOZART'S REALISATION OF THE PIANO CONCERTO IN C MAJOR K246

Few discoveries relating to composers of the Classical period have incited greater controversy than the discovery in 1920 of Mozart's autograph additions to an eighteenth-century keyboard part belonging to a complete set of orchestral parts of the Piano Concerto in C major K246. Recently, Robert D. Levin has concluded that this document 'does not shed light on Mozart's own continuo playing'.[50] The basis of Levin's pronouncement is his agreement with Ferguson's theory that Mozart's additions do not represent a continuo realisation but rather an *ad hoc* arrangement for a performance on two pianos.[51]

Although Ferguson's theory can be refuted on purely musical grounds, this is no longer necessary thanks to the discovery of a second eighteenth-century manuscript copy of the Piano Concerto K246 containing Mozart's additions.[52] That Mozart's additions were copied into the keyboard part belonging to a second, complete set of orchestral parts for this concerto (produced for the Mozart family at some expense, one supposes) strongly suggests that the additions were not prepared for a performance on two pianos but for a performance with orchestra where an amateur soloist was being assisted in the task of providing a continuo realisation.

A preliminary assessment of the second set of orchestral parts shows it to have been used by one of Mozart's Parisian students who entered not only 'improvements'

47 In full-score autographs, Mozart interdicted keyboard activity by entering rests into the left-hand staff of the keyboard system, as in: K238, 2/84–5; K242, 1/190–2 and 2/end of bar 64 and beginning of bar 65; K271, 1/63–4 and 66–7, 3/79–82 and 352–5; K415, 1/167.

48 Szász, 'Figured Bass in Beethoven's "Emperor" Concerto', pp. 44–54.

49 See Szász, 'Figured Bass in Beethoven's "Emperor" Concerto', pp. 42–3.

50 Robert D. Levin, 'Instrumental Ornamentation, Improvisation and Cadenzas', in Howard Mayer Brown and Stanley Sadie, eds., *Performance Practice*, (2 vols., London 1989), II p. 288.

51 Ferguson, '*Col Basso* and *Generalbass* in Mozart's Keyboard Concertos', pp. 13–4 and 25–7; and Linda Faye Ferguson, 'Mozart's Keyboard Concertos: Tutti Notations and Performance Models', *Mozart-Jahrbuch* (1984/85), pp. 32–9.

52 I found this document in a large collection of manuscript copies of works by Mozart preserved in the Bibliothèque nationale in Paris. The orchestral parts of the Concerto in C major K246 are catalogued as D. 11.980. Title of keyboard part: Concerto. Del Sig.~or Amadeo Wolgango Mozart./Cembalo.

to his teacher's continuo realisation but also an unmistakably French-styled figured bass to one of the 'improved' bars.[53] Interestingly, the manuscript contains a loose leaf bearing a hitherto unknown cadenza to the first movement of K246 that seems to represent a hurried (and later corrected) copy of a now lost Mozart autograph.[54]

As to whether Mozart's notated realisation sheds light on his own continuo playing, the answer is a qualified 'yes'. The argument that Mozart would have played a more virtuosic realisation is flawed, because it is based on the mistaken assumption that the student's technical deficiency prevented the composer from creating an elaborate accompaniment. In fact, nothing prevented Mozart from elaborating his realisation with trills, arpeggios, scales, Alberti basses and other ornamental, figurative or virtuosic passages, since any amateur capable of playing the solos would have obviously been capable of incorporating their stylistic and technical features into a continuo realisation. In addition, a comparison of Mozart's realisation with the nearly seventy Classical realisations known to this writer shows it to be similar in every essential detail to the most elaborate of these. The only exception is the doubling of the oboes in 2/9–12 which suggests that the realisation was conceived with two alternatives in mind: when only strings were available, the soloist would play the oboe doubling;[55] but when winds were also available, the soloist would leave out the oboe doubling. When placed in the context of eighteenth-century performance practices, Mozart's full-score autographs and his realisation of K246 suggest the following guidelines for the performance of continuo with full orchestra.

(1) As a rule, the soloist plays continuo only when the double-basses are playing, and only if not excluded by rests entered in the left-hand staff of the keyboard part. If the cellos and the double-basses play *divisi*, the soloist reinforces the double-bass line (at the notated rather than the actual pitch).

(2) When not otherwise excluded, the soloist plays non-stop in the middle register of the keyboard: mostly with both hands, occasionally with the left hand alone.

53 Entered in longhand, the amateur's realisation ignores Mozart's appropriate *t.s.* choice during four thinly orchestrated bars: 1/20, 22, 30 and 31. In 1/20, the student's realisation is a harmonic abomination. Figures complement the realisation at 1/22, where the third and the first inversions of the dominant seventh chord in C major are notated as a slashed '4' and '5' respectively. In French notation, these slashed figures indicate the presence of the tritone (the intervals of the augmented fourth 'f–b' or the diminished fifth 'b–f') in the aforementioned chords. See Michel Corrette's *Le Maître de clavecin* (Paris 1753), p. 17, 'Leçon en ut.', and the note on the bottom: 'Les François chiffrent le Triton ainsi', followed by a slashed '4'.

54 The orchestral parts (and perhaps the cadenza, too) may have been copied already in Salzburg (i.e. prior to Mozart's arrival in Paris).

55 The money-making potential of K246 as a teaching piece *par excellence* may have given Mozart the incentive needed to compose an accompaniment that could accommodate student performances using the reduced forces of a small string ensemble or even a string quartet (see Mozart's *a quattro* performing alternative for his piano concertos K413, K414, K415 and K449). The Paris copy contains two sets of fingerings in the solos of the three movements: one by the copyist, the other by the amateur.

First movements require a special approach: in long ritornellos, the soloist plays mostly with both hands, and occasionally with the left hand alone; in short tuttis within solo blocks, the soloist plays mostly with the left hand alone or, rarely, not at all.[56]

(3) Under no circumstances should the soloist play anything that could distract the audience from concentrating on the orchestral parts. The main exception is a few beats before the cadenza – here the soloist may overstep the boundaries by playing with the right hand thickly textured chords in a higher-than-normal continuo register; meanwhile, the left hand may descend to a lower-than-normal *col basso* register by playing in octaves.[57]

(4) The soloist should never try to complement the wind section – the keyboard's sole allegiance is to the string section, of which it is an inseparable part.

(5) Under all circumstances, the soloist should adapt the string-bass line to the keyboard idiom.[58]

Interestingly, some of the guidelines deduced from Mozart's autographs are corroborated by the printed and manuscript sources of Beethoven's piano concertos. However, the Piano Concerto No. 4 in G major Op. 58 constitutes an exception that must be discussed separately.

THE CASE OF BEETHOVEN'S PIANO CONCERTO IN G MAJOR OP. 58

Ferguson has made a convincing case for the keyboard's total silence in the tuttis of this concerto's Andante con moto. Indeed, in this movement, Beethoven seems to have turned every accepted rule of Classical continuo practice on its head. Rather than casting the soloist in the traditional role as supporting member of the string section, Beethoven here created the first truly Romantic model of the soloist *v* the orchestra (or, what is even more iconoclastic, soloist *v* string section).[59]

It seems, however, that the keyboard–string orchestra polarity is operational in all three movements. By applying the first guideline above to the concerto's first movement, it becomes obvious that the keyboard–string-section polarity is fully activated already at the very beginning of the piece.[60] Hence, accompaniment should be started no earlier (and no later) than at the double-bass *arco* entrance at 1/15 (and even here, only as *t.s.*). In the third movement, too, the keyboard–string-section polarity is in effect during every tutti prior to the subito fortissimo (3/32).

---

56 See Szász, 'Figured Bass in Beethoven's "Emperor" Concerto', pp. 42–3.

57 See, among others, Mozart's K365, 3/463–5. The thicker texture may have provided the means of controlling the ritenuto that signals the soloist's imminent cadenza on the tonic 6–4 chord.

58 Szász, 'Figured bass in Beethoven's "Emperor" Concerto', p. 11, n. 14.

59 The opening of Mozart's Piano Concerto in E♭ major K271 does not qualify, since the keyboard is treated as a member of the string section (the soloist plays *all'unisono*).

60 Double-bass exclusion in 1/6–13 implies the concomitant exclusion of keyboard continuo.

But even this climactic reunification of the two forces is exceptional: for nine consecutive bars (3/32–40), the soloist is called upon to support the uninterrupted syncopations of the string basses doubled by the bassoons.

Reinforcing the string bass with concomitant chordal syncopations in the right hand produces a stylistically unacceptable effect, because the keyboard becomes a separate body of sound set in opposition to the downbeats of the other orchestral instruments.

This exceptional and unparalleled continuo fragment in the Classical concerto literature allows only one stylistically correct solution: as in Mozart's realisation of the Concerto K246, 2/4, the right hand must precede the off-beat activity of the left hand by providing chordal support on the downbeats (shown in this author's realisation, which includes the adaptation of the string bass to the keyboard idiom) (Ex. 1.1).

Ex. 1.1   Beethoven: Piano Concerto in G major Op. 58, third movement, bars 32–41

But after this brief joining of forces, the keyboard and the orchestra part ways again by resuming their playful dialogue at the downbeat *sforzando* (3/41).[61]

Unfortunately, the proverbial carelessness of engravers makes it impossible to ascertain Beethoven's continuo intentions in the G major concerto. Even the existence of a separate cue system in the second movement (unique among the original editions of the piano concertos) does not clarify the composer's intent: probably as a result of the engraver's unthinking habit of translating all pitches played by cellos and double-basses into large-size noteheads, the soloist appears to be instructed to play not only the solos but also the string-bass line engraved with large-size noteheads in the cue system.

61 For a hypothetical programmatic basis for Beethoven's radical departure from continuo practices, see Owen Jander, 'Beethoven's "Orpheus in Hades"', *Nineteenth-Century Music*, 8/3 (1985), pp. 195–212. Performers may, however, choose to follow the model of mainstream realisations such as Mozart's K246 and Beethoven's 'Emperor', where the Rondo theme is played by the keyboard player in the dual capacity of soloist and accompanist.

THE SIGNIFICANCE OF NOTATED CONTINUO FRAGMENTS IN CONCERTOS AND SYMPHONIES

A major problem for today's musician is the scarcity (though not total absence) of continuo realisations in full-score autographs and manuscript copies of concertos and symphonies: in J. S. Bach's Triple Concerto in A minor BWV 1044, five bars of continuo at the beginning of the third movement;[62] among Joseph Haydn's hundred plus symphonies, eleven bars of right-hand activity at the close of his Symphony No. 98;[63] in Mozart's original piano concertos, two bars of continuo near the end of his penultimate concerto (K537);[64] in Beethoven's Piano Concerto Op. 15, two bars of figured bass towards the end of the second movement.[65]

The common denominator in these examples is that they represent unusual solutions, often exceptions to the then current performance conventions; and whenever performance conventions were violated, the notational conventions encouraged that the exceptions be recorded in longhand. Unawareness of this notational principle leads to two errors of interpretation: the explicitly notated fragment is held up as a model to be emulated elsewhere; or its absence is interpreted as implying the absence of keyboard continuo in Classical concertos and symphonies.[66]

In addition to these authentic fragments, a sizeable number of extant printed and manuscript realisations deserve separate consideration.

METHODS FOR IDENTIFYING BONA FIDE CONTINUO REALISATIONS IN EIGHTEENTH- AND NINETEENTH-CENTURY SOURCES

In their continuo realisations, late-eighteenth- and early-nineteenth-century musicians employed either figures[67] or notes on a staff. Because the use of figures as the

---

62 In the opening bars of the third movement, a string bass-line is absent, its place taken by the viola line and its realisation by the *cembalo*; as soon as the situation returns to normal (i.e. the string bass enters), Bach discontinues the realisation, its place taken by shorthand figured bass notation.

63 The right hand does not play chords in the middle register of the keyboard – it plays chords broken successively in upward and downward direction, with the fifth finger repeatedly depressing the highest pitch available on Haydn's fortepiano.

64 At 3/185–6, the keyboard bass has more notes than the string bass; the right hand does not play downbeat chords in the middle register but off-beat sixths in the high register; bar 187 is not realised because here everything returns to normal (see the editorial suggestions in the *Neue Mozart Ausgabe*).

65 Ferguson has already pointed out that at 2/84–5 the cellos and double-basses play *divisi*, hence Beethoven was compelled to clarify that it was not the cello but the double-bass line that was to be fitted out with figures in the piano part.

66 James Webster, 'On the Absence of Keyboard Continuo in Haydn's Symphonies', *Early Music*, 18/4 (1990), pp. 599–608.

67 The importance for performance practice of continuo realisations that employ figured bass as their exclusive notational symbol was discussed by Ellwood Derr in his lecture 'Basso Continuo Realisation in Mozart's Piano Concertos' (Michigan MozartFest, The University of Michigan in Ann Arbor,

absolute equivalent of longhand notation is little known nowadays, a brief explanation is in order.

The distinctive feature of figures used for the purposes of continuo realisations is their scrambled appearance. Such scrambling is, of course, intended, the relative position of figures representing their relative distance from the bass pitch. The most systematic use of this notational alternative is found in Jean-François Dandrieu's *Principes de l'accompagnement du clavecin* (*c.* 1719).[68] When applied literally, this longhand notational alternative yields an unambiguous figured-bass realisation such as that found in the fragments below, taken from the original edition of Mozart's Piano Concerto in A major K414.[69]

Ex. 1.2   Mozart: Piano Concerto in A major K414, first movement, bars 41–7, Artaria edition

Ex. 1.3   Mozart: Piano Concerto in A major K414, second movement, bars 1–3, Artaria edition

The misplaced horizontal dashes in Ex. 1.3, 2/2–3 belong between the last beat of bar one and the first beat of bar two (shown in square brackets).

Unfortunately, this type of longhand figured-bass notation was used inconsistently in Classical realisations. The cause of this inconsistency is not too difficult to guess. Because the system did not offer any time-saving alternatives, performers would at best realise the more problematic passages with the longhand numerical

---

(67 contd.) 18 November 1989). But since I am not familiar with the nature of Derr's conclusions other than from belated firsthand reports, I am summarising here the results of my independent research.

68   Every exercise is notated in three versions: figured with the longhand numerical alternative, figured traditionally (shorthand) and unfigured. I am indebted to Akira Ishii for having brought this treatise to my attention.

69   Published in Vienna by Artaria (plate number 41). The lower staff reproduces the original figures; the upper staff represents this writer's translation of their pitch equivalent. Without explanation, the original figures were 'unscrambled' in the *Neue Mozart Ausgabe*.

alternative, then revert to the traditional (shorthand) figured bass for the less problematic ones. The result is a smorgasbord of notations that offers no enviable task for twentieth-century sleuths in search of authentic realisations: they have no alternative but to attempt to separate the figures intended as longhand from those intended as shorthand notation.

It would appear that no such problems could possibly plague the extant realisations that use notes on a staff as their exclusive notational device. Nevertheless, various ways were found to circumvent the tedious process of writing out full realisations. Let us take a later edition of Mozart's Piano Concerto K414.[70] The first movement's opening tutti (not reproduced) contains no realisation; it is notated with the traditional string bass-line in the left-hand staff (large-sized figured bass unadapted to the keyboard idiom),[71] and the violin cue in the right-hand staff (small-sized noteheads).[72] But the opening tuttis of the second and third movements do contain realisations printed in small-size notes. No confusion can arise from using this notational system as long as the realisations are carried out consistently throughout the rest of the movement. This, however, was not accomplished in the opening tutti of the third movement where, it appears, a problem arose about how to accompany properly the appoggiaturas of the first violins. Rather than solve the problem on the spot, the realisation was abandoned momentarily, its place taken by the violin-cue pitches, as seen in Ex. 1.4.

Ex. 1.4   Mozart: Piano Concerto in A major K414, third movement, bars 1–8, Schmitt edition

---

70 GRAND CONCERT/ pour le/ CLAVECIN ou FORTE PIANO/ [etc.]/ W: A: MOZART./ Liv; I. Prix f2–10–/ à Amsterdam/ chez J. Schmitt./ [etc]. [No plate number].

71 Beethoven's painstaking adaptation of the string bass to the keyboard idiom in the 'Emperor' remains the supreme model for *col Basso* practices.

72 Note, however, that the violin cue is interrupted whenever the soloist is not to play continuo, as in bars 13–14, 58, and 60.

Only later, at the return of the Rondo theme, was the problem of correct keyboard accompaniment solved, as seen in Ex. 1.5.[73]

Ex. 1.5   Mozart: Piano Concerto in A major K414, third movement, bars 96–103, Schmitt edition

The consequences of these inconsistent notational practices are similar to the problems created by mixing longhand and shorthand figured bass: today's musician has no alternative but to attempt to sort out the small-sized notes intended as violin cues from the small-size notes intended as *bona fide* keyboard continuo. For this reason, the only advice that can be given to those in search of realisations is this: look out for them anywhere and everywhere, for they may appear in the least expected places.

Yet it would be a mistake to assume that no consistently prepared realisations were produced in the Classical era. Mozart's Piano Concerto K414 was published around 1802 in an edition that provides realisations for every long and short tutti.[74] Though not without flaws, the overall quality of this realisation is excellent, and it is hereby recommended as one of the most representative models for 'authentic' realisations.[75]

But no publication measures up to the quality and scope of a little-known British venture: forty-eight Haydn symphonies arranged as quintets with keyboard continuo.[76] Significantly, the keyboard part is referred to by terms that are borrowed from Baroque terminology. Two of the three arrangers – the violinist and

73 The *all'ottava sopra* indications in square brackets in the left-hand staff represent this writer's suggestions for adapting the string bass to the keyboard idiom (see n. 87).

74 GRAND CONCERTO/ pour le/ Piano-Forte/ [etc.]/ W. A. Mozart,/ Oeuvre 4me./ L. [1]./ (Edition faite d'après le manuscrit original/ de l'auteur)./ A Offenbach s/m chez J. André. Prix f 2 $\frac{3}{4}$ [plate number 1554].

75 My main reservations are that this realisation perpetrates the Baroque concept of keyboard continuo (right hand plays in all short tuttis), and that the bass is unadapted for the keyboard idiom.

76 Arranged for flute, string quartet and keyboard, the four sets of twelve symphonies were published in London. Two sets were arranged by Johann Peter Salomon. The first set (catalogued as h. 655. qq. in

Kapellmeister Johann Peter Salomon and the cellist Frederick William Crouch – call the keyboard part an 'accompaniment' (a term encountered in the first bar of J. S. Bach's full-score autograph of the Brandenburg Concerto No. 5). The third arranger, Salomon's violin pupil Dr Charles Hague, 'Professor of Music in the University of Cambridge', gives the keyboard adaptation the unabashed name of 'thorough bass'.

Nevertheless, the only realisations that may be termed consistently genuine continuo are those by Salomon, for both Crouch and Hague have overstepped the bounds of accepted continuo practices by occasionally assigning to the keyboard player's right hand obbligato orchestral parts. Salomon consistently avoids this temptation. Nevertheless, Salomon had to grapple with notational problems caused by non-musical (i.e. commercial) interests. One such concern was to make these arrangements available at an affordable price; for this purpose, the keyboard part's left-hand staff was deliberately conceived as string- and, concomitantly, keyboard-bass.[77] This money-saving device is prominently displayed in German engravings of Salomon's arrangements; in a copy of Haydn's Symphony No. 98 issued in Berlin, the absence of a bass part is explained as follows: '*PIANOFORTE. Die untern Stimme zugleich VIOLONCELLO*'.[78] Naturally, any of the adaptations that were originally conceived with this money-saving alternative in mind cannot provide any insight into how keyboard players were expected to adapt the string bass to the keyboard idiom. Similarly, symphonies published without a separate keyboard part cannot provide any insight into how keyboard players were expected to support the string section of the orchestra.

The obsession with time- and money-saving devices reaches new heights in manuscript copies and the original edition of Beethoven's masses. The single staff of the organ part, or the left-hand staff of the organ system, is occasionally called upon to accommodate any of the following situations, sometimes simultaneously: the cellos and double-basses playing separate bass lines with either the arco or the

(76 contd.) the British Library's Catalogue of Printed Music – hereafter CPM) contains the 'London' symphonies (Nos. 97, 93, 94, 98, 95, 96, 104, 103, 102, 99, 101 and 100) that received their world premieres in London under the combined leadership of Haydn (fortepiano continuo) and Salomon. The second set, published by Birchall (g. 455. v. (2.) in CPM), contains symphonies Nos. 85, 83, 90, 92, 51, 91, 48, 64, 88, 82, 80 and 73. A third set, arranged by Dr Charles Hague, was published by Preston (h. 2872. b. in CPM – the flute part is missing) and contains symphonies Nos. 66, 69, 74, 44, 63, 75, 70, 41, 71, 47, 77 and 53. The last set, arranged by Frederick William Crouch and published by Welsh and Hawes (Mus. 14. 76–81 in the Cambridge University Library Catalogue), contains symphonies Nos. 56, 76, 81, 67, 78, 79, *Gruppe* I:G3, 43, 57, 55, *Gruppe* I:B2, 61.

77   Robert Birchall's re-engraving of Salomon's arrangements (dated [1820?] in the CPM) offers this costlier alternative: 'NB. a Separate Bass [cello] part to these Quintetts may be had. Price 2.ˢ6.'

78   QUINZE QUINTUORS/ pour la/ Flûte, 2 Violons, Alto & Violoncelle/ No. 1 à 6/ avec accompagn: de Piano Forte ad libitum/ arrangé des grands Symphonies/ composées pour les Concerts de Mr Salomon/ à Londres/ par/ Joseph Haydn . . . / Chez N. SIMROCK à BERLIN. [plate number 85].

pizzicato option;[79] figured bass unadapted to the organ idiom that indicates the left- and the right-hand activity of the organist plus the activity of the feet on the pedals; figured bass adapted to the organ idiom; longhand realisation of the organist's right- hand activity; pitches played by the *contrafagotto*; instrumental cues of various instru- ments entered with the same size noteheads as the organ part; long stretches where the organ supports the vocal ensemble's contrapuntal activity part by part; and figured bass to cue in the orchestral activity during *senza Organo* and *t.s.* stretches. Of course, today's organist is rarely aware of any of this, for the new organ parts are usually printed on an independent, two-staff system. Therefore it must be remem- bered that, with few exceptions, the pitches that appear in the single or left-hand staff of Beethoven's masses may have very little if anything to do with how the bass line ought to be adapted to the organ idiom.

Finally, some closing remarks on figured bass in general. It may surprise many a musician today to find out that figured bass *per se* was not considered to be a foolproof method of ensuring proper harmonic, rhythmic and melodic accom- paniment. Figures were too often faulty, and it is instructive to see the harmonic monstrosities committed by an amateur who, in 1806, produced a complete manuscript realisation of Mozart's Piano Concerto in G major K453 based on the faulty figures and the corrupt use of *t.s.* as published in the original edition of this work.[80] A more effective means of assisting performers in the production of correct accompaniments was to provide them with an unadapted and unfigured string bass plus the first-violin cue (a notation adopted in Beethoven's Piano Concertos Opp. 19 and 37, and the Triple Concerto Op. 56). This method was also employed by *Kapellmeisters* who, thanks to the visual and aural proximity of the first violinist, were able to improvise keyboard accompaniments from what to the uninitiated must have appeared to be a bare string-bass part.

POSTSCRIPT: SUGGESTIONS FOR REALISING BEETHOVEN'S FIGURED AND UNFIGURED BASS

For organists, the model for the realisation of Beethoven's figured and unfigured bass ought to be self-evident: the realisation of the *Missa solemnis* as published in the

79 Apparently unaware that arco and pizzicato must be treated differently by the keyboard accompanist, Willy Hess has mistakenly concluded that the occurrence of *pizz.* in an organ part implies that the affected bass notes represent string-bass cues (see his Eulenburg pocket score No. 951 edition of the *Missa solemnis*, p. XX); the rules of adapting *pizz.* are quoted in Szász, 'Figured bass in Beethoven's "Emperor" Concerto', p. 25, n. 27.

80 See especially 1/233, and 3/12. In its corrupt use, *t.s.* is a generic term that denotes the absence of harmonic activity, i.e. it can be interpreted at will as *all'ottava*, as *unisono*, or as genuine *t.s.*. I found this realisation among the papers of George Frederick Bristow (catalogued as JOB 76–9 in the New York Public Library) and I am indebted to John Shepard for his help. The year 1806 is inscribed under the name I. H. Blum on the covers of both the fortepiano and the *Violino I^{mo}* parts.

original edition. For pianists, I do not know of a better initiation into Classical continuo practices than performing Haydn's London Symphonies as arranged by the co-conductor of the celebrated Salomon concerts.

True, Johann Peter Salomon's keyboard accompaniments cannot be taken at face value in all aspects. As a rule, the bass line is unadapted for the keyboard idiom, and occasionally the realisations provide harmonies even where the orchestral bass is carried by instruments other than the string basses. To be sure, precedents for such practices exist in the Baroque repertoire.[81] But it would be a mistake to make routine practice out of such exceptional cases.[82]

Nevertheless, if Salomon's arrangements were disseminated in modern editions,[83] performers would gain access to quality realisations representative of mainstream continuo practices from the end of the eighteenth and the beginning of the nineteenth centuries. When utilising Salomon's realisations as models for tutti accompaniment in piano concertos, soloists should provide a similar keyboard support, but only when the string basses are playing. Given Beethoven's thicker orchestration, it would seem plausible to play occasionally thicker textures with the right hand than those found in Mozart's realisation of the Piano Concerto K246.[84]

As to the problem of adapting the string bass to the keyboard idiom, I suggest the following expedient solutions.

(1) Repeated notes in quick succession: leave out the notes that are not occurring on main beats and/or play tremolo.[85]
(2) Figurative or ornamental string bass: play only the pitches that are essential for the harmonic perception of the passage.[86]
(3) Any unadapted pitches occurring in the left-hand staff may be played either as written, or *all'ottava sopra*, or *col ottava sopra*, or *all'ottava bassa*, or *col ottava bassa*.[87] But whatever one plays, it should be comfortable for the hand, and it should not take hours on end to learn.

---

81 See n. 62 in this chapter.

82 The figures accompanying the viola bass line in 1/1–6 of Haydn's Concerto in D major Hob. XVIII:11 as engraved by J. J. Hummel (Berlin and Amsterdam) represent cues (note the qualifying symbol 'Viola'); by contrast, the figures starting at 1/7 represent continuo (note the qualifying symbol *Cem: [balo]*).

83 According to H. C. Robbins Landon, Salomon's autograph quintet arrangement of the 'London' symphonies is in private possession in Hollywood, California.

84 See Szász, 'Figured Bass in Beethoven's "Emperor" Concerto', p. 10, n. 13.

85 See Mozart's adaptation of the string bass in the Piano Concertos K37, 1/12–15; K453, 3/270–2; and K466, 3/370.

86 See Mozart, Piano Quartet in G minor K478, 2/128–9. In Beethoven's Op. 58, 1/56–7, play only every fourth note (i.e. play only the pitches on beats 1,2,3,4 – not as single notes, but *col ottava bassa*).

87 See Szász, 'Figured Bass in Beethoven's "Emperor" Concerto', Exs. 1–7, 16a and 17. The term *all'ottava sopra* represents the left hand's activity of playing single pitches one octave higher than the cello line (not to be confused with the right hand's *all'ottava* activity defined earlier).

For those interested in the wider implications of this topic, a few closing remarks are appended. Experience has shown that the modern concert grand piano can function effectively in both solo and continuo capacities.[88] If, however, one chooses 'original' instruments for performing Classical concertos, it should be remembered that, in probably most of the standard Classical repertoire, the term '*Cembalo*' no longer refers to the harpsichord (Beethoven still retains this term in his full-score autograph of the 'Emperor'). It is, on the one hand, fallacious to assert that all music by Beethoven's contemporaries should be played with continuo: written about the time of the 'Emperor', the full-score autograph manuscript of Carl Maria von Weber's Piano Concerto Op. 15 contains enough evidence to support the conclusion that its composer preferred the soloist to be silent in all tuttis.[89] But, on the other hand, it is equally wrong to suggest that Beethoven was the last composer to expect his works to be performed with continuo: if the first-hand testimony of the great music theorist Adolph Bernhard Marx is of any import, then Mendelssohn still conducted his string symphonies of the early 1820s from the keyboard, 'which Felix played in discreet accompaniment, and mostly or entirely as thoroughbass'.[90] Nor do these concerts of Mendelssohn represent the swan song of keyboard continuo, for this author has dated the only known nineteenth-century full-score manuscript copy of the 'Emperor' as having been prepared no earlier than 1841 and no later than 1843.[91] In this score, the orchestral cues present in the original piano part's right- and left-hand staves were consistently eliminated, yet Beethoven's keyboard adaptation of the string bass together with its figures, *tasto solo* and *all'ottava* episodes were fully retained. About a decade and a half later, the 'Emperor' was finally engraved in what became the first full-score edition of this work: the idiomatic keyboard bass – and the figures – and the *tasto solos* – and the *all'ottavas* – had all vanished into thin air.

88 See Szász, 'Figured Bass in Beethoven's "Emperor" Concerto', p. 63, n. 76.
89 Catalogued as Add. MS 47853 in the British Library.
90 A. B. Marx, *Erinnerungen aus meinem Leben* (Berlin 1865), vol. I, trans. in 'From the Memoirs of Adolf Bernhard Marx', *Mendelssohn and His World*, ed. R. Larry Todd (Princeton 1991), p. 207.
91 Catalogued as X. 232 in the Bibliothèque nationale, Paris. My methodology for dating this manuscript will be recounted in a forthcoming issue of *Early Keyboard Journal*.

2

BEETHOVEN'S REVISIONS TO HIS FOURTH PIANO CONCERTO

BARRY COOPER

No autograph score is known to survive for Beethoven's Fourth Piano Concerto, and the best source for its outer movements is a manuscript score, containing his corrections and annotations, in the Gesellschaft der Musikfreunde, Vienna.[1] Such corrected copies are known for many of Beethoven's works,[2] and their importance is sometimes overlooked; it is interesting to observe, for example, that although several of his sketchbooks, autograph scores and original editions have been reproduced in facsimile in recent years, not a single substantial corrected copy has yet been given the same distinction. Yet their significance for performers is obvious when one bears in mind the route by which a large number of his works came into print. Normally he wrote only one autograph score, which usually contains many alterations. A fair copy was then made by a professional copyist, and Beethoven looked through this, correcting minor errors and adding occasional dynamics, etc., before sending the copy to the printers to use for the first edition. The corrected copy was therefore likely to be in places the most accurate source, since it might contain additional indications omitted from the autograph, as well as notes that were misprinted in the original edition.

The score for the Fourth Piano Concerto corresponds broadly to this pattern, but has certain idiosyncrasies that have long been known but never fully appreciated. It was first described by Gustav Nottebohm over a century ago, and has since been discussed briefly by Willy Hess and Paul Badura-Skoda.[3] The most striking feature about the score is the presence, in the outer movements, of numerous sketch-like annotations in Beethoven's hand, written on or near the staves allocated to the piano part. Also notable is the fact that the second movement is a much later manuscript that clearly does not belong with the rest of the score and was presumably inserted simply to make the work complete.

1　A82B

2　A list of them is provided in *The Beethoven Compendium*, ed. Barry Cooper (London 1991), pp. 191–2.

3　Gustav Nottebohm, *Zweite Beethoveniana* (Leipzig 1887), pp. 74–8; Willy Hess, 'Varianten zum Solopart von Beethovens G dur Konzert', *Schweizerische Musik-Zeitung und Sängerblatt*, 85 (1945), pp. 348–50; Paul Badura-Skoda, 'Eine wichtige Quelle zu Beethovens 4. Klavierkonzert', *Österreichische Musikzeitschrift*, 13 (1958), pp. 418–26.

The remaining features of the score are less remarkable. The outer movements were written in black ink (in contrast to the brown ink of Beethoven's sketchy annotations) by one of Beethoven's principal copyists – Copyist D.[4] Beethoven's ordinary corrections are in his customary *Rötel*, or red pencil, and relate to minor (though sometimes important) errors, such as the fact that the clarinets are in C, not B♭. Such corrections are quite distinct from the brown-ink annotations. There are also various pencil marks – mainly numbers – not in Beethoven's hand; their distribution indicates that they almost certainly relate to the original engraving of the parts – thus confirming Badura-Skoda's suggestion that the score was used for preparation of the original edition, which appeared in August 1808.[5]

Where the piano part does not have soloistic material it is marked 'Tutti' and contains a reduction of the orchestral parts, usually considerably simplified. This common convention provided several advantages: the piece could be played privately without orchestra as a satisfactory whole; the pianist could familiarise himself with the orchestral passages; he could direct a performance from his piano part, and could fill in orchestral notes as and when necessary if there were deficiencies or if the orchestra needed continuo-like reinforcement. The disadvantage of this layout was that mistakes could easily be made as to whether certain notes were part of a tutti and omitted in a full performance, or were genuine solo material. Badura-Skoda drew attention to certain places where most modern editions are incorrect in this matter; two places in particular are worth repeating here, since many performances even today are still incorrect. In bar 253 of the first movement, many editions show a crotchet rest for the first beat, instead of bass Gs (see Appendix to this article, item No. 12). Similarly bar 402 of the Finale in modern editions begins with a quaver rest, producing an incorrect diminished triad in second inversion, instead of a dominant seventh based on G (Appendix, No. 26). Both cases resulted from the word 'Solo' being printed above the second note of the bar instead of the first note. In the Finale the word 'Solo' is correctly positioned in the Vienna manuscript, as shown, and the pedal mark is also applied to the first note of the bar. On the other hand, the manuscript itself is wrong in the first movement, with the word 'Solo' on the second beat; but as the first beat is not a reduction of the orchestral part but a soloistic gesture, the manuscript must have been miscopied from Beethoven's autograph, and the mistake overlooked by Beethoven.

It is the sketch-like annotations, however, that are of greatest importance. They affect over a hundred bars altogether, and indicate variants that are in some cases very different from the published version. The full significance of these variants can only be appreciated from careful examination. Yet they are extremely difficult to

---

4   See Alan Tyson, 'Notes on Five of Beethoven's Copyists', *Journal of the American Musicological Society*, 23 (1970), pp. 439–71.

5   Georg Kinsky (completed Hans Halm), *Das Werk Beethovens* (Munich 1955), pp. 136–7.

decipher, and an adequate text of them has not previously been available. Nottebohm published only 'the most important of the legible alterations and additions',[6] while Badura-Skoda described some of them as 'illegible', 'almost illegible' or 'scarcely decipherable'.[7] Nottebohm's transcriptions are, as usual, fairly reliable, but Badura-Skoda had difficulty even with several annotations not described by him as illegible. The transcriptions presented here were made with great care from the original manuscript, and only in a very few places was there much doubt about Beethoven's intentions. They are appended at the end of the article and have been numbered for convenience. They show the text that results when Beethoven's annotations are combined with the notes originally present. Each annotation is worth discussing individually (readers wishing to compare the original version should consult a standard edition).

First movement

No. 1 (bars 148–51).   The third and fourth semiquavers in bar 148 have been marked with staccato dashes in place of the slur originally present. This new articulation pattern – slur plus two staccatos – is clearly meant to apply throughout this and the following bars. The staccato marks are reasserted at the third and fourth semiquavers in bar 150. Additionally, notes 3–6 and 11–12 in this bar are marked with an 8va sign beneath them; the one for notes 11–12 is clearly intended to apply to notes 11–14, so that the intended new text for bars 148–51 is as given here. The result is a more complex and imaginative articulation than before, with some interesting new antiphonal effects between different registers. Similar articulation was presumably intended for the corresponding place in the recapitulation (bars 315–18), perhaps also with the octave leaps, although there are no annotations here.

No. 2 (bars 155–61).   In bar 155 the second and third triplets show the middle note rising instead of falling a third, giving a pattern that is more elegant melodically and harmonically. This pattern was clearly intended to continue for the rest of the bar; meanwhile the left-hand quavers are marked with staccato signs (the last one accidentally omitted). The right-hand triplet pattern is restated on the first triplet of the next bar, where it is joined by the left hand an octave lower; both hands then evidently continue the triplet pattern for the rest of the bar. In the following bar, the direction of the right-hand triplets is reversed from the original, giving an overall pattern that sounds more complex but is actually easier to play and also avoids the awkward repeated note at the start of bar 158. Again it is only the first triplet that is annotated – this was obviously sufficient to indicate what was to

6   Nottebohm, *Zweite Beethoveniana*, p. 75.
7   Badura-Skoda, 'Eine wichtige Quelle', pp. 421–5.

happen throughout the bar, and also presumably in bars 159 and 161, where the figuration reappears. In the recapitulation, there is in bar 324 an annotation similar to bar 157 (see No. 17 below); bars 322–3 were left untouched in the MS, but should probably also be altered, to match bars 155–6.

No. 3 (bars 166–74). There are several very remarkable changes here. The initial left-hand triplet is written an octave lower, and its first note is now a chord. The entire chromatic scale for this bar and the next must therefore be played an octave lower than originally. Meanwhile the right hand, instead of sitting on a double trill for four bars, keeps jumping to different notes, each with a trill (presumably a double trill, though there is only one 'tr' sign over each note). The left-hand figuration in bars 170–3 is altered to give a richer sound, and the right hand is given a series of at least thirty-two tiny crotchets in bar 173. The last six of these in the transcription are slightly uncertain and there could possibly be an extra e^2 and d^2 at the end; but the suggested version makes very good sense, for the thirty-two notes then fall into four groups of demisemiquavers, for which Beethoven did not bother to write in the beams. Such short note values might be scarcely playable, had Beethoven not inserted a prominent 'ri – tar – dan – do' covering this and the previous bar, cancelled by an implied 'a tempo' in bar 174. This rapid scale and the previous group of splashing trills greatly increase the drama and energy of this passage, while the ritardando heightens the emotional intensity and expressiveness, resulting in a much improved overall effect. Bar 173 is the first of several passages where the annotations make use of an extended keyboard compass, whereas the standard version never exceeds c^4.

No. 4 (bars 192–4). Here Beethoven has improved the continuity of the music by filling in the silence in bar 193 with an answering left-hand figure, which is then intensified through chromatic alteration in the following bar. He has also changed the *piano* to *forte* in bar 192, reserving the soft dynamic level until bar 195 when the string bass enters.

No. 5 (bars 198–9). The right hand is given an extra chord at the second note of bar 198, converting a duplet into a triplet; the left hand is presumably to have the same rhythm. In the rest of the bar slurs have been added, giving a more imaginative, syncopated rhythm to what was previously a rather bland scale. It is possible that matching alterations were also intended in bars 200–1, but more likely these were intended to stand as before, to provide contrast and variety. At any rate, bars 202–3, which had formerly presented the original pattern a third time, are annotated differently again (see below).

No. 6 (bars 202–17). In bar 202 the first right-hand triplet is altered to form a sextuplet, with the lower and higher notes of the chord alternating and slurred in pairs. Again it can be presumed this pattern continues into the next bar. Then in bars 204–5 some entirely new figuration is added. Although it consists, like the original version, of a series of sextuplet semiquavers, it requires a more agile technique and therefore creates a much more spectacular effect. This new figuration is written out up to the middle of bar 205, but is clearly meant to continue, presumably up to the end of bar 213. It takes little skill to work out what notes are needed in order to continue the pattern in the most effective way, and so the version presented here is probably precisely what Beethoven intended. At bar 214 a new figuration is annotated, written out just for the first two beats, but obviously intended to continue into the next bar. This contrast of figuration produces added variety, whereas the figuration in the original version has become somewhat stale by this point. In bar 216 the left hand is provided with a pair of semiquaver triplets that match those in the right hand, and again the pattern must continue for the following two triplets and be repeated in the next bar.

No. 7 (bars 221–4).   In bar 221, right-hand triplets are changed to duplets to provide rhythmic contrast with the left hand. In the next two bars Beethoven has written unbeamed arpeggios, whose details are clear enough (Ex. 2.1) but whose implications are slightly uncertain. The version suggested here combines these notes with the original notes of beats 3–4 in both bars, and must be close to what Beethoven intended. In bar 224, the first right-hand arpeggio is written out in full (though unbeamed and with accidentals missing), and the second can be deduced by analogy.

Ex. 2.1   Beethoven: Piano Concerto No. 4 Op. 58, first movement, bars 222–3

Nos. 8–9 (bars 226–31, 235).   Most of the figuration here has been rewritten completely. Although this is the central part of the development, we find here, as in No. 3 (which formed part of the second group), chromatic scales, leaping trills, and a ritardando added at the part marked dolce. Far more notes are crammed into the scale than in the standard version, giving a more virtuosic effect. The ritardando is this time cancelled explicitly, at bar 235, which is otherwise unaltered.

No. 10 (bar 243).   The fifth to seventh notes (right hand) are altered from b^2–$a\sharp^2$–b^2 to $c\natural^3$–b^2–a^2, giving a smoother melodic line; a matching change is made to the left hand later in the bar. Although this is not an obvious improvement when the bar is considered on its own, the revised version is motivically closer to the semiquaver scale figuration of bars 239 and 241; and bar 243 as a whole functions as a kind of variation of bar 239, so that the closer motivic relationship creates greater overall cohesion.

No. 11 (bars 248–50).   Revisions in the second half of bar 248 demand greater agility from the pianist. Bar 249 is not annotated, but as the piano part is identical to the previous bar, one must presume the same alterations were intended. In bar 250 the standard version has the two hands in parallel motion throughout, but the revisions make the pattern less predictable.

No. 12 (bar 253).   See above, p. 24.

No. 13 (bar 256).   Here Beethoven has inserted a delightful rocketing arpeggio in place of demisemiquaver figuration that tends to sound rather scrambled.

No. 14 (bar 281).   The right hand is altered from triplet quavers to a dactylic rhythm that is more incisive and helps to accentuate the sforzandos. The same rhythm must be intended for the left hand.

No. 15 (bars 286–8).   This was originally a tutti passage where the piano was silent after the initial b^2. Beethoven has added semiquavers in the right hand in bar 286 as shown (the initial b^2 must be reduced from quaver to semiquaver to accommodate them). The left hand is similarly annotated, except that the fifth to seventh semiquavers are not written in and the rests are omitted. The figuration should clearly continue in the next bar, and it presumably stops at the sforzando in bar 288, although it is possible that Beethoven intended it to continue further still, right up to the next solo passage in bar 290. This added figuration reflects his increasing desire to see recapitulations as opportunities for further variation and elaboration rather than as mere restatement. (Note, for example, the use of a similar variation principle in the recapitulation of the Finale of *Les Adieux*, composed the year after the concerto was published.)

No. 16 (bars 300–1).   Again Beethoven has introduced spectacular leaping trills, this time to replace a chromatic scale. These trills also make use of the extended compass first exploited in No. 3.

No. 17 (bars 324–9).   Bar 324 is annotated with just the first beat of the revised figuration as in the exposition (bar 157); but it must, as before, apply to the rest of the bar and the ensuing bars too. Bars 322–3 should probably also be amended to match the exposition, as mentioned earlier; and the first two beats of bar 329, previously restricted by the limited compass of Beethoven's earlier piano, could be made to match the exposition (bar 162) rather than as shown here.

No. 18 (bars 335–6).   As in the exposition, leaping trills are added to heighten the drama, but the precise details are different, and Beethoven does not bother to insert most of the beaming for the quavers. Bars 337–40 should probably be left unaltered, despite what happens in the exposition, since the passage returns in decorated form after the cadenza.

Ex. 2.2   Beethoven: Piano Concerto No. 4 Op. 58, first movement, last two chords of cadenza

No. 19 (bars 347–57).   The cadenza is not indicated except for the last two chords (Ex. 2.2), which are remarkable harmonically but do not correspond with any of the known cadenzas. After the cadenza Beethoven produces an extraordinarily beautiful, ethereal effect by transposing the tune an octave higher than originally, and adding trills beneath it, creating a texture similar to that in the Finale of the 'Waldstein' Sonata (bars 485–506) and the coda of the 'Prometheus' Variations, Op. 35, where again the right hand has a trill and melody simultaneously while the left plays arpeggio figuration. The effect is particularly striking here, however, since the melody exceeds the old limit of the keyboard compass several times. Beethoven was evidently so delighted with this new effect that, instead of adding increasingly elaborate figuration in bars 349–53 as he had done originally, he continued the same texture for seven whole bars. In bars 354–5 he added double trills for the right hand, although these collide with the left-hand arpeggios in a way that makes the music virtually unplayable as it stands; perhaps the trills were meant to be omitted in the second half of these two bars. Bars 356–7 contain further use of pairs of triplet quavers syncopated across the beat to increase rhythmic interest, as in No. 5. It is possible that this figuration was intended to continue in the following bars, but probably the original text was resumed at this point.

No. 20 (bars 361–8). The scales of bars 361–2 are replaced by virtuosic broken octave figuration, and those in bars 363–6 are substantially revised. The details of this revision are not wholly clear. Again all the beaming is omitted; in one place the scale is represented just by its first note and a diagonal line (bar 364), and in another even the diagonal line is omitted. But the original text is still visible, and something combining it with the annotated scales was certainly intended. In bar 367 the first beat of the right hand originally consisted of four semiquavers, but it is annotated with a six-semiquaver sextuplet figure that was evidently intended to apply to both hands for the whole of this bar and the first half of the next. The result of all these changes is a more impressive and brilliant conclusion to the movement as a whole.

Third movement
No. 21 (bar 19).   Trills are added to the right hand to match the previous bars and enhance the decorative effect.

No. 22 (bar 30).   The right-hand melody is annotated as a triplet – a rhythm obviously intended for both hands. This three-note motif had appeared in quavers in each of the previous two bars, and appears in the orchestra in semiquavers in the second half of bar 30; thus the triplet provides both contrast and an effective way of making a written-out acceleration that is less jerky and abrupt than in the original version. This alteration and the preceding one were perhaps meant to be reused at the reprise of the same material at bars 178 and 189.

No. 23 (bars 134–41).   As in the first movement, Beethoven enlivens the rhythm by inserting two-note slurs for the first five triplets, and the effect is by implication continued. Then in bar 138 the brilliance is heightened still further by the addition of trills as well as the two-note slurs (which are reasserted in this bar).

No. 24 (bars 159–60).   The rapid scale begins on a^3 in the original copy, although this first note has been omitted – probably by mistake – in the printed editions. At the end of the scale Beethoven has inserted some extra chords before the tutti resumes the rondo theme. The rhythmic detail of these chords is slightly unclear towards the end, but is probably as shown. The insertion increases the feeling of suspense, and also has the practical advantage of ensuring that the orchestra enters at exactly the right moment, which is more difficult to accomplish at the end of a rapid scale.

No. 25 (bars 364–8).   Beethoven has added trills and two-note slurs to the right hand in each of these five bars, in place of the continuous slurs in the original. Their absence in the left hand at this point probably indicates that this was to remain unaffected. Similarly there is good reason for ceasing the trills at bar 369, even though the right-hand figuration continues: at this point, after a long diminuendo, the piano finally reaches *pp* and attention shifts to the viola part (marked dolce). Piano trills here would draw attention away from the important viola melody.

No. 26 (bar 402).   See above, p. 24.

No. 27 (bars 412–5).   The first note of bar 412 is annotated with a written-out turn, which is presumably to recur in bars 413–14. In bar 415 Beethoven writes a new cadenza, longer and more unorthodox than the original one – again keeping the audience in suspense and terminating in such a way that there will be no ensemble problems for the orchestra when it enters at bar 416.

No. 28 (bars 451–8).   Again Beethoven inserts more irregular and detailed articulation marks, making the music much more interesting than the bland effect in the original. Bar 458 is also altered to produce a more effective preparation for the ensuing melody.

No. 29 (bars 486–91).   In bar 486 Beethoven exploits the extended compass by putting the right hand (and by implication the left hand) up an octave. This high pitch is then maintained in a trill for the next four bars (which were previously a tutti passage), creating a delightful bell-like effect above the orchestra.

No. 30 (bar 553).   As in Nos. 24 and 27, a pause before a new section is given additional decoration, this time in the form of written-out trills that prolong the suspense.

No. 31 (bars 566–8).   Here the right hand is extended to the very top of the new keyboard compass (f^4) for the first time, before landing on the two–note chord that plays such an important role in the thematic material of the movement. The original version, by contrast, seems awkwardly constrained by the limited compass, and ends unsatisfactorily on a chord with c^4 at the top.

No. 32 (bars 579–81).   The last annotation is one of the least remarkable, but again it increases the brilliance by replacing plain crotchet chords with pairs of shooting quavers (the annotations of bars 579–80 apply by implication to bar 581 as well).

It has been necessary to list all the annotations in a systematic and perhaps pedestrian manner, in order to obtain a clear overall picture of their character and function. From this their purpose can be deduced more confidently. They were obviously not present in the score when the music was being printed, as they would have been a considerable distraction to the engraver, but must have been intended for a performance either by Beethoven or by someone else, after publication. Yet no one but Beethoven himself could have performed from such tiny, almost illegible, annotations as these. And they could not have been intended for a copyist. Even the best copyist would have had difficulty with many of them, and of course some are not fully notated; copyists were well trained in copying, but not in editing and amplifying incomplete notations. Beethoven could have been planning to write out an entirely fresh piano part – perhaps for his patron Archduke Rudolph, the work's dedicatee, or, as Nottebohm suggests, for a performance by Ferdinand Ries or Friedrich Stein in January 1809;[8] but this seems improbable.

It is almost certain, then, that the annotations were for Beethoven himself to perform, and the only suitable opportunity was his great concert of 22 December 1808, which included this work and the premieres of the Fifth and Sixth Symphonies. This occasion was, in fact, the first public performance of the concerto, which had until then been heard, if at all, only in a semi-private performance in March 1807.[9] Czerny relates that at the public concert Beethoven played the concerto very 'mutwillig' (mischievously, capriciously), inserting in the decorative passages many

---

8 Nottebohm, *Zweite Beethoveniana*, p. 75.

9 Kinsky, *Das Werk Beethovens*, p. 136. Despite Kinsky's assertion, it is by no means certain that the concerto performed by Beethoven at the 1807 concert was this one, although it could have been, since the score was evidently completed the previous year.

more notes than were written.[10] Although Beethoven was capable of adding such material on the spur of the moment (witness the many reports of his unprepared improvisations), he seems to have preferred to jot down some preparatory ideas when playing concertos. Many sketches are known for cadenzas for the first four piano concertos, and although such cadenzas were traditionally improvised, pianists by this date often prepared them in detail beforehand, as did Ries when he performed Beethoven's Third Piano Concerto.[11] Thus one would expect Beethoven to have made some sketches for the passages Czerny referred to, and indeed to have inserted them in a manuscript score. For although the work had been published in parts in August 1808, no score had been printed, and Beethoven would have wanted one for conducting the work. The only score in existence, apart from a presumably messy autograph, would have been the printer's score, which was no doubt retrieved from the local publisher (the Bureau des Arts et d'Industrie) after publication. Thus Badura-Skoda's hypothesis that a single score was used both as printer's copy and conducting score, and that the outer movements of this score survive in Vienna, with annotations for the December 1808 concert, must be correct.

What happened to the score of the middle movement, and did it also contain annotations? The first thing to note about the movement is its extreme brevity: in the Beethoven *Gesamtausgabe*, for example, the first and last movements occupy thirty-seven and twenty-eight pages respectively, but the middle one occupies only three. Moreover the movement is very simple technically, and provides almost no scope for the kind of increased decoration characteristic of the outer movement annotations. It is more than likely, therefore, that Beethoven left the movement as it was. Without any such autograph annotations, there would have been much less incentive to preserve the manuscript, and this may well be the reason why this movement became separated and discarded (before being replaced years later by a fresh manuscript).

Thus the version deciphered and reconstructed here must as a whole be a very close approximation to what Beethoven actually played at the concert of December 1808. He may not have kept to the annotations absolutely rigidly, but they certainly represent the version he was intending to play.

The version has still further importance, however, since it postdates the published one and represents Beethoven's latest-known thoughts on the work (excluding the cadenza he wrote for Archduke Rudolph in 1809). Czerny's account seems to imply that the alterations were mere fanciful ideas – perhaps no worse than the published version but not necessarily any better. The above analysis of them, however, demonstrates that most, if not all, were palpable improvements – as usual,

10 In Nottebohm, *Zweite Beethoveniana*, p. 75.
11 See Franz Wegeler and Ferdinand Ries, *Remembering Beethoven*, trans. Frederick Noonan (London 1988), p. 101.

Beethoven's last thoughts were his best. Similar improvements can be found in the autograph score of the Third Piano Concerto – improvements made either between the autograph and the printed edition or between the three stages of the autograph represented by three different inks.[12] Examples can be found of additional trills (1/195–6), staccato signs (1/211–4), changes to utilise a wider keyboard compass (1/225, 504–5), and insertion of more highly decorative figuration (2/27, 40). The difference between the two concertos is that the Third Piano Concerto was not published until some time after the first (and indeed the second) performance, whereas Beethoven performed the Fourth four months after its publication.

Post-publication alterations such as these undermine any notion of a fixed and immutable text. It is not just that they contain occasional ambiguities in the notation, which allow more than one possible realisation (see No. 17, for example). They also indicate that the work was never absolutely fixed in Beethoven's mind. The same applies, for example, to his last piano sonata, Op. 111, where different but equally authentic sources are at times contradictory, so that one has no final text but a number of variants where editorial choice must ultimately be the deciding factor. The variants in the concerto appeared for different reasons, but even if they had been introduced merely to surprise the audience on a particular occasion, they would demonstrate the instability of the received, published version.

I have argued elsewhere that Beethoven did not regard his published texts as representing perfection, and was capable of revising and improving them almost indefinitely.[13] It was only the law of diminishing returns, and the need to produce some form of the work without too much delay, that caused his works to be published in the form they were, rather than in an improved version. And once they had been published, it was uneconomical for the publisher, and too time-consuming for Beethoven, to issue revised versions, even though he would have wished to do this. I have also argued that, in his Second Piano Concerto, where again there are some amendments postdating the published version, these ought to be restored if one wants to hear the work at its very best.[14] The same applies to the Fourth Piano Concerto. It seems extraordinary that such a widely admired work could be improved in so many places, even by Beethoven himself. But it is even more extraordinary that, although he did so and the results have been known about for over a century, it is still always the original, unimproved version that is performed, and that nobody has hitherto attempted to incorporate all the changes in a new edition or recording. The main barriers have been the decipherability of some of the annotations, and a lack of appreciation of their full significance. Now that they

12 See Anne-Louise Coldicott, 'A Source Study of Beethoven's Concertos', (PhD diss. University of Manchester 1986), pp. 165–73 and Appendix IV.

13 Barry Cooper, *Beethoven and the Creative Process* (Oxford 1990), pp. 173–4.

14 *ibid.*, pp. 302–3.

are all available, performers should be encouraged to take up the challenge of a version that not only approximates very closely to what Beethoven played on the only occasion he performed the work in public, but is also more virtuosic, sophisticated, sparkling and original than the standard one.[15]

15 I am grateful to David Fanning for giving the first performance of this concerto incorporating my edition of the revisions, and for making several useful observations. A recording of this version is being issued in 1994 by Conifer Records.

APPENDIX

Beethoven's Fourth Piano Concerto: corrections and revisions to the piano part

In the list below, Nos. 12 and 26 are original correct readings misprinted in the editions. The remaining numbers are revisions made after publication. The text given is derived from combining the manuscript score with Beethoven's annotations. Where the annotations imply continuation of the new material into the following notes or bars, it has been added editorially. Standard conventions such as square brackets and crossed ties are used for editorial additions.

No. 1

No. 2

No. 3

No. 4

No. 5

No. 6

No. 8

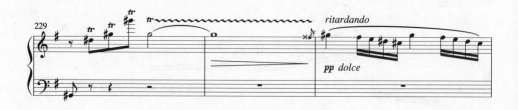

No. 9

No. 10

No. 11

No. 12

No. 13

No. 14

No. 15

No. 16

No. 17

No. 18

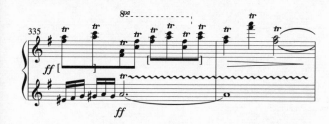

No. 19

No. 20

No. 21   No. 22

Third Movement

No. 23

No. 24

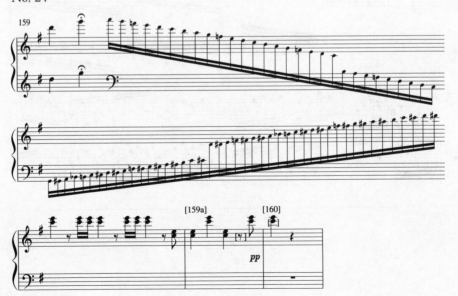

No. 25

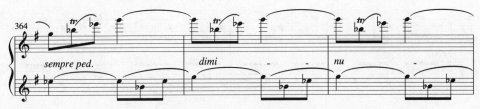

No. 26

No. 27

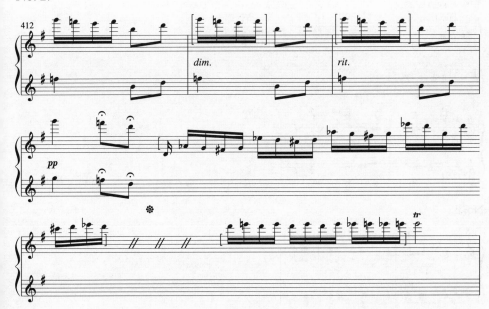

No. 28

No. 29

No. 30

No. 31

No. 32

3

BEETHOVEN'S PIANOFORTE PEDALLING

DAVID ROWLAND

Beethoven's pedalling indications raise a number of questions for performers on both modern and historical instruments. Which stops, levers, or pedals did he use? This is difficult to answer since it is not always possible to be certain which instruments Beethoven had at his disposal; and there was no such thing as a standard disposition of pianos throughout Beethoven's lifetime. The number and type of tone-modifying devices differed according to the period in which a piano was made and the particular practices of individual makers. Beethoven's indications for the levers and pedals pose further problems. He was only in the habit of marking them in his music from the early years of the nineteenth century; before then we can only guess which devices he may have used, and how often he may have used them. Furthermore, after *c.* 1800 it appears that his directions represent only some of the occasions on which he used the levers and pedals.

Given these problems, can Beethoven's technique be reconstructed? Only in part. It is obviously not possible to discover precisely what Beethoven did in all of his works, but by assembling information about his instruments and collecting accounts of his playing, as well as comparing his performance style with that of his contemporaries, we can at least gain a little more insight into his style of pedalling than the indications in the scores alone provide.

BEETHOVEN'S PIANOS AND THEIR KNEE LEVERS/PEDALS

Little is known with certainty about the instruments Beethoven played in his youth. The 1770s were years of transition in which keyboard players were content to play the harpsichord, clavichord, or piano, depending on which was available. Dr Burney's observations during his tour of Germany and Austria in 1772, for example, show how the piano had become common in some areas, but that audiences in a number of important cities were still used to performances on the older instruments.[1] Precisely what the situation was in Bonn is impossible to tell,

---

1 Charles Burney, *The Present State of Music in Germany, the Netherlands and United Provinces* (London 1773), ed. Percy Scholes (London 1959). A summary of some of Burney's comments on keyboard instruments can be found in David Rowland, *A History of Pianoforte Pedalling* (Cambridge 1993), chapter 1.

but it is likely that Beethoven would have been used to playing all three keyboard instruments in his earliest years.

Pianos such as those which Beethoven might have played as a child, and which may have determined his early attitudes to performance, had a variety of tone-modifying devices. Knee levers were common on grand pianos of the 'Viennese' design in Germany and Austria by this time,[2] although some makers persisted in the use of handstops.[3] Square pianos in these countries, on the other hand, rarely had knee levers before 1780, relying almost exclusively on handstops for changes in registration.[4] (Pedals were virtually unknown on any pianos in Europe before the nineteenth century, with the notable exception of English instruments.) Almost all German and Austrian pianos, of whatever design, had a knee lever or handstop for raising the dampers, and some instruments had an additional device for muting the sound; this was done by the introduction of a strip of material between the hammers and strings (the 'moderator'). The *una-corda* device was unknown on 'Viennese' instruments before the nineteenth century.

Whilst it is not known which instruments Beethoven played in his early years, it is possible to conjecture that an aspiring keyboard player of his abilities would have taken every opportunity to perform on the best available pianos. In Beethoven's case this would probably have meant the latest grand pianos by the Augsburg maker, Stein. Indeed, by the 1780s, there are clear indications that he was beginning to favour Stein's pianos. A letter by Neefe dated 8 April 1787 appeared a little over two months later in Carl Friedrich Cramer's *Magazin der Musik* in which he extols the virtues of music in Bonn and continues: 'The love of music is increasing greatly among the inhabitants. The clavier is especially liked; there are here several *Hammerclaviere* by Stein of Augsburg, and other correspondingly good instruments'.[5] Beethoven almost certainly visited Stein in Augsburg four years later on his return journey from Vienna in the spring of 1787.[6] Later still, in 1791, an article by Carl Ludwig Junker appeared in which he described events at Mergentheim, where Beethoven had gone with the Elector Max Franz:

I heard also one of the greatest of pianists – the dear, good Bethofen [sic], some compositions by whom appeared in the Speier Blumenlese in 1783, written in his eleventh year.

2 The term 'Viennese' piano is used in this chapter to refer to those instruments with the hammer action mounted on the key shaft as typified in pianos by Stein and his successors.

3 The Viennese maker Walter, for example, seems to have been more conservative than Stein in this respect; see Rowland, *Pedalling*, chapter 2.

4 See Rowland, *Pedalling* chapter 2.

5 Carl Friedrich Cramer, *Magazin der Musik* (Hamburg 1787), p. 1386; trans. in *Thayer's Life of Beethoven*, 2nd edn (Princeton 1967), ed. Elliot Forbes p. 86. 'Die Musikliebhaberey nimmt unter den Einwohnern sehr zu. Das Clavier wird vorzüglich geliebt; wir haben hier mehrere Steinische Hammerclaviere von Augsburg, und andern denen entsprechende Instrumente.'

6 Thayer/Forbes, *Beethoven*, pp. 87–8.

True, he did not perform in public, probably the instrument here was not to his mind. It is one of Spath's make, and at Bonn he plays upon one by Stein.[7]

Beethoven's relationship with the Stein family continued after he moved to Vienna. Nanette Stein married Johann Andreas Streicher in 1794 and shortly afterwards the couple moved their business to Vienna. Beethoven must have ordered a piano from them soon afterwards, because on 19 November 1796 he wrote to Streicher: 'I received the day before yesterday your fortepiano, which is really an excellent instrument.'[8]

It would be difficult to avoid the conclusion from these sources that Beethoven preferred Stein's pianos in the 1780s and 1790s, and it is therefore important to know which tone-modifying devices they had.

Stein's pianos from the 1770s to the 1790s often had two knee levers which operated the damper-raising mechanism. Each lever operated one end of the damper rail which remained undivided (unlike some later pianos, where the damper rail was split – see below). This meant that the performer could raise the treble and bass dampers more or less independently, although there was no distinct point in the middle of the keyboard which differentiated between these two registers. Alternatively, all of the dampers could be raised together. These were the only 'pedal effects' that could normally be produced on Stein's pianos, since there was generally no device for muting the sound – a fact which may account for Beethoven's apparent reservations concerning the use of the 'moderator', to which we will return later. Although the moderator was seldom found on Stein's pianos, it was common on those of Stein's main rival, Walter, one of whose pianos both Mozart and Beethoven possessed.[9]

Precisely when Beethoven acquired his Walter piano is uncertain. Czerny, writing in 1842, recounted his first visit to Beethoven (in 1801): 'The room looked very disorderly; papers and clothing were scattered everywhere, several trunks, bare walls, hardly a chair except for the rickety one at the Walter pianoforte (which instrument was the best of its time).'[10] There is also a letter dating from November

7 Alexander Wheelock Thayer, *Ludwig van Beethoven's Leben* (Berlin 1866), I, p. 213; trans. in Thayer/Forbes, *Beethoven*, p. 105. 'Noch hörte ich einen der größten Spieler auf dem Klavier, den lieben guten Bethofen; von welchem in der speierischen Blumenlese vom Jahr 1783, Sachen erschienen, die er schon im 11. Jahr gesetzt hat. Zwar ließ er sich nicht im öffentlichen Konzert hören; weil vielleicht das Instrument seinen Wünschen nicht entsprach; es war ein Spathischer Flügel, und er ist in Bonn gewohnt, nur auf einem Steinischen zu spielen.'

8 Oscar G. Sonneck, *Beethoven Letters in America* (New York 1927); trans. in *The Letters of Beethoven* (London 1961), ed. and trans. Emily Anderson p. 24. 'Vorgestern erhielt ich ihr forte piano, was wahrlich vortrefflich gerathen ist.'

9 Mozart's Walter piano had knee levers for the damper-raising mechanism and a handstop for the moderator.

10 Carl Czerny, *Über den richtigen Vortrag der sämtlichen Beethoven'schen Klavierwerke*, (Vienna 1963), ed. Paul Badura-Skoda p. 10: 'Ein sehr wüst aussehendes Zimmer, überall Papiere und Kleidungsstücke verstreut, einige Koffer, kahle Wände, kaum ein Stuhl, ausgenommen der wackelnde beym Walterschen Fortepiano damals die besten.'

of the following year in which Beethoven appears to be negotiating for a new Walter piano:

since the time when people began to think that my relations with Walter were strained, the whole tribe of pianoforte manufacturers have been swarming around me in their anxiety to serve me . . . you may give Walter to understand that, although I can have pianofortes for nothing from all the others, I will pay him 30 ducats, but not more than 30 ducats, and on condition that the wood is mahogany. Furthermore, I insist that it shall have the *register with one string*.[11]

Beethoven's remarks about his relationship with Walter suggest that the two men had known each other for some time. Perhaps the piano which Czerny saw in 1801 had been in Beethoven's possession for a few years. Whether or not it was replaced by a new one by the same maker in 1802 or 1803, following the negotiations, is uncertain.

Beethoven's letter is particularly interesting in one further respect. He was clearly anxious to have an *una corda* device, which was only just beginning to appear on 'Viennese' instruments. Beethoven's interest in the *una corda* may have stemmed from his acquaintance with English and French pianos, particularly Haydn's.[12] In any event, it proved to be very popular with him from around this time.

Walter's pianos cannot have been the only ones familiar to Beethoven at this stage in his career. He must have used a variety of instruments in concert halls and private houses. His familiarity with pianos by a number of makers is reflected in his correspondence, which also mentions the makers Jakesch (1802), Pohack and Moser (1803).[13] In assessing which tone-modifying devices Beethoven might have used it is therefore necessary to survey general trends amongst makers. Before the end of the eighteenth century this is straightforward enough: 'Viennese' pianos had one or two knee levers to raise the dampers (the damper rail remaining undivided) and many had the moderator lever described above. During the 1800s, new devices came into fashion. The *una corda* has already been mentioned; there was also the bassoon – a strip of parchment that was brought into contact with the strings in the bass register. In addition, knee levers began to be replaced by pedals. Some makers did this earlier than others, but by 1810 the pedals had become more or less standard on all pianos.

11 *Ludwig van Beethovens sämtliche Briefe* (Leipzig 1923), ed. J. Kapp; trans. in *Letters of Beethoven*, p. 82, except for the text in italics; Beethoven here wrote 'den Zug mit einer Saite' which is mistranslated by Anderson as 'the tension with one string': 'dann aber drängt sich seit den Tagen, wo man glaubt, ich bin mit Walter gespannt, der ganze Klaviermacher Schwarm und will mich bedienen . . . Sie geben ihm also zu verstehen, daß ich ihm 30 ♯ bezahle, wo ich es von allen anderen umsonst haben kann. Doch gebe ich nur 30 ♯ mit der Bedingung, daß es von Mahagoni sei und den Zug mit einer Saite will ich auch dabei haben.'

12 Haydn's Longman and Broderip piano which he brought back from London in 1795 and his Erard piano of 1801 would both have had the *una corda*.

13 *Letters of Beethoven*, pp. 83 and 101.

By the early years of the nineteenth century Beethoven's fame had spread abroad. At the same time, piano manufacturers were looking increasingly to the leading pianists to endorse their instruments. It is hardly surprising therefore that Beethoven received the gift of a French Erard piano in 1803. It had the standard French arrangement of four pedals: *una corda*, moderator, lute and damper-raising.[14] The significance of this piano for the performance of Beethoven's music is limited, however. He disliked its action[15] and regarded the piano as 'quite useless' by 1810.[16]

Beethoven's complaints about his Erard piano were voiced in a letter to Streicher. Indeed, by this time, the instruments made by the Stein/Streicher family seem to have been back in Beethoven's favour, so much so that he wrote in 1817: 'Perhaps you are not aware that, although I have not always used one of your pianos, since 1809 I have always had a special preference for them.'[17] William Newman has made a strong case for Beethoven preferring Streicher's instruments after this date despite the arrival of a Broadwood piano from London in 1818.[18] It is therefore the disposition of Streicher's pianos that is of most relevance to the last twenty or so years of Beethoven's life. Throughout this period the 'standard' arrangement of pedals on Streicher's pianos was four: *una corda*, bassoon, moderator and damper-raising. Some more lavish instruments included 'Turkish music' devices,[19] but, as we shall see, these effects tended to be ridiculed by serious-minded pianists. Even the bassoon was viewed with suspicion, and it is significant that Hummel's Streicher piano had no such device.[20]

Exactly how many of Streicher's pianos were used by Beethoven is not known. What is clear, however, is that, at the same time that he corresponded regularly with the Streichers, he received or played instruments by other makers; yet, as we have seen, they do not seem to have much significance for the performance of his music. Only one more instrument deserves comment – the Graf piano which he received on loan in 1825. Graf was arguably the most important maker in Vienna at the time whose pianos had the same standard four-pedal arrangement as Streicher's.[21] The piano that Beethoven received from Graf did not, however, have

---

14 The lute was common on pianos in Europe at this time. It comprised a strip of leather or cloth which was brought into permanent contact with the strings for as long as the stop, lever, or pedal was engaged.

15 See William Newman, *Beethoven on Beethoven* (New York 1988), pp. 45–64.

16 *Letters of Beethoven*, p. 300.

17 *Ludwig van Beethovens sämtliche Briefe*, ed. J. Kapp, p. 423; trans. in *Letters of Beethoven* p. 686: 'vielleicht wissen Sie nicht, daß ich, obschon ich nicht immer ein Piano von Ihnen gehabt, ich die Ihrigen doch immer besonders vorgezogen seit 1809.'

18 Newman, *Beethoven*, pp. 45–64.

19 Such as bass drum, cymbal and triangle effects.

20 George Ludwig Kinsky, *Katalog des Musikhistorischen Museums von Wilhelm Heyer in Cöln* (Cologne 1910), I, p. 193.

21 Deborah Wythe, 'The Pianos of Conrad Graf', *Early Music*, 12 (1984), pp. 447–60.

the normal disposition: it only had three pedals, omitting the bassoon – evidence perhaps that Beethoven, like Hummel, had little time for novel effects.

GENERAL CHARACTERISTICS AND INFLUENCES

During Beethoven's years in Vienna there were two distinct types of piano – the English and the Viennese. These types of instrument gave rise to two distinct styles of playing. Kalkbrenner observed:

The instruments of Vienna and London have produced two different schools. The pianists of Vienna are especially distinguished for the precision, clearness and rapidity of their execution; the instruments fabricated in that city are extremely easy to play, and, in order to avoid confusion of sound, they are made with mufflers up to the last high note; from this results a great dryness in sostenuto passages, as one sound does not flow into another. In Germany the use of the pedals is scarcely known. English pianos possess rounder sounds and a somewhat heavier touch; they have caused the professors of that country to adopt a grander style, and that beautiful manner of *singing* which distinguishes them; to succeed in this, the use of the loud pedal is indispensable, in order to conceal the dryness inherent to the pianoforte.[22]

Like the instruments themselves, the two distinct styles of playing which Kalkbrenner described had existed before the end of the eighteenth century. English and French pianists were using the pedals regularly at least by the mid 1790s, and were beginning to include markings for them in editions of their music.[23] Their style of writing for the instrument was consequently changing, and figuration which relies heavily on the damper-raising pedal is common in their music before the end of the century. Performers on 'Viennese' pianos were much more cautious, however. Printed pedal markings are very rare in their music until the nineteenth century and many German writers remained extremely conservative on the subject for several decades.[24]

The prevailing style of piano performance in Vienna emphasised neatness, clarity and refinement. Hummel epitomised this style and, in his piano tutor, warned

22 Frédéric Kalkbrenner, *Méthode pour apprendre le pianoforte*, 2nd edn (Paris 1830); trans. S. Novello (London 1862), p. 10. 'Les instrumens de Vienne et ceux de Londres ont produit deux écoles. Les pianistes de Vienne se distinguent particulièrement par la précision, la netteté et la rapidité de leur exécution; aussi les instrumens fabriqués dans cette ville sont extrêmement faciles à jouer, et afin d'éviter la confusion des sons, ils ont des étouffoirs jusqu'au dernier *fa* en haut; il en résulte une grande sécheresse dans les traits de chant, un son ne se liant pas à l'autre. On ne connaît presque pas l'usage des pédales en Allemagne. Les pianos anglais ont des sons plus ronds et un clavier un peu plus lourd; ils ont fait adopter aux professeurs de ce pays un style plus large et cette belle manière de chanter qui les distingue; il est indispensable pour y parvenir de se servir de la grande pédale, afin de cacher la sécheresse inhérente au piano.'

23 Rowland, *Pedalling*, chapter 5.

24 *ibid.*, chapters 5 and 8.

against the over-use of the pedals.[25] It was against Hummel's style of playing that Beethoven's was judged: 'Hummel's partisans accused Beethoven of mistreating the piano, of lacking all cleanness and clarity, of creating nothing but confused noise the way he used the pedal.'[26] It is clear that Beethoven's style was very different from that of other 'Viennese' pianists of his day. His insistence on a sonorous and legato style had more in common with his 'London school' contemporaries, despite the fact that he had reservations about their pianos.[27] Indeed, there is strong evidence to suggest that Beethoven was influenced by certain members of the 'London school' in a variety of ways. Beethoven apparently owned much of Clementi's music and agreed to offer Clementi's publishing firm some first editions of his music when Clementi visited Vienna in 1807.[28] Of greater significance to Beethoven's performance style than Clementi, however, is J. B. Cramer. Cramer impressed Beethoven with his playing when he visited Vienna in 1799.[29] This was an immensely important period in the history of pedalling, and Cramer had been among the first to introduce indications for the pedals into his music just two years previously in London.[30] His playing in 1799 must have used the most advanced pedalling techniques in Europe – a fact which would not have escaped Beethoven's notice. Indeed, Cramer's visit may have inspired Beethoven to begin marking the pedal in editions of his music, which he began to do shortly afterwards. Whether or not this was so, Beethoven offered him a rare tribute by quoting some of his music in his own compositions.[31] Czerny also noted of Beethoven's Sonata Op. 26 that 'This Finale is in that uniform, perpetually moving style, as are many of the Sonatas by Cramer, whose sojourn at Vienna prompted Beethoven to the composition of this work.'[32]

The Sonata Op. 26 contains further interesting material concerning the history of pedalling. This is one of Beethoven's first works with pedal markings, and in the *Marcia funèbre* the damper-raising pedal is used to accompany several passages of rapidly-repeated notes (Ex. 3.1).

25 Johann Nepomuk Hummel, *Ausfürlich, theoretisch-practische Anweisung zum Pianoforte-spiel* (Vienna 1828); Eng. trans. (London 1828), Part III, p. 62.

26 Carl Czerny, *Erinnerungen aus meinem Leben*, ed. Walter Kolneder (Strasbourg 1968), p. 19: 'Hummels Anhänger warfen dem Beethoven vor, daß er das Fortepiano malträtiere, daß ihm alle Reinheit und Deutlichkeit mangle, daß er durch den Gebrauch des Pedals nur konfusen Lärm hervorbringe.'

27 The principal members of the so-called London School were foreigners who spent varying amounts of time in the capital: Clementi, Cramer, Dussek and Field.

28 Leon Plantinga, *Clementi: His Life and Works* (London 1977), pp. 196–9.

29 Thayer/Forbes, *Beethoven*, p. 209.

30 Cramer's Second Concerto (1797) was probably the first music published in London with pedalling. See Rowland, *Pedalling*, chapter 5.

31 Alexander Ringer, 'Beethoven and the London Pianoforte School', *The Musical Quarterly*, 56 (1970), p. 754.

32 Carl Czerny, *Supplement (oder vierte Theil) zur grossen Pianoforte Schule* (Vienna 1842), p. 50: 'Dieses Finale ist in jener gleichmässig bewegt fortlaufenden Manier, wie in manchen Sonaten Cramers (dessen damalige Anwesenheit in Wien auch Beethoven zur Composition dieser Sonate anregte).'

Ex. 3.1   Beethoven: Piano Sonata Op. 26, third movement (Marcia funèbre), bars 31–2

This *tremolando* style was one of the characteristic uses of the damper-raising pedal in the first music with printed pedal markings published in Paris by Steibelt in 1793. The *tremolando* style quickly became popular in that city, particularly in more trivial works such as potpourris made up of the favourite operatic melodies of the day. Despite the fact that the *tremolando* style failed to impress the 'London school' when Steibelt arrived there in the mid 1790s, he persevered with it, and it was one of the prominent features of his playing when he came to Vienna in 1800:

When Steibelt came [from Paris] to Vienna with his great name, some of Beethoven's friends grew alarmed lest he do injury to the latter's reputation. Steibelt did not visit him: they met first time one evening at the house of Count Fries, where Beethoven produced his new Trio in B♭ major for Pianoforte, Clarinet and Violoncello (Op. 11), for the first time. There is no opportunity for particular display on the part of the pianist in this Trio. Steibelt listened to it with a sort of condescension, uttered a few compliments to Beethoven and felt sure of his victory. He played a Quintet of his own composition, improvised, and made a good deal of effect with his tremolos, which were then something entirely new.[33]

Steibelt irritated Beethoven. Eight days later, the two pianists met again:

[Beethoven] went in his usual (I might say, ill-bred) manner to the instrument as if half-pushed, picked up the violoncello part of Steibelt's quintet in passing, placed it (intentionally?) upon the stand upside down and with one finger drummed a theme out of the first few measures. Insulted and angered he improvised in such a manner that Steibelt left the room before he finished, would never again meet him and, indeed, made it a condition that Beethoven should not be invited before accepting an offer.[34]

33 Franz Gerhard Wegeler and Ferdinand Ries, *Biographischen Notizen über Ludwig van Beethoven* (Coblenz 1838; rpr 1972), p.81; trans. in Thayer/Forbes, *Beethoven*, p. 257. 'Als Steibelt mit seinem großen Namen von Paris nach Wien kam, waren mehrere Freunde Beethoven's bange, dieser möchte ihm an seinen Rufe schaden.

   Steibelt besuchte ihn nicht; sie fanden sich zuerst eines Abends beim Grafen Fries, wo Beethoven sein neues Trio in B-dur für Clavier, Clarinette und Violoncello (Opus 11) zum erstenmale vortrug. Der Spieler kann sich hierin nicht besonders zeigen. Steibelt hört es mit einer Art Herablassung an, machte Beethoven einige Complimente und glaubte sich seines Sieges gewiß. – Er spielte ein Quintett von eig'ner composition, phantasirte und machte mit seinen Tremulando's, welches damals etwas ganz Neues war, sehr viel Effect.'

footnote 34 on opposite page

Despite this clash of personalities Beethoven was sufficiently concerned to appear up-to-date with the latest fashions in the pianistic world that he included passages of tremolando not only in Op. 26, but also in the Third Piano Concerto.

At a time when pedalling techniques were developing rapidly, Beethoven was clearly interested in pianistic styles other than those which were current in Vienna. The extent to which it is possible to discuss influences is limited; but it at least seems likely that Beethoven was attracted to elements both in Cramer's style and, ironically, in the playing of his much-loathed rival, Steibelt.

BEETHOVEN'S PEDAL MARKINGS – SOME GENERAL OBSERVATIONS

In a frequently-quoted remark concerning the damper-raising pedal, Czerny observed that 'BEETHOVEN, in particular, employed it in the performance of his pianoforte works much more frequently than we find it indicated in those compositions.'[35] Taken at its face value, this comment suggests that the modern performer may be justified in using the pedal more liberally than is indicated in many of Beethoven's works. Indeed, Czerny reinforces this view by suggesting pedalling for some of Beethoven's music that was printed before Beethoven (or any other Viennese composer) was in the habit of marking it in printed scores, such as in the Op. 2 Sonatas.[36] Czerny, however, had lessons from Beethoven in the years 1801–3, and therefore can hardly be regarded as an authority on the latter's performance in the closing years of the eighteenth century when creating a reputation for himself as a performer. Furthermore, since the 1790s appear to have been the most crucial decade in the development of pedalling, when techniques were advancing very rapidly,[37] it cannot be assumed that Beethoven's performance at the time when Czerny was his pupil reflected his style of five or ten years previously. For reliable evidence concerning these earlier years we must look elsewhere.

In the *Kafka* sketch miscellany there is a marking by Beethoven for the sustaining lever which dates from the period 1790–2. This is the earliest known direction for the damper-raising device by any composer (Ex. 3.2), although there are several accounts of earlier keyboard players using similar devices.[38]

34 *ibid.*, pp. 81–2; trans. in Thayer/Forbes, *Beethoven*, p. 257. '[Beethoven] ging auf seine gewöhnliche, ich möchte sagen, ungezogene, Art an's Instrument, wie halb hingestoßen, nahm im Vorbeigehen die Violoncell=Stimme von Steibelt's Quintett mit, legte sie (absichtlich?) verkehrt auf's Pult und trommelte sich mit einem Finger von den ersten Tacten ein Thema heraus. – Allein nun einmal beleidigt und gereizt, phantasirte er so, daß Steibelt den Saal verließ ehe Beethoven aufgehört hatte, nie mehr mit ihm zusammenkommen wollte, ja es sogar zur Bedingung machte, daß Beethoven nicht eingeladen werde, wenn man ihn haben wolle.'

35 Czerny, *Supplement* p. 4; trans., p. 2. '*Beethoven* benützte es beim Vortrag seiner *Clavier*-Werke sehr häufig – weit öfter als man es in seinen *Compositionen* angezeigt findet.'

36 *ibid.*, p. 37.

37 See Rowland, *Pedalling*, Part II.

38 *ibid.*, chapter 3.

Ex. 3.2   Beethoven 'Kafka' sketchbook folio 96r

Whilst it is certainly evidence that Beethoven was aware of the damper-raising lever, however, its significance for his performance in other works is more difficult to assess. The function of the damper-raising lever in Ex. 3.2 is to sustain a bass note while chords are played in a higher register. This was to become a very popular texture from the end of the 1790s, especially when it was adapted so that the right hand played a melody above a left-hand part which included both bass notes and chords. Yet this sort of keyboard writing is scarcely used in Beethoven's earlier piano works. It is not possible, therefore, to use Ex. 3.2 as unequivocal proof of Beethoven's extensive use of the damper-raising device in performance during the 1790s.

Perhaps of greater relevance to Beethoven's early works than the *Kafka* miscellany example is the evidence of 'pedalling' in the piano concertos Op. 15 and Op. 19. These were among the earliest works to be published with indications for the knee levers in Vienna and Leipzig in 1801. Manuscript sources of these concertos as early as *c.* 1795 contain preliminary indications for the levers, showing that Beethoven used them in some of the first performances of these works.[39] Whilst this is evidence that Beethoven used the damper-raising mechanism before regularly indicating it in printed scores, the extent to which he did so remains unknown.

Once Beethoven began to indicate tone-modifying devices regularly in his music published from 1801, he used terminology that was common at the time. *Senza sordini* and *con sordini* (meaning 'without dampers' and 'with dampers') were the terms customarily used in Vienna for the damper-raising levers in the early years of the nineteenth century, and occur in works by several other composers. The change from this terminology to the more commonly-used 'ped.' with an appropriate release sign (which originated in England) occurred within a few years,[40] coinciding with the abandonment of knee levers in favour of foot pedals by piano manufacturers. Nowhere in his music does Beethoven specify the separate use of treble or bass dampers. In this respect he simply followed common practice of the time – though there is a somewhat curious indication in the autograph of the 'Waldstein'

39 Joseph Schmidt-Görg and others, eds., '*L. van Beethoven: Werke – neue Ausgabe sämtlicher Werke*' (Munich and Duisberg, 1961–), III/2, *Kritischer Bericht*, pp. 83–4.

40 R. Kramer, 'On the Dating of Two Aspects in Beethoven's Notation for Piano', in Rudolf Klein, ed., *Beethoven Kolloquium 1977* (Kassel 1978), pp. 160–73.

Sonata Op. 53. At the beginning of the first movement occurs the direction: 'Nb. Wherever "ped." occurs, the whole damping, that is, treble and bass, should be raised. "O" signifies that it should be allowed to fall again.'[41] The first actual pedal marking occurs in the final movement (Ex. 3.3).

Ex. 3.3 Beethoven: Piano Sonata Op. 53 third movement, bars 1–12

Perhaps Beethoven thought that a performer might raise only the bass dampers in order to sustain the low C at the beginning of the first bar unless otherwise instructed. Whatever his reason for such a precise indication, it at least shows that he took into account the divided damping mechanism, perhaps suggesting that he used it on occasion himself.

The only other pedal marking found in Beethoven's music is that for the *una corda*. This is indicated in the Fourth Piano Concerto, published in 1808, but not again until the last five piano sonatas. Beethoven's markings for this pedal are much more detailed than almost any other contemporary composer's. Many pianists were sceptical of its value, and most did not bother to mark it specifically. Beethoven's idiosyncratic use of the *una corda* will be discussed in greater detail below.

---

41 'Nb. Wo ped. steht wird die ganze Dämpfung sowohl vom Bass als Dißkant aufgehoben. O bedeutet, daß man sie wider fallen laße.'

BEETHOVEN'S USE OF THE DAMPER-RAISING LEVERS OR PEDAL

The effects which Beethoven created with the damper-raising levers/pedal have been studied by several authors. Newman offers a useful classification: 'Beethoven seems to have had seven uses of the damper pedal particularly in mind. These include sustaining the bass, improving the legato, creating a collective or composite sound, implementing dynamic contrasts, interconnecting sections or movements, blurring the sound through harmonic clashes, and even contributing to the thematic structure'.[42] Some of these categories reflect common usage and require little or no comment. 'Creating a collective or composite sound', for example, by means of arpeggios, or the cumulative effect of successive chords played in various registers of the keyboard, is a feature of numerous works of the period, as is the creation of dynamic contrasts by means of the pedal.

Others of these categories might at first sight appear to be peculiar to Beethoven, but were in fact common at the time. One of these is the use of the damper-raising pedal to contribute to the thematic structure. An example of this occurs in the final movement of the 'Waldstein' Sonata Op. 53, where the pedal is used to characterise the rondo theme each time it occurs. Czerny noted this: 'this Rondo, of a pastoral character, is entirely calculated for the use of the pedal'.[43] This practice had in fact become quite common in the closing years of the eighteenth century. In the first published music with pedalling, Steibelt's *6me Pot pourri* (1793), the composer had characterised a recurring theme in this way and he went on to do so in more substantial works such as sonatas and concertos. Other composers followed suit, so that by the time Beethoven's 'Waldstein' Sonata was composed this had become one of the accepted uses of the damper-raising pedal.

The damper-raising pedal had also been used to sustain bass notes. Indeed, this was arguably the most important use of this pedal, since it enabled composers to write entirely new textures. The most common of these has already been mentioned – a bass note followed by chords or broken chords in a higher register played by the left hand, while the right hand performed a decorated melody above. This sort of writing was extremely popular with certain members of the 'London school', and became an important element of the nocturne style in the hands of John Field, whose earliest Nocturnes were published in 1812.[44] This texture was not so popular among composers in Vienna, however, perhaps because of the different sound of the 'Viennese' piano. It occurs in Beethoven's music, but not to the same extent as

---

42 Newman, *Beethoven*, p. 236.

43 Czerny, *Supplement* p. 59; trans., p. 57. 'Dieses *Rondo* von pastoralem *Character* ist ganz auf den Gebrauch des Pedals berechnet.'

44 For a detailed examination of the emergence of this style see David Rowland, 'The Nocturne: Development of a New Style', in Jim Samson, ed., *The Cambridge Companion to Chopin* (Cambridge, 1992), pp. 32–49.

in the music of his 'London school' contemporaries. Moreover, when it does occur, it is not always accompanied by pedal markings, as for example in the Sonata Op. 109 (Ex. 3.4).

Ex. 3.4   Beethoven: Piano Sonata Op. 109, third movement, variation 1

It is unlikely that passages such as this should be played without the pedal. Perhaps this is an illustration of Czerny's observation that Beethoven used the pedal 'much more frequently than we find it indicated in those compositions',[45] although Czerny does not comment on this particular example.

Newman's observation that the damper-raising pedal was used by Beethoven for 'improving the legato' requires some examination. Passages such as the beginning of the slow movement from the Sonata Op. 57 ('Appassionata' – Ex. 3.5) and many other similar moments might benefit greatly from the use of the pedal, not only for legato, but also for the enriching of the tone that is an inevitable consequence of using that pedal.

Yet these passages do not have pedal markings, and neither does Czerny suggest the addition of the damper-raising pedal in these places. Indeed, comments which Czerny made elsewhere indicate that perhaps these passages should be played with a legato produced by the fingers alone:

[Beethoven] understood remarkably well how to connect full chords to each other without the use of the pedal.[46]

Many players have so accustomed themselves to employ the [damper-raising pedal], that a pure and classical performance with the fingers only, has been almost totally neglected; –

45 See n. 35.

46 In Gustav Nottebohm, *Zweite Beethovenia* (Leipzig 1887), p. 356; trans. Newman, *Beethoven*, p. 239. 'Er verstand es ausserordentlich, volle Accorde, ohne Anwendung des Pedals, an einander zu binden.'

that some are scarcely in a position to perform a simple four-part, connected passage duly legato without the pedal.[47]

Ex. 3.5   Beethoven: Piano Sonata Op. 57, second movement, bars 1–8

Ex. 3.6   Clementi: Fantasia Op. 48, p. 3

The use of finger-legato rather than the damper-raising pedal was common in the first half of the nineteenth century.[48] Pianists of that period evidently did not try to use the pedal for legato and for a richer tone as much as their successors. Nevertheless, there were occasions when composers such as Clementi indicated the pedal in this way (Ex. 3.6).

---

47 Czerny, *Supplement*, p. 31; trans., p. 29. 'Viele Spieler haben sich dasselbe so sehr angewöhnt, dass der reine, klassische Fingerspiel beinahe ganz versäumt worden ist; – dass Mancher kaum im Stande wäre, einen einfachen, vierstimmigen, gebundenen Satz gehörig *legato* ohne Pedal vorzutragen . . . '

48 See Rowland, *Pedalling*, chapter 8.

The precise placing of the pedal markings suggests that Clementi intended syncopated pedalling here – the technique whereby the pedal is raised on the beat and depressed immediately afterwards, so as to create the effect of constant pedal. Whether or not Beethoven had adopted a similar technique in equivalent places is uncertain; perhaps this is another case where he might have used the pedal 'more frequently than we find it indicated in those compositions'.[49] But in view of the strength of support for finger-legato, pianists should hesitate before using the pedal in all such circumstances.

The most controversial of all Beethoven's pedal markings are those which, as Newman observes, blur 'the sound through harmonic clashes'.[50] The most notable is the first movement of the Sonata Op. 27 No. 2. In this case, the directions 'Si deve suonare tutto questo pezzo delicatissimamente e senza sordino/ sempre pp e senza sordino' seem to suggest that the damper-raising pedal should be depressed through-out changes in harmony and melody, thereby producing a confused sound on the modern piano, and some blurring on an early instrument. Did Beethoven really intend these effects? Czerny is ambiguous on the subject. In his comments on Op. 27 No. 2 he says that 'the prescribed pedal must be re-employed at each note in the bass'.[51] It is not clear from these remarks whether Czerny is relating Beethoven's own practice, or simply suggesting a way of coming to terms with the pedal marking on a more modern piano. In a similar instance from the beginning of the slow movement of the Third Piano Concerto, however, Czerny explicitly states that Beethoven held down the damper-raising pedal throughout a lengthy passage with several changes of harmony:

Beethoven (who publicly played this Concerto in 1803) continued the pedal during the entire theme, which on the weak-sounding pianofortes of that day, did very well, especially when the shifting pedal [*una corda*] was also employed. But now, as the instruments have acquired a much greater body of tone, we should advise the damper pedal to be employed anew, at each important change of harmony.[52]

This account is also interesting in that it shows how Beethoven used the *una corda* pedal alongside the damper-raising pedal to minimise the resonance of the instru-ment, so as to reduce the resultant harmonic blurring. The *una corda* pedal was also used in Op. 27 No. 2, according to Czerny, who observed: 'The bars 32 to 35

49 See n. 35.   50 See n. 42.

51 Czerny, *Supplement*, p. 51; trans. p. 49. 'Das vorgezeichnete *Pedal* ist bei jeder Bassnote von Neuem zu nehmen.'

52 *ibid.*, pp. 109–10; trans. pp. 107–8. 'Beethoven (der dieses *Concert* 1803 öffentlich spielte) liess das *Pedal* durch das ganze Thema fortdauern, was auf den damaligen schwachklingenden *Clavieren* sehr wohl anging, besonders, wenn auch das Verschiebungspedal dazu genommen war. Aber jetzt, wo der Ton weit kräftiger geworden, würden wir rathen, das Dämpfungspedal bei jedem bedeutendern Harmoniewechsel immer wider von Neuem zu nehmen.'

remarkably *crescendo* and also *accelerando* up to *forte*, which in bars 36 to 39 again decreases. In this *forte*, the shifting pedal is also relinquished, which otherwise Beethoven was accustomed to employ throughout the whole piece.'[53] (Beethoven was not in the habit of marking the *una corda* at this date.)

The evidence of Beethoven's markings and Czerny's remarks suggests that Beethoven probably did hold down the damper-raising pedal for lengthy passages, and even whole movements in the case of Op. 27 No. 2. If this was indeed the case, then Beethoven was simply following established practice. Similar passages can be found in the music of many composers around the turn of the century, in Vienna and elsewhere. Ex. 3.7 by Gelinek is a late instance, where the effects of harmonic blurring are reduced by the direction *piano* in bar 2.

Ex. 3.7   Gelinek: Variations set No. 47, variation 7 (1809)

A similar passage by Clementi, published over a decade earlier, is even more cautious with its use of a drone bass throughout (Ex. 3.8).

Even in these examples it would be just conceivable to argue that the composer might have intended the pedal to be released in the middle of the passage. This can

53   *ibid.*, p. 51; trans. p. 49. 'Die Takte 32 bis 35 bedeutend *crescendo* und auch accelerando bis zum *Forte*, welches in den Takten 36 bis 39 wider abnimmt. Bei diesem *Forte* wird auch das Verschiebungspedal weggelassen, welches sonst Beethoven durch das ganze übrige Stück zu nehmen pflegte.'

hardly have been the case in Ex. 3.9, however, where the direction for the damper-raising pedal (the *Grande pedalle*) is for the whole variation, but that for the lute (the *Sourdine*) only for the quaver chords.

Ex. 3.8   Clementi: Piano Sonata Op. 37 No. 1, first movement

Beethoven seems to have been following a common trend in his use of the damper-raising pedal for lengthy passages including changes of harmony. It was a relatively short-lived fashion, however, because of the increasing resonance of pianos in the early years of the nineteenth century. Markings such as those described above had virtually disappeared in music intended for the heavier, English-style piano by the year 1800; it was only in music for the 'Viennese' instrument that similar indications persisted for the first few years of the new century.

BEETHOVEN'S USE OF THE UNA CORDA AND OTHER PEDALS

Pianists at the beginning of the nineteenth century were divided in their opinions over the usefulness of the *una corda* pedal for a number of reasons. Some commentators complained that it put the piano out of tune, among them Czerny: 'In making use of this pedal we must take care not to play too hard, as the single strings are easily put out of tune or even broken.'[54] Most grand pianos of the early

---

54 Carl Czerny, *Vollständige theoretisch-praktische Pianoforteschule* Op. 500 (Vienna 1838–9), Part 3, p. 42; Eng. trans. (London 1838–9), p. 57. 'Man hüthe sich beim Gebrauch dieses *Pedals* stark zu spielen, weil die einzelne Saite leicht verstimmt oder gar abgeschlagen werden könnte.'

nineteenth century allowed the hammer to strike one, two, or all three strings
(unlike the modern mechanism, which can only be reduced to the two-string position). When the one-string position was in use, tuning was particularly vulnerable.

Ex. 3.9   Boieldieu: Piano Concerto No. 1, p. 14

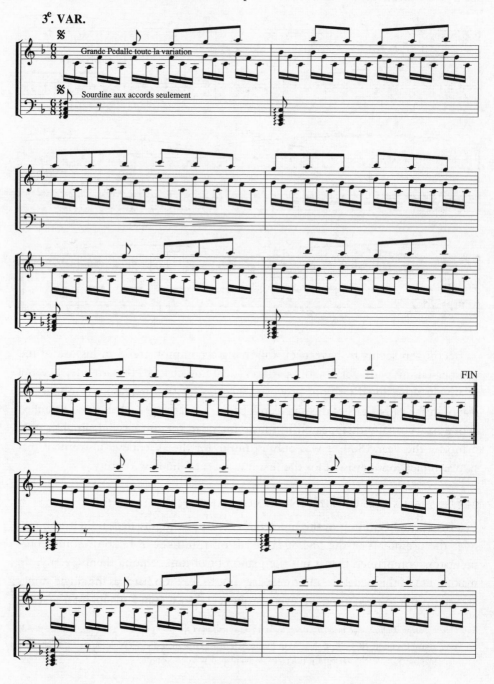

Some pianists seem to have used the *una corda* for a change in tone quality, but not in order to increase the dynamic capabilities of the instrument. John Field was evidently very particular in this respect: 'His use of the pedal was moderate. He never used the una-corda to play *pp* or diminuendo. The fingers did these.'[55] Others, such as Cramer, allowed a more extensive use: 'the left hand Pedal serves to move the Keyboard from Left to Right, and takes off one or two strings from the hammers; it is chiefly used in Piano, Diminuendo, and Pianissimo passages . . . As the Left hand Pedal is only used in soft passages, it does not require any particular mark.'[56]

Since each pianist had his or her own peculiar way of using the *una corda*, it is perhaps not surprising that it is seldom marked in scores. Some composers never indicate it and others seem only to do so when a particular effect is intended. It is against this background that Beethoven's use of the *una corda* must be assessed.

We have already seen how Beethoven requested the *una corda* on an instrument by Walter in 1802[57] and how, according to Czerny, he used it in the Third Piano Concerto and the Sonata Op. 27 No. 2.[58] However, it was not until the Fourth Piano Concerto (*c.* 1806) that he indicated its use in the score. Having done so on this occasion, no further markings for it occur until the last five piano sonatas. The sporadic nature of these markings need not surprise us – no other composer was any more consistent than Beethoven, and most were considerably less so. What the evidence seems to suggest is that Beethoven used the *una corda* throughout his

55 Related by Field's pupil Dubuk in Heinrich Dessauer, *John Field, sein Leben und seine Werke* (Langensalza 1912), p. 49. 'Im Pedalgebrauch war er mäßig. Nie benutzte er die Verschiebung, um "pianissimo" oder diminuendo zu spielen. Dies hatten allein die Finger zu machen.'

56 Johann Baptist Cramer, *Instructions for the Pianoforte*, 3rd edn (London 1818), p. 43.

57 See n. 11.

58 See ns. 52 and 53

career from the early years of the nineteenth century onwards. But how exactly did Beethoven use the *una corda*, and how did his technique compare with that of his contemporaries?

Beethoven's use of the *una corda* can be seen at its most extensive in the 'Hammerklavier' Sonata Op. 106, particularly in the slow movement, where there are about twenty directions for it. These include lengthy passages during which the pedal remains depressed, short sections for as little as one-and-a-half bars and, most idiosyncratic of all, passages where there is a gradual shift from the one-string to the three-string position. These markings are much more detailed than those of any other nineteenth-century composer. They demonstrate a lack of concern for the changes in timbre that result from the use of the pedal in this way – especially if the shift from the one- to the three-string position is effected on an instrument where the hammers are worn, and therefore where the strings are alternately struck by compressed and soft leather. Perhaps Beethoven was less concerned about this than other pianists on account of his deafness in later years; but it would be misleading to suggest that Beethoven only used the *una corda* in this way when he was at his most deaf. The markings in the Fourth Piano Concerto include progressive use of the pedal from the three- to the one-string position, and Czerny's description of Beethoven's performance of the Sonata Op. 27 No. 2 suggests that he may have employed the technique at an even earlier date.[59]

Was the *una corda* the only soft pedal used by Beethoven? We saw earlier that the so-called moderator pedal would have been available to him on some of the pianos he played in the eighteenth century and almost all in the nineteenth. Yet there is no indication either in his music or in descriptions of his playing to suggest that he ever used it. Indications for it in some of Schubert's sonatas and songs show that some at least of his contemporaries found a place for the moderator,[60] and even in the 1830s Czerny advocated a restricted use of it:

This pedal is much seldomer used, even in Germany (where it is chiefly to be met with), than either of the two preceding kinds [the damper-raising and una corda]; and it is advantageously applicable only in a very soft *Tremolando* on the lower octaves of the instrument, in conjunction with the Damper pedal, when it produces an imitation of distant thunder.[61]

However, any use of the moderator in Beethoven's music remains entirely conjectural.

What of the other pedals with which Beethoven would have been familiar? Several points are relevant here. First, devices such as triangles, drums and cymbals

---

59 See n. 53.

60 See, for example, Schubert's song 'Der Tod und das Mädchen' D531, the slow movement of the Piano Sonata in A minor D784, and the first movement of the Piano Sonata in D♭ major D567.

61 Czerny, *Pianoforteschule* Op. 500, Part 3, p. 48; Eng. trans. (London 1838–9), III, p. 65. 'Dieses *Pedale del* Piano wird noch weit seltener gebraucht, und ist eigentlich nur bei einem sehr leisen *Tremolando* in den tiefen Octaven, in Verein mit dem Dämpfungs=Pedal, völlig an seinem Platze, um eine Art von fernem Donner hervorzubringen.'

were only included on a relatively small number of expensive pianos – and there is no evidence that Beethoven owned or played such instruments. Secondly, the fact that Beethoven's Graf piano had the rather unusual disposition of three, rather than four pedals (omitting the bassoon) suggests that Beethoven required no more than the damper-raising, *una corda* and moderator pedals in 1825. Thirdly, a number of important writers on pianoforte performance were outspoken in their condemnation of additional pedals, among them Hummel and Czerny.[62] Thus in the absence of any evidence to the contrary, it seems most unlikely that Beethoven had any use for pedals other than the damper-raising, *una corda*, and perhaps the moderator.

62 Hummel, *Anweisung*, trans. III, p. 62; and Czerny, *Pianoforteschule* Op. 500, trans. III, p. 65.

4

BEETHOVEN AND THE DEVELOPMENT OF WIND INSTRUMENTS

COLIN LAWSON

INTRODUCTION: THE CURRENT REVIVAL OF BEETHOVEN'S WIND INSTRUMENTS

Beethoven's career coincided with a particularly dynamic period in the history of musical instruments, which has been reflected in a vast organological literature, documenting a period of remarkable change in both the woodwind and brass families during the fifty years following the death of Mozart. For each of the instruments, it is now possible to chart the progression of mechanical developments which radically transformed the tone-colours of the eighteenth-century orchestra. The clarinet serves as the most radical example of the woodwinds; at the beginning of Beethoven's career it was a five-keyed boxwood instrument, whereas a mere fifteen years after his death it was available to adventurous players in the Boehm system we know today. Keys were gradually added to the woodwinds, partly to facilitate the available range of trills, but increasingly to enable notes which had been cross-fingered to be produced with more accurate intonation and with greater security. The elimination of weaker-sounding cross-fingerings tended to produce instruments which were stronger in tone, and this development was encouraged by increasing bore diameters and other aspects of design, such as the thickness of the wood itself. Orchestral demands encouraged louder instruments and ensured that voices which could not compete, such as the basset horn, were confined to music-making of a domestic nature. With the addition of mechanism, all the wind instruments became comfortable in a wider range of tonalities, and the production of wind and brass instruments which were virtually omnitonic became for many manufacturers a recognised aim.

In an age which, in terms of musical equipment, was far less standardised than we can imagine, players varied a great deal in their degree of enthusiasm for new types of instrument. Such differences in outlook are reflected throughout the nineteenth century, on the one hand by writers who felt that the new versatility of wind instruments was indispensable, and on the other by those who felt that something of the individuality of tone-colour was lost as a result of mechanical developments. Even in the later nineteenth century, regret was expressed in some circles that the true qualities of older instruments had been lost. As William Stone observed in the first edition of Grove's *Dictionary of Music*:

hardly any wind instrument, except the flute, has been so altered and modified . . . in its mechanism as the oboe . . . It has thus become by far the most elaborate and complicated of reed instruments, and it is a question whether a return to an older and simpler pattern, by lessening the weight of the machine, and the number of holes breaking the continuity of the bore, and by increasing the vibratory powers of the wooden tube, would not conduce to an improved quality of tone.[1]

Stone was even more vehement with regard to the bassoon: 'Various attempts have been made to give greater accuracy and completeness to its singularly capricious scale; but up to the present time all these seem to have diminished the flexibility of the instrument in florid passages, or to have impaired its peculiar but telling and characteristic tone.'[2]

However, the general view well into the twentieth century was that instrumental design had been subject to continual progress. Such an approach to Classical and Romantic music was nicely documented as late as 1969 in the second edition of the *Harvard Dictionary of Music*: 'In the period after Bach the problems of performance practice largely disappear, owing to the more specific directions of composers for clearly indicating their intentions.'[3] Even in 1980 this attitude still prevailed, as is evident in the *New Grove* article 'Performing Practice' by Howard Mayer Brown: 'there has been no severance of contact with post-Baroque music as a whole, nor with the instruments used in performing it'.[4] In fact, any apparent continuity of tradition has turned out to be a somewhat dangerous image, for superficial similarities between early-nineteenth-century instruments and today's counterparts can in practice act as a barrier to a true appreciation of the earlier models. Mayer Brown suggested that 'to hear Beethoven's symphonies played with the same degree of authenticity [as the Horn Sonata] would be no less revealing in sound quality, but the practical difficulties of assembling and equipping such an orchestra are almost insuperable'. In fact, the 1980s saw period performance of Beethoven's orchestral music move well past the experimental stage, becoming part of the musical establishment through its widespread popularity.

Recently, however, Clive Brown has warned that some of today's instruments would not have been familiar to the musicians of Beethoven's Vienna.[5] In respect

1 *A Dictionary of Music and Musicians*, ed. G. Grove (London 1879–89), II, p. 486, art. 'Oboe'.

2 *ibid.*, I, p. 151, art. 'Bassoon'.

3 Willi Apel, *Harvard Dictionary of Music*, 2nd edn (Cambridge, Mass. 1969), pp. 658–9.

4 *The New Grove Dictionary of Music and Musicians*, ed. Stanley Sadie (London 1980) XIV, p. 388, art. 'Performing Practice'.

5 Clive Brown, 'Historical Performance, Metronome Marks and Tempo in Beethoven's Symphonies', *Early Music*, 19/2 (1991), p. 248.

of consolidation of appropriate playing styles, 'there is serious concern that where a search to rediscover the sounds and styles of nineteenth-century music conflicts with the exigencies of the recording studio and the need to obtain a neat and tidy assimilable product, it is the latter that are regarded as paramount . . . The public is in danger of being offered attractively packaged but unripe fruit.' How can the fruit be ripened? Clearly it is essential to become as knowledgeable as possible in relation to historical compromises. In any period, nationality of instrument and playing technique is highly significant, and this factor needs to be assigned its proper weight. Difficulties relating to equipment have arisen partly because of the sheer variety ideally required, and partly because of the status of today's period orchestras as freelance operations.

The problems of balancing twentieth-century aspirations with earlier elements in a broader musical context have been brought into focus in another article by Clive Brown,[6] in which he produces evidence of a sharp decline in musical standards from a peak at the end of the eighteenth century, which 'came at the end of an era when the material stability and stylistic certainty which lay at its root were already under threat from powerful external and internal forces'. He attributes the problem to a lack of adequate rehearsal or efficient direction, and to the absence of a conservatoire which could produce players with a common style. Since Viennese orchestras amounted to collections of individuals of highly varying ability, any notion of a distinctive style of orchestral playing is misguided. Brown's entire article acts as a timely reminder as to the degree of choice and taste that today's period performers are called upon to exercise. Significantly, he believes that any idea of how an orchestra actually played remains highly speculative. It should be noted that inflection and nuance receive great attention in the many instrumental tutors published during Beethoven's lifetime, and were a clear priority of the players themselves. On the other hand, it is still true that detailed research into historical playing techniques, which could pave the way for a real differentiation between the sound and articulation of the wind sections known to, say, Beethoven, Cherubini and Rossini, is still in its infancy. The New Grove Handbook, *Performance Practice* invites further research into various areas of this type of study, whilst of all the treatises dealing with wind instruments in the Beethoven era, Froehlich's *Vollständige theoretisch-praktische Musikschule* (Bonn, 1811–12) in particular deserves further investigation.

THE SCORES AS EVIDENCE

Beethoven's 'classicising' period

Organological work has tended to be conducted with insufficient attention to the music played by the very instruments under discussion. Scores can begin to

6 Clive Brown, 'The Orchestra in Beethoven's Vienna', *Early Music*, 16/1 (1988), pp. 4–20.

illuminate a variety of important issues, such as the relative importance of each of the woodwinds within the orchestra, the role of instruments such as the C clarinet (with implications for the desirability of its retention in modern performance), the inhibiting effect of upper range limits and the tailoring of idiom to suit contemporary instruments (e.g. the hand-horn). Of course, tutors give some idea of how instruments were used, together with a range of technical possibilities, though these latter were not infrequently exceeded by composers. Surviving instruments cannot *per se* give a clear idea of the contexts in which they were used, though occasionally some specifications of a soloist's instrument are known, as with Heinrich Baermann's ten-keyed clarinet, on which he played the concertos of Weber. In Beethoven's dealings with wind instruments his ideals had to be tempered by a knowledge of their characteristics and (by comparison with some other instruments) their limitations. He demanded of his wind players a radical increase in volume (and endurance) allied to a technical fluency over a wide range of idioms and dynamics, and also the ability to play in a much wider variety of tonalities than hitherto. Virtuoso wind writing had been an important feature of the later eighteenth century (the Mannheim composers producing some spectacular examples), but with few exceptions there had remained a clear distinction between solo and orchestral practice. All the eighteenth-century woodwinds were fluent in certain keys, as illustrated in Mozart's various wind concertos. The clarinet was treated with particular caution in this respect, and certainly the interval of a twelfth between its registers was a limiting factor; in 1764 as many as seven sizes of clarinet had been reported,[7] and although Mozart restricted himself to the four pitched in A, B♭, B♮ and C, he instructed Thomas Attwood to write parts for the instrument only in the keys of F and C. Naturally, Mozart's own practice was somewhat more flexible than this might imply. The clarinet is an instrument which underwent a radical development in virtuoso capabilities during Beethoven's career, but individual players must have been taken aback by the sheer variety of expression increasingly demanded in orchestral contexts. Beethoven was at the forefront of developments rather than following them, and his writing undoubtedly hastened manufacturers' efforts to produce winds and brass of omnitonic possibilities.

Nonetheless, it was only in orchestral contexts that wind instruments contributed to Beethoven's stylistic innovations, for although he often carried his technical demands to the very limit of what was possible, he undoubtedly came to recognise that wind instruments were more limited in scope than, say, the piano or string quartet. Wind chamber music was thus only an attractive proposition to Beethoven during what Charles Rosen has called his 'classicising' period, where his treatment of tonality posed scarcely any new technical problems; works such as the Septet or the Quintet for piano and wind 'are reproductions of classical forms based upon

7   Valentin Roeser, *Essai d'instruction à l'usage de ceux qui composent pour la clarinette et le cor* (Paris 1764), p. 2.

the exterior models, the results of the classical impulse rather than the impulse itself'.[8] Rosen further observes that it cannot have been easy for Beethoven to abandon such facility for a more experimental approach. This was the moment at which the role of wind instruments underwent radical change, with the orchestral writing (especially for clarinet) at first remarkably cautious by comparison with his chamber music.

Beethoven's earliest use of wind instruments reveals an absorption of eighteenth-century idioms and the gathering of experience which was later to play an important part in his orchestral writing. During his period as viola player in the Bonn orchestra he came into contact with individual wind virtuosos, such as the horn player (later publisher) Nikolaus Simrock. Among Beethoven's early teachers, Schindler noted the oboist and conductor Pfeiffer[9] – and the oboe was the only wind instrument to inspire Beethoven to embark upon a concerto. Its surviving sketches, couched in the idiomatic key of F, may have been preparatory material for a completed work, since Haydn included it in a list of Beethoven's music in a letter to the Elector at Bonn.[10] The tailoring of works for individual circumstances is illustrated by the Trio WoO 37 for piano, flute and bassoon, written for the family von Westerholt, and with a particularly agile part for the bassoonist Count, ascending to b^1, a semitone higher than Mozart's Concerto K174, and actually higher than Beethoven's own later upper limit for the instrument. Fashionable combinations of instruments were an important influence, as illustrated by the Trio Op. 87 for two oboes and cor anglais and its companion Variations on 'Là ci darem la mano', composed after Beethoven heard a trio by Wendt performed at the Vienna Tonkünstler-Sozietät on 23 December 1793. Chamber music including cor anglais was cultivated extensively by composers such as the Haydn brothers, Fiala, Reicha and Triebensee. Here the virtuosity lies firmly within eighteenth-century bounds, with an upper oboe limit of d^2, rather than the f^3 exceptionally required by Mozart.

Fashionable effect is again illustrated in the Rondino WoO 25, with its prominent parts for duetting horns, a combination which was highly acclaimed by late-eighteenth-century audiences throughout Europe. Gerber commented that when a pair of horn virtuosos appeared in a concert the effect was that of a flute accompanied by a gamba;[11] he was probably referring to the famous duo Johann Palsa and Carl Thürrschmidt, the latter the inventor of a chromatic non-transposing mute

8   Charles Rosen, *The Classical Style* (London 1971), p. 380.

9   Anton Schindler, *Biographie von Ludwig van Beethoven* (Münster 1860), trans. Donald W. MacArdle as *Beethoven As I Knew Him* (London 1966), p. 39.

10 Alexander W. Thayer, *Ludwig van Beethovens Leben*, trans. and rev. Elliot Forbes as *Thayer's Life of Beethoven* (Princeton 1964), p. 144.

11 Ernst Ludwig Gerber, *Historisches-Biographisches Lexicon der Tonkünstler* (Leipzig 1792), art. 'Spörken', quoted in Horace Fitzpatrick, *The Horn and Horn-Playing and the Austro-Bohemian Tradition from 1680 to 1830* (London 1970), p. 225.

which enabled instant echo effects (including stopped notes) to delight the audience. It was probably at the hands of the Bohemian brothers Anton and Ignaz Beck that Beethoven first heard this effect, since they played frequently in Vienna and were described in a 1787 review as being among the few artists who played this seldom well-played instrument to perfection.[12] Like so many of the wind instruments, the horn's affinity with the human voice attracted especial critical acclaim. The *Jahrbuch der Tonkunst von Wien und Prag* (1796) remarked that, as far as the actual number of its notes was concerned, this instrument was poor, but that the composer who knew how to use the horn well could arouse remarkable sensations with it, including love's complaints, repose, melancholy, horror and awe. The virtuoso, continued the writer, had much to overcome in the way of embouchure and pitching, but also had at his command a wonderful array of melting, floating and dying-away effects.[13]

From the outset, Beethoven's horn writing reflects an understanding of the respective roles of high and low players, in which the *cor basse* was in no way inferior; indeed, some of the principal virtuosos such as Thürrschmidt were low players, with legendary hand-stopping technique and the ability to cover wide leaps. The role of the second horn is a vital element in Beethoven's scoring and his knowledge of associated idioms finds an early illustration in the Sextet Op. 81b, which has long retained a reputation as a formidable challenge: the first edition of Grove's *Dictionary of Music* stated baldly that it was so difficult as to be never played.[14] This comment is in itself a reflection of the subsequent decline in specialised hand-horn technique; whilst the Sextet's first horn part demonstrates agility in the high register, the second is characterised by the use of pedal notes, brisk arpeggios including leaps, and a variety of stopped notes (Ex. 4.1). Arpeggios were something of a second horn visiting card, as for example towards the end of the opening movement of the Octet Op. 103. This kind of writing is typical of the figures illustrated in tutors of the period, such as Domnich's *Méthode de premier et de second cor* (Mainz 1808), in which the author recommends that a pupil should elect from his first lesson which register he will adopt. The Piano Quintet illustrates even in its introduction the characteristic leaps and arpeggios of the *cor basse*, and in the slow movement the horn solo episode is an effective example of a melodic passage integrating stopped notes, whose dramatic use recurs throughout the finale. Beethoven's horn writing is inextricably bound up with the nature of the instrument; when the Horn Sonata was premiered by Giovanni Punto on 18 April 1800, critics enthused in particular over Punto's voice-like quality and his equal command of both high and low registers. Here again are arpeggios and leaps, free use of melodic stopped notes and, in the first movement, a daring use of the factitious G between the fundamental

12 Fitzpatrick, *The Horn*, p. 204.   13 In *ibid.*, p. 180.
14 *Dictionary*, ed. G. Grove, I, p. 750, art. 'Horn'.

Ex. 4.1   Beethoven: Sextet Op. 81b, first movement, bars 88–100 (horns)

and first partial of the horn's bass sub-octave, pointing to a prowess in this register remarkable even for a second horn. The Septet also has a true *cor basse* part, with a chromatic solo in the Adagio, featured triplet arpeggios in the Trio of the Menuet (described in the first edition of Grove's *Dictionary of Music* as 'a trying passage'),[15] and a solo chromatic scale in the introduction to the Finale. Knowledge of Beethoven's early solo use of the hand-horn is essential for an understanding of the procedures in his orchestral parts. The introduction of valves, which became widespread only some considerable time after Beethoven's death, remained controversial throughout the nineteenth century, and the substantial nature of this very change meant that by comparison with early-nineteenth-century woodwinds, the older type of horn was never quite forgotten.

In relation to the double-reed instruments, Beethoven proved himself to have completely absorbed the Viennese serenade tradition. In the Octet, the oboe takes the leading role until the Finale, and is clearly differentiated in character and idiom from the clarinet. The Piano Quintet invites comparison with its supposed model, Mozart's K452, but differs from it not only in the integration of its musical style, but in its symptomatic choice of clarinet rather than oboe as carrier of the principal material. The low accompanying oboe writing which results was not unknown to Mozart, as shown at the beginning of the Adagio of his Serenade K361, but the relationship of oboe and clarinet in Beethoven's Quintet was undoubtedly a new

15 *ibid.*

departure. His bassoon writing in chamber music retains Mozart's freedom, with flexible melodic writing for the principal player up to ab^2, anticipating later virtuoso orchestral contexts such as the Violin Concerto. The early chamber music with wind all lies within convenient tonalities, of crucial importance in the case of the clarinet, where Beethoven's orchestral practice is at first absurdly cautious. Of course, Mozart's special relationship with Anton Stadler had borne fruit not only in solo works but also in orchestral parts – a project such as his arrangement of Handel's *Acis and Galatea* illustrates the extent to which the clarinet was taking over from the oboe as the principal woodwind colour in Mozart's palette. Haydn's conservative clarinet parts are much more typical of the period, though he did become more daring in *The Creation* and *The Seasons*, intended for Viennese rather than English clarinettists.

Beethoven's fluent clarinet writing in the Octet and Rondino is couched within the amenable keys of Eb and Bb – F and C for Bb clarinet. The Rondino includes an exercise in the use of the chalumeau register – an area of the instrument he generally used with caution, particularly in comparison with contemporaries such as Weber. The Sextet Op. 71 belongs to an important tradition of ensemble writing for clarinets, horns and bassoons, discussed as early as 1764 by Roeser. In the 1760s the operas of J. C. Bach had made a feature of this texture, and Mozart later used it for the original version of his Serenade K375 and in the garden scene of *Così fan tutte*. It remained important to Beethoven throughout his life, in orchestral contexts ranging from the C major Piano Concerto to the Ninth Symphony. Clarinet parts in the Quintet and Septet reveal a similar concentration on the upper register, with melodic idioms which were sometimes chromatic within essentially grateful tonalities; occasionally a relatively plain usage of the chalumeau register occurs. The popularity of the Septet within Beethoven's lifetime is well known, and it won immediate enthusiasm from clarinettists: Weber's friend Baermann wrote of the slow movement solo that the artist who managed to perform this beautiful motif with the same intimacy and warmth which Beethoven thought and felt should grip and inspire every listener.[16] In terms of tonality this movement is significant for being in the subdominant of Ab rather than the dominant of Bb preferred in the wind ensemble pieces; clarinet tutors of the period agree that flat keys rather than sharp were easier to negotiate. More revealing of Beethoven's growing confidence in the clarinet is his decision to frame the solo around the 'break' of the instrument, a part of the compass which Mozart had also not been afraid to explore. Overall, Beethoven was already aware of the dramatic and lyrical qualities of the clarinet, which are nicely illustrated in the Variations of the Trio Op. 11. In terms of sheer power and dramatic potential, the clarinet alone of the woodwinds was well placed

16 Baermann's contribution to Gustav Schilling's *Beethoven-Album* of 1846, quoted in Pamela Weston, *Clarinet Virtuosi of the Past* (London 1971), p. 148.

to respond to Beethoven's increasing range of expression, though the question of whether it could also cope with shifts of tonality and extreme keys seems to have posed a problem for the composer which never completely receded.

Beethoven's orchestra

Orchestral music was immediately a more controversial area for the winds, as was shown by the performance difficulties surrounding the *Cantata on the Death of Joseph II* of 1790 – Wegeler's *Notizen* remarked that this cantata was supposed to be performed in Mergentheim, but that several places were so difficult for the wind players that some musicians explained that they were unplayable and the performance was cancelled.[17] Thayer notes that the premiere, scheduled to take place at a memorial celebration on 19 March, was also cancelled, minutes of a preparatory meeting two days earlier stating that for various reasons the proposed cantata could not be performed. Even assuming an innate conservatism among members of the Bonn orchestra, it is worth speculating upon what aspects of the score might have thrown the wind players into confusion. In the chorus which opens and closes the work, the shifting tonality would have been quite unfamiliar; indeed, Brahms later commented admiringly upon all the typical characteristics which could be observed and associated with Beethoven's later works.[18] Thus, more than any of Beethoven's other works of the 1790s, this was effectively a taste of things to come; difficulties for the wind lay not so much in executing demanding solos, as in coping with an unfamiliar, wide-ranging tonal idiom allied to variable rhythms in recitative style. In the actual recitative which follows the opening number, the tonality indeed shifts to such a degree that Beethoven omits any key signature, even for the B♭ clarinets – a notational device rare at this time but more common later.

Increasingly, Beethoven's choice of keys took into account the capabilities and characteristics of wind instruments only as part of the overall equation. Schindler noted Beethoven's enthusiasm for Daniel Schubart's observations on the characters of the various keys, even though Beethoven was not always in full agreement;[19] his admiration for *Die Zauberflöte* derived partly from Mozart's use of various keys according to their specific psychical qualities. All the woodwinds had to cope with a much wider range of tonalities than hitherto; in addition, Beethoven's interim use of extreme keys posed special problems for the clarinet and its notation, particularly in late works such as the Ninth Symphony. Another difficulty was the overall demand for more dynamic intensity and sheer stamina, reflected in the provision of doubled wind for some large-scale performances, e.g. in programmes of 1813 and

17 In Thayer/Forbes, *Beethoven*, p. 101.
18 *ibid.*, p. 102.
19 Schindler, *Biographie*, p. 366.

1814 including the premieres of the Seventh and Eighth Symphonies. Reports of performance difficulties in Beethoven's music were legion and often single out the wind instruments; an early example was the celebrated review of the premiere of the First Symphony in the *Allgemeine musikalische Zeitung*, which reckoned that its only flaw was that the wind instruments were used too much, so that there was more *Harmonie* than orchestral music as a whole. In the second part of the symphony the players became so lax that despite all efforts on the part of the conductor no fire whatsoever could be got out of them, particularly from the wind instruments.[20] Elsewhere, plenty of specific difficulties were cited: Schindler noted of the allegro in the Overture 'Leonora' No. 2 that a considerable portion of this version was always spoiled by the woodwinds, while of 'Leonora' No. 3 that the strings as well as the woodwind were unable to perform the running passage at the end of the overture to the satisfaction of the composer.[21] In each case clarity of execution was surely the deficient element. Among reports of early performances of the symphonies, Carse notes of the 'Eroica' that in Leipzig in 1807, Rochlitz willingly gave extra rehearsals gratis in order to master what he regarded as the most difficult of all symphonies, even in terms of merely playing the right notes. Two years later the Fifth was not very successful, on account of the great difficulties.[22]

From a strictly technical viewpoint, Beethoven's symphonies remained playable on the Classical woodwinds known to Haydn and Mozart, though the delicacy of such instruments rendered them increasingly inappropriate, and craftsmen such as Grundmann and the Grensers designed instruments that were essentially more powerful, whatever the complexity of their keywork. As we have noted, there was much controversy as to the benefits of extra mechanism; in France, the earliest oboe professors at the Paris Conservatoire, Sallantin and Vogt, maintained an allegiance to the four-keyed instrument, the latter arguing against contemporary nine-keyed German instruments on the grounds that they were liable to leakage, and also that the keys tended to endanger the stopping of adjacent finger-holes. Vogt's pupil Brod, on the other hand, set about improving the instrument with delicate, practical keywork, and won high praise for his submission. The clarinet exhibited a wide variety of approach: in 1813 Müller submitted to the Paris Conservatoire a thirteen-keyed 'omnitonique' B♭ clarinet, but found the judges loath to abandon the various colours of existing clarinet sizes, whereas in Italy the virtuoso Cavallini (1807–70) reputedly used a six-keyed clarinet throughout his career. Leakage of pads seems to have been a constant threat to players: the virtuosos Stadler and Backofen both lay some emphasis on the importance of maintenance.[23] In 1808 an anonymous

---

20 Thayer/Forbes *Beethoven*, p. 255.
21 Schindler, *Biographie*, p. 128.
22 Adam Carse, *The Orchestra from Beethoven to Berlioz* (Cambridge 1948), p. 133.
23 See discussion in Colin Lawson, 'The Basset Clarinet Revived', *Early Music*, 15/4 (1987), pp. 487–501.

contributor to the *Allgemeine musikalische Zeitung* recommended at least nine keys on the clarinet to avoid dull and scarcely usable notes in the chalumeau register and addressed the usual counter-arguments by stating that his own new clarinet had been played daily for nine months without needing a single repair.

Beethoven frequently discussed instrumental capabilities with players: Schindler records that Joseph Friedlowsky taught Beethoven the mechanics of the clarinet, and Carl Scholl similarly the flute. As for general developments in instrument manufacture, the principal outlets for discussion (in addition to tutors) were journals such as the *Allgemeine musikalische Zeitung* and *Cäcilia* in Germany and the *Harmonicon* in England. Of particular importance were articles on the acoustics of wind instruments, on improvements to the bassoon, and on the clarinet and basset horn published in *Cäcilia* by its founder Gottfried Weber during the 1820s. Of all Beethoven's orchestral instruments, the clarinet shows an unparalleled development from poor relation to a positively favourite tone-colour. Its first contributions tend to be in association with bassoons and horns within amenable tonalities, rather than as an integrated member of the woodwind section. As already noted, this type of serenade texture occurs in the central movement of the First Piano Concerto (where the outer movements are restricted to cautious tutti parts, playing virtually no part in woodwind dialogue) and together with flute in the scena and aria, 'Ah! perfido'. For the clarinets, the Triple Concerto is a direct parallel to the Piano Concerto, with a change from C to B♭ instruments for the A♭ slow movement. (Changes of clarinet immediately prior to solos were a new difficulty, arising from the more distant wide-ranging key relationships between movements.) For a further period, Beethoven's confident handling of the clarinet was restricted to a variety of contexts with bassoons and horns, as in the second subject of the first movement and in the slow movement of the Second Symphony. The Third Piano Concerto presents related combinations such as oboe with clarinets and bassoons, and during woodwind dialogue the clarinet at last begins to achieve a certain prominence. However, the C major recapitulation of the second subject in the first movement excludes the (B♭) clarinets in order to avoid the written key of D, a tonality consistently warned against in tutors. Much more remarkable is the wholesale abandonment of the clarinets during the coda to the finale, again in C major. D major was was certainly an ungrateful key for the clarinet, but Beethoven exhibits here an extraordinary caution: almost twenty years previously Mozart had ventured into this tonality for the coda of the Serenade K388 and later for the whole of his overture to *La clemenza di Tito* (Ex. 4.2), and in both cases the two sharps were notated as accidentals in the score.

Beethoven's caution in the Third Piano Concerto illustrates the continued reputation of the clarinet as highly limited in relation to tonality, despite its virtuoso ability in amenable keys. It also explains why the C clarinet continued to flourish –

Ex. 4.2   Mozart: Overture *La clemenza di Tito* K621, bars 2–4 (clarinets)

this instrument was specifically recommended for the keys of C, F and G in Backofen's tutor of 1802, provided the music was suited to its particular tonal properties. Whereas Mozart had instinctively taken account of different orchestral colours in each key during the process of selection, with Beethoven, the technical solutions were perhaps of secondary importance. The 'Eroica' was formulated in a key which was eminently suitable for clarinets, and along with this came a more confident and integrated approach, though always with restrictions imposed by the prevalent tonality in any given passage. The slow movement of the Fourth Symphony has a new type of texture featuring long cantabile solos in the upper register, which had been something of a rarity in Mozart's orchestra, where the clarinets are generally in pairs. Meanwhile, the question of Beethoven's tonality continued to produce some unusual solutions in respect of notation; the first 'Leonora' overture indicates a willingness to include B♭ clarinets in C major (to avoid a change of instrument within the piece), but not to write an actual key signature of two sharps for them. In fact, Beethoven retains a quite false signature of one flat to the end of the overture, again proving his exaggerated dread of D major for clarinet parts. The decision not to ask for a change of instrument within a single movement is confirmed in the second and third 'Leonora' overtures: C clarinets are now preferred and, as a result, the solo in the introduction falls in A♭. From a purely technical point of view, B♭ clarinets would have been a more obvious choice. The need to use clarinets in the overall key of G, which occurs in the Fourth Piano Concerto, scarcely arose at all in Mozart's music, a sole exception being the Notturno K437, for which he used A clarinets with a signature of two flats. Mozart never writes parts in G: in F major contexts he uses C clarinets, and in E major (in *Idomeneo* and *Così fan tutte*) he resorts to the rare clarinet in B.

Beethoven's G major Piano Concerto has prominent C clarinet parts in a wide range of tonalities, including in the first movement a B minor passage of the type tutors explicitly recommended to be avoided (Ex. 4.3). The G major slow movement of the Violin Concerto provides a parallel instance, with a change from A to C clarinets which is difficult to explain except as a matter of convention, since

Ex. 4.3   Beethoven: Piano Concerto No. 4 Op. 58, first movement, bars 124–6

the more incisive tone-colour is hardly more appropriate. The Sixth and Eighth Symphonies represent an important departure from eighteenth-century practice in preferring B♭ clarinets for the key of F; both works are of course also significant for the sheer virtuosity of the solo writing, in particular the control demanded at the top of the compass. The Trio of the Eighth Symphony expands the working compass upwards from d^2 through to g^3, Mozart's orchestral limit having been e^3; however, in 1829 Gottfried Weber was still recommending an upper limit of c^3 or d^3 for orchestral players. The sheer flexibility and range of dynamics demanded in this solo presumably shows the influence of Friedlowsky, and henceforward g^3 became Beethoven's upper limit. He soon came to expect quiet legato playing in this part of the compass, as for example at the end of the 'Credo' of the *Missa solemnis*. The effectiveness of this register was already a matter for debate in Mozart's day; Süssmayr's concerto sketch for Stadler ventures to c^4, though in 1808 the anonymous writer in the *Allgemeine musikalische Zeitung* praised Mozart's restraint in this respect.

In terms of tonality, Beethoven's later clarinet parts reflect the situation set out in Gottfried Weber's article 'Ueber Clarinett und Bassetthorn' in *Cäcilia* of 1829. Weber recommends avoidance of tonalities with more than two accidentals, and notes that some offer a choice of clarinet; highly significant is his point that further alternatives were increasingly available because every size of clarinet could now play in every key, though with varying degrees of difficulty. Thus, considerations of colour increasingly come to play a part, as in the B♭ march in *Fidelio*, which employs C, rather than B♭, clarinets. The D major 'Gloria' of the *Missa solemnis* has C clarinets, which in tone-quality suit the overall character more than a more conventional choice of A clarinets. The G major 'Benedictus' has C clarinets, which would also have been Beethoven's choice earlier in his career; we have already noted his reluctance to use a signature of two flats for A clarinets, though his increased confidence in the instrument would surely not have prevented their use here. In other words, this was a tonality which presented two radically different alternatives in terms of colour, and the use of B♭ clarinets in Weber's Mass in G indicates that a third option was rapidly becoming available. Colour is surely the primary consideration for the change to C clarinets in the D minor Scherzo of the Ninth Symphony.

Besides illustrating the traditional combination of clarinets, horns and bassoons, the slow movement of the Ninth Symphony illustrates an astonishing unwillingness to write correct but complex key signatures for the clarinets. When the tonality is D, accidentals occur before individual notes, for example. The Finale presents further examples: at bar 76 the music moves from D minor to D major and, since there is no time to change clarinets, B♭ instruments continue for fifteen bars, though without signature. The Presto at bar 208 has a single flat instead of four. Another concealment of the true key signature appears at bar 493 when, in an overall signature of two sharps, Beethoven prefers to write accidentals in front of individual notes in the clarinet parts. From a historical viewpoint, this indicates the rapidity with which the clarinet had been liberated. It has been suggested with some justification that the wide-ranging tonality of the Ninth Symphony contrasts sadly with Beethoven's hesitancy in notating the music for clarinets. One also needs to ask to what extent the different colours of various clarinets mattered to him at various stages of his life, and to bear in mind that a number of important writers such as Gottfried Weber and Berlioz, as well as the players Berr and Baermann, emphasised that the choice of clarinet should always be the responsibility of the composer rather than the player. As Beethoven's last works show, he seems to have maintained a clear view of appropriate contexts for the C clarinet at a time when, for contemporaries such as Schubert, it had become virtually restricted to usage in its home key. Schubert's Ninth Symphony, for example, retains it for the three of its movements in C, even though the Scherzo and Trio modulate at various times to both sharp and flat tonal areas. However, Mendelssohn gravitated towards the A clarinet for C major works (a practice noted in the first edition of Grove's *Dictionary*) and, notwithstanding a few C clarinet parts in the music of Liszt and Brahms, this weakened its position at a time when developments in mechanism enabled A and B♭ clarinets to be more fluent in a wider variety of keys.

The status of other woodwinds during Beethoven's lifetime was largely reflected in the demands of composers for louder and more brilliant sounds in ever larger concert rooms. In these circumstances, the clarinet was likely to remain pre-eminent as a solo instrument, and indeed there were no other woodwind concertos to match the works of Weber and Spohr, though a great number of virtuosos (particularly on the flute) had distinguished careers during the period. In the later eighteenth century the flute had lost something of the specialised emotional association it had enjoyed in Bach's works, tending to become purely an orchestral voice. The colourful if technically treacherous flat keys no longer contained the singular effect achieved in *The St Matthew Passion* and *The Musical Offering*. In Beethoven's time, the flutes most in favour ranged from four- to eight-keyed instruments (though even the one-keyed flute continued to flourish), whilst there were also instruments of very considerably greater mechanical complexity. A host of 'improvements' was developed by different players and makers: the treatise by J. G. Tromlitz *Ueber die Flöten mit mehren Klappen* (Leipzig, 1800) discusses an eight-keyed instrument, even though the author himself preferred a Quantz-type instrument. The mechanism is described in a detailed and laboured way, with a discussion of newly-available tonalities as extreme as F♯ major, but also a warning of the new obligations of maintenance implied by the new design. Significantly, when Boehm eventually came to explain his motivation for a remodelling of the flute in 1832, he claimed to have been inspired by the difficulties encountered in orchestral, rather than solo, music. He specified defects of uncertain sounding notes, problems of intonation and (significantly for performance of Beethoven) notes in which crescendo and diminuendo were problematic. He realised that the placement of holes still derived from the keyless flute, when convenience of finger-position rather than acoustical principles was a crucial factor. Nonetheless, something of a dilemma remains as to whether the Boehm flute entirely satisfies Beethoven's intentions.

The tone of the classical flute came to be regarded as its primary asset: Weber's well-known review in the *Allgemeine musikalische Zeitung* (1811) of Capeller's nine-keyed flute shows an appreciation of its improved intonation and greater facility for trills, describing the invention as perfecting the flute to an extent that hardly left anything to be desired. In other words, tone was a colour which did not need discussion. Tulou, professor at the Paris Conservatoire from 1826–56, refused to make use of the Boehm system, and in his tutor (*c.* 1835) emphasised the importance of preserving the flute's passionate and expressive tone. He reckoned that to play what was difficult with ease was doubtless a merit, but by no means the final goal. The wide range of musical character which Beethoven demanded of the flute can be well illustrated by comparing the sombre chording in the Fifth Symphony with the evocative bird-song in the 'Pastoral'. In general, his flute writing tends to be high, though the solo which begins at bar 328 of 'Leonora' No. 3 is an ambitious exception. The upper part of the range became one of the most controversial aspects of all Beethoven's wind writing. In the First Symphony, the Andante cantabile con moto at bar 51 shows an avoidance of the awkward $g^{\#3}$, and later (bar 153) the flute is silent during a doubling passage with violins, in order to avoid a^3 and $b\flat^3$ (Ex. 4.4). By the 'Eroica' the range is essentially g^1 to g^3, with occasional $a\flat^3$ and $a\natural^3$ in the first movement. Even by the Eighth Symphony $b\flat^3$ was studiously avoided, with the top of the texture distorted (e.g. at bars 186 and 387) to take account of this. Charles Nicholson's *Preceptive Lessons* (1821) provided fingerings for c^4 and d^4, claiming that he was first to introduce them in print; in fact, Francoeur's *Diapason général* had cited the range as d^1 to c^4 as early as 1772. Schubert, who wrote boldly for the flute's highest register, made an important feature of $b\flat^3$ in his Second Symphony, though it never again occurred in his work in quite so insistent a fashion. In Beethoven's Ninth Symphony the Scherzo brings problems of melodic continuity, well illustrated in bars 343 and 348 but evident throughout (Ex. 4.5). Wagner's realisation of Beethoven's intentions involved changing such passages, on the grounds that musical logic was compromised to accommodate the technologically limited instruments. His entirely responsible attitude (involving no attempt to add to the coherence or subtlety of the musical content) brings to mind the familiar argument about whether composers would have written their music in the same way, had later instruments been available to them. For Wagner, Beethoven transcended such arguments.

Ex. 4.4   Beethoven: Symphony No. 1 Op. 21, second movement, bars 152–4

Ex. 4.5   Beethoven: Symphony No. 9 Op. 125, second movement, bars 338–48

Mozart had tended to treat oboe and clarinet as alternatives, a notable example being the various dramatic situations in *Così fan tutte*. The clarinet's further dimension in terms of dynamics and expressive power enhanced its position in most areas of music-making, leaving the oboe within Beethoven's wind section in a more static role. In the 'Eroica', the delicacy of the oboe writing is paramount, the slow movement in particular illustrating this emotional area, and such contexts continued to be a valuable resource, notably in the Scherzo of the 'Pastoral' Symphony. During Beethoven's lifetime, the two-keyed oboe gradually developed into an instrument which frequently had a minimum of eight keys; this could better provide the sheer volume now demanded, as Beethoven and his contemporaries expanded the oboe's expressive range. Indeed, in 1807–8 oboes with eleven and with nine keys were procured for the Vienna Hoftheater.[24] As with the clarinet, national styles of playing were already in evidence, a French sensitivity and refinement contrasting with German warmth and robustness. Virtuosity in orchestral oboe parts was not of course the province of Beethoven alone; Haydn had been inspired by the skills of visiting artists, for example in the Scherzo and Finale of his Symphony No. 38. Schubert produced some awkward passages, for example in the Scherzo and Trio of his Sixth Symphony, including fluent writing in E major. In the Scherzo of Beethoven's Ninth Symphony, the wide-ranging tonalities within the movement demand great flexibility and virtuosity. However, it is Florestan's highly emotional aria in Act 2 of *Fidelio* which seems to extend the dramatic range of the oboe, with its highly-charged passage-work and ascents to f^3 at the word 'Freiheit'; the general possibility of this note was admitted only in Choron's *Traité général*

24   Roger Hellyer, 'Some Documents Relating to Viennese Wind-Instrument Purchases, 1779–1837', *Galpin Society Journal*, 28 (1975), pp. 51–61.

(Paris, 1813). Overall, this aria indicates Beethoven's perception of a manic side to the oboe's personality, which never really finds a parallel elsewhere in his music.

The bassoon elicited a wide variety of responses from writers, in terms both of its character and musical potential. Ozi's tutor of 1802/3 listed as many as eight troublesome notes, though he noted that it had become one of the most perfect of wind instruments thanks to recent developments, and that it could now play in all keys. Froehlich, on the other hand, describes a situation in which as many as three *corps-de-rechange* wing joints and crooks were necessary to cope with the different pitches likely to be encountered. Most bassoons still had only one or two extra keys in addition to the standard equipment of the classical instrument; different notes tended to be out of tune on different instruments, so standard fingerings were of limited value. Almenraeder's treatise (1822) noted that complicated fingerings on the old bassoon militated against flowing execution. He thus added certain keys and relocated others to improve evenness of tone and intonation; and reports of these improvements published in *Cäcilia* became known to Beethoven. Nonetheless, criticism of the bassoon continued apace; as late as 1836 Hogarth wrote of the fifteen-keyed English instrument: 'Many of the notes are false, and can only be corrected to a certain extent by the skill of the player.'[25] Berlioz wrote in 1843 (of the French bassoon) that its sonority was not very great and that its timbre, absolutely without brilliance or nobility, leaned towards the grotesque. However, from Beethoven's confident handling of the bassoon in his orchestral scores, there is no hint that this was a transitional period in its history. He follows Haydn in his extrovert solo writing, as in the coda of the slow movement of the Fifth Symphony and throughout the Violin Concerto, while expecting great fluency as early as the Introduction to the Second Symphony. The Fourth Symphony in particular illustrates a wide variety of character, with one or two extremely taxing moments. Thus, the bassoon is another instrument whose erratic organological history tends to be disguised within the pages of Beethoven's scores.

In the case of brass instruments, Beethoven distanced himself from the developments in manufacture which took place during his lifetime, writing exclusively for valveless instruments. Of these, the horn is used for the most striking effects, whereas the limitations of the natural trumpet led to its inevitable omission from climaxes in inconvenient keys, despite some idiomatic effects elsewhere. The trombone was used by Beethoven in a manner closer to French than Viennese practice, though his extremes of range make for more difficulties in performance. Notwithstanding some idiomatic effects such as its pianissimo use in the 'Benedictus' of the *Missa solemnis*, Beethoven's treatment of the trombone is overall more conservative than either Weber's or Schubert's, though he played an important part in expanding

25 George Hogarth, 'Musical Instruments: the Oboe, Bassoon and English Horn', *Musical World*, 3/38 (1836), pp. 178–81.

its sphere of operations beyond opera and church music. In the later nineteenth century the main issue of performance practice was whether to use valved trumpets and horns; Wagner was in no doubt that they should be substituted and the parts rewritten to remove any supposed limitations. On the other hand, Berlioz described the use of valves for stopped notes as a dangerous abuse, and in 1853 Gleich claimed that the use of valves in Weber and Beethoven was a 'vandalismus'.[26] Comparing the natural and valved horn, the first edition of Grove's *Dictionary* merely noted that each had its advantages. Beethoven's orchestral horn parts are only comprehensible with reference to the valveless instrument of his time, and in relation to the clearly defined roles for each player. Not surprisingly, second horn solos abound in Beethoven's scores, for example in the Allegro of the Overture *Fidelio* and in the 'Et vitam venturi' of the 'Credo' of the *Missa solemnis* (Ex. 4.6). Significantly, the 'Sanctus' has three horn parts, for second horn in E and a pair in D. Berlioz reckoned Beethoven exceedingly reserved in his horn writing, except in solos or for occasional striking effects. Even of these latter, the chromatic writing à 4 in the Priest's aria 'Will unser Genius' in *The Ruins of Athens*, with its second horn leaps and arpeggiated figures, was by no means the first quartet of its type, the Serenade K131 providing an isolated example in Mozart's music. The use of three horns in the 'Eroica' is innovatory, though the Trio is actually rather conservative in terms of hand-horn technique and musical style. Beethoven's attraction to the traditional elements in the character of the horn is well displayed in the alphorn melody which begins the last movement of the 'Pastoral' Symphony. However, it is perhaps *Fidelio* which represents a turning point in terms of the endurance and facility demanded of the players, notably in the trio of horns which accompanies the aria 'Komm Hoffnung'. Later on, chromatic solos became more common in Beethoven's music and, in assessing their effectiveness on the modern horn, one might recall Gerber's comment in 1792 that in the space of a hundred years the instrument had already been brought to a degree of perfection which left nothing more to be desired.

Ex. 4.6 Beethoven: *Missa solemnis* 'Et vitam venturi', bars 36–51

26 Ferdinand Gleich, *Handbuch der modernen Instrumentirung für Orchester und Militairmusikcorps* (Leipzig 1853), p. 37.

The manner in which Beethoven utilised each instrument to its utmost capacity is illustrated most potently in the fourth horn solo in the Adagio of the Ninth Symphony. Domnich's horn tutor cites the scale of A♭ as an exercise for both first and second horn, and although he remarks that in terms of intonation and hand-horn technique it presents some difficulties and could only be executed at moderate speed, he shows nonetheless that it clearly fell within the training of Beethoven's day. In fact, by 1823 scales in all keys on a given crook were required of horn students. Blandford's series of articles (1925) makes the point that Beethoven was here exploiting the hand-horn to its harmonic and colouristic limit; in its ultimate fulfilment of what was possible, the solo actually posed the need for the valved instrument and prepared the way for it.[27] However, as for Beethoven's own practice, his deafness makes it highly unlikely that he would have renounced his carefully acquired technique of hand-horn writing for an instrument with valves which he had never heard. It is also true that the horn writing contains fewer infractions of accepted practice than the solo voice parts. Beethoven here (as elsewhere) wrote for two pairs of horns of equal standing, the second pair pitched in a key other than the tonic, in accordance with normal convention. The tonality of the passage ensures that it is the second pair of horns which is involved, whilst the tessitura and idiom ensures that the solo will be the responsibility of the *cor basse*; indeed, Beethoven's score specifically directs 'sempre corno secondo'. In these circumstances our own notions of the role of the fourth horn player are certainly at odds with early-nineteenth-century practice. A complete understanding of this celebrated solo demands that evidence from organological and documentary research be linked to an appreciation of stylistic and technical developments within the composer's scores. Of course, this interdisciplinary approach can usefully be applied more generally throughout Beethoven's music, in order to enhance our appreciation of the various practical aspects of performance ideals current at that time.

27 Walter F. H. Blandford, 'The Fourth Horn in the Choral Symphony', *Musical Times*, 66 (1925), pp. 28–32, 124–9 and 221–3.

5

BEETHOVEN'S SONATAS FOR PIANO AND CELLO: ASPECTS OF TECHNIQUE AND PERFORMANCE

DAVID WATKIN

In 1796 Beethoven visited the Court of Friedrich Wilhelm II at Berlin, where he composed the two sonatas 'for Harpsichord or Pianoforte and Violoncello Obbligato' Op. 5. Often described as the earliest examples of Beethoven's fully emerged individual style, these sonatas were also among the first works of a new genre. The role of the cello in such works as the piano trios of Haydn and Mozart had been essentially to underpin the piano in its weak lower register. However, Mozart, on his visit to Berlin, had transformed a long-established instrumental combination in his 'Prussian' Quartets (K575, K589 and K590) by giving the King's first cellist, Jean-Pierre Duport (1741–1818) an unusually prominent role. In similar fashion Beethoven, writing for Jean-Pierre's younger brother Jean-Louis Duport (1749–1819), who had become first cellist at the court in 1789, transformed the sonata for piano and accompanying instrument into a whole new genre.

Jean-Pierre Duport, whose teacher Martin Berteau (c. 1700–71) had originally been a gamba player, was appointed first cellist at the Prussian court and cello teacher to Friedrich Wilhelm in 1773 and became one of Europe's most celebrated cellists.[1] Jean-Louis Duport freely acknowledges the influence of his elder brother in the introduction to his *Essai sur le doigté du violoncelle et sur la conduite de l'archet* (Paris, c. 1806), which was one of the first thorough and systematic methods for the cello. A rich source of information on matters of technique and style, it represented the culmination of a French school of cello playing founded by Berteau, but its influence on successive generations was considerable.

In January 1797, Beethoven performed the Op. 5 Sonatas in Vienna with Bernhard Romberg (1767–1841), a former colleague from the Bonn Court opera orchestra and the chief inspiration for a German school of cello playing which was dominant throughout most of the nineteenth century. Romberg was also a composer of some distinction, one Leipzig reviewer comparing his abilities as composer and performer to those of Mozart.[2] Romberg's career successfully spanned nearly fifty years, during which he was appointed professor at the Paris Conservatoire

---

1 Mozart wrote a set of Variations K573 for piano on a minuet by Jean-Pierre Duport.
2 *Allgemeine musikalische Zeitung*, 9 (1806–7), 543.

(1801–3), and solo cellist (1805) and *Kapellmeister* (1815–19) at the Prussian court. He completed his *Violoncell Schule* in 1839.

Another important cellist in Beethoven's circle was Anton Kraft (1749–1820), the author of a technically spectacular cello concerto (*c.* 1790), which Beethoven may have heard him play in Vienna in 1804. Also believed to be a collaborator in Haydn's D major concerto (Hob. VIIb: 2), Kraft came into contact with Beethoven as a member of Schuppanzigh's Quartet, and he was the cellist Beethoven had in mind for the Triple Concerto Op. 56. However, it was J. J. Friedrich Dotzauer (1783–1860), a founder-member of the nineteenth-century German school, who eventually took the cello part in the first public performance of the Triple Concerto (May 1808). Dotzauer had studied with J. L. Duport's pupil, Krieg, and may have had some contact with both Romberg and Beethoven. The French translator of his *Violoncellschule* (*c.* 1825) claims categorically that the treatise was based on Romberg's fundamental principles.

In 1808 Schuppanzigh founded the famous Razumovsky Quartet which, with Joseph Linke (1783–1837) as cellist, was renowned for its performances of Beethoven's works. Little is known about Linke's playing, but he appears to have frequently made himself available to try out certain passages for Beethoven,[3] most notably when the two Sonatas Op. 102 were written during a retreat to the Countess Erdödy's country residence. Along with the Duports, Romberg, Kraft and Dotzauer, he was one of the principal cellists in Beethoven's circle during a period of remarkable musical, organological and technical change. It is the aim of this essay to establish some of this circle's approaches to technique and style, so that these may be taken into consideration by cellists who are contemplating performances of Beethoven's sonatas and indeed, other works for the instrument.

An article in the *Allgemeine musikalische Zeitung* (1809) discussed 'an unusual fingerboard which some cellists use, namely where the C string can lie higher from the fingerboard than the other three strings'. The writer cautiously dismisses the new 'invention' claiming that 'one can do just as well without this, what one can do with it'.[4] Romberg, who experimented extensively with the arrangement and repair of instruments,[5] is believed to have developed this invention (Fig. 5.1a), a predecessor of the modern fingerboard.[6] He explains that 'many players find it inconvenient to play with grooves in the fingerboard, and yet without them the G,

3 *The Letters of Beethoven* (London 1961), ed. and trans. Emily Anderson, p. 482.

4 *Allgemeine musikalische Zeitung*, 11 (1808–9), 593: 'Verschiedene Violoncellisten bedienen sich eines andern Griffbretts als des gewöhnlichen; eines solchen nämlich wo die C Saite vom Griffbrett angerechnet, höher liegen kann, als die drei übrigen Saiten . . . So viel ist gewiss, dass man auch ohne dieselbe alles das leisten kann, was man mit dieselben leist.'

5 Bernhard Romberg, *Violoncell Schule* (Berlin 1840), trans. (London 1840), p. 2.

6 Spohr credits Romberg with this development in his *Violinschule*, p. 10. See also Louis Spohr, *Selbstbiographie*, (2 vols., Kassel and Göttingen 1860–1), trans. (1865; rpr. 1969), I, p. 78.

5.1a   Romberg's fingerboard (shown in cross-section): Bernhard Romberg, *Violoncell Schule* (Berlin 1840), frontispiece

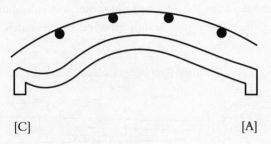

[C]   [A]

5.1b   A typical Baroque cello fingerboard (cross-section)

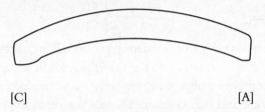

[C]   [A]

5.1c   A typical modern cello fingerboard (cross-section)

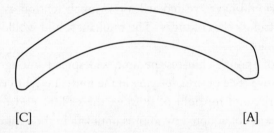

[C]   [A]

D and A strings cannot lie in proper proportion. The C string should lie higher, otherwise it would jar when played with a strong bow.'[7] Dotzauer, whose finger-board was also grooved, adds that it is also of great benefit when playing in the higher registers of the G string.[8] It would certainly facilitate, for example, playing the opening four bars of the A major sonata Op. 69 on the G string and executing with greater attack the *sf* C-string bass notes which accompany the second subject (bars 25–6). Apart from the end-pin, Romberg's fingerboard was the final significant adjustment the cello underwent. By comparison with the flatter fingerboard of the typical eighteenth-century cello (Fig. 5.1b) it had three advantages: first, it allowed the strings to lie more closely together, facilitating high cross-string passagework; it also allowed the curvature of the bridge to be steep enough for the middle strings

7   Romberg, *Violoncell Schule*, trans., p. 2.
8   J. J. Friedrich Dotzauer, *Violoncellschule* (Mainz *c.* 1825), p. 59.

to be played with the bow one at a time; and, most importantly, it maintained each string's perpendicular angle of depression onto the fingerboard. The more easily made modern fingerboard (Fig. 5.1c) uses the same principle, but it is flat rather than grooved under the C string (although grooved fingerboards were still in use well into the current century).

5.2   Romberg's string gauge: Bernhard Romberg, *Violoncell Schule* (Berlin 1840), frontispiece

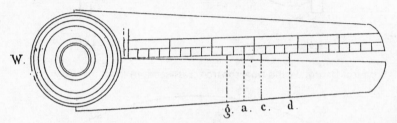

Some of Romberg's strings were evidently very thick, a quality which required them to be pressed straight down on to the fingerboard. His string gauge (Fig. 5.2) shows very thick top two strings (gut) and relatively thin bottom two (wound gut).[9] The very thick d and thin G strings allowed for a smoother change of tone-colours between these middle strings. As the elevation of the neck in Romberg's detailed plans of his own instrument differs little from most modern cellos, these thick top strings would have created at least as much tension as that exerted on most wound gut-strung cellos of today. The resultant sound would have been both powerful and resonant.

While the use of Spohr's chin-rest became widespread among violinists, along with a more expressive style of string playing in the mid nineteenth century, allowing them greater security and freedom of shifting, the cellist's end-pin, though long used by amateurs, was not adopted by soloists until late in the century. The manner of holding the cello described in Duport's *Essai*, as in most nineteenth-century methods, required the instrument to be held securely, 'so that the lower left-hand corner of the back may fall into the hollow of the left knee, and the weight of the instrument may be borne on the calf of the left leg, the foot being brought forwards . . . The right leg must be placed against the lower side of the instrument to keep it steady'[10] (see, for example, Fig. 5.3). Without the security of an end-

---

9 Romberg's gauge results in the following approximate measurements for the thickness of strings: a – 1.50mm gut; d – 2.00mm gut; G – 1.25mm wound gut; C – 1.75mm wound gut. A less accurate gauge of Dotzauer gives: a – 1.15mm; d – 1.95mm. 'Medium-gauge' strings in use today (in period instrument performance) are most commonly a – 1.2mm. gut; d – 1.45mm. gut; G – 1.425mm. wound gut; C – 1.9mm. wound gut.

10 Jean-Louis Duport, *Essai sur le doigté du violoncelle et sur la conduite de l'archet* (Paris c. 1806), p. 5: 'de façon que le coin de l'échancrure inférieure d'en bas à gauche, se trouve dans la jointure du genou gauche, afin que le poids de l'instrument soit porté sur le mollet de la jambe gauche; et le pied gauche en dehors . . . La jambe droite se pose contre l'éclisse d'en bas de l'instrument, pour le maintenir en sûreté.'

5.3   Bernhard Romberg, *Violoncell Schule* (Berlin 1840), facing p. 9

pin, cellists had to rely on the contact of the left hand with the neck and strings for certainty of intonation, and a continuous, fierce vibrato was less practicable. They sought instead to produce as much resonance as possible from their instruments.

5.4   The resonant notes of the cello according to Duport: Jean-Louis Duport, *Essai sur le doigté du violoncelle et sur la conduite de l'archet* (Paris c.1806), trans. (London 1840), p. 141

TABLE OF THE SOUNDS WHICH HAVE SEVERAL PERCEPTIBLE RESONANCES.

2 Resonances By the unison of the G string.	2 Resonances By the octave of the C string.	2 Resonances By the unison of the D string.	3 Resonances By the octave of the G string and the 12th of the C string.
2 Resonances By the unison of the A string.	2 Resonances By the double octave or 15th of the C string.	3 Resonances By the 8th of the D string and the 12th of the G string	2 Resonances By the 17th of the C string.
3 Resonances By the 15th of the G string and the 19th of the C string.	2 Resonances By the 12th of the D string.	2 Resonances By the 17th of the G string.	2 Resonances By the triple octave of the C string.
3 Resonances By the 15th of the D string and the 19th of the C string.	2 Resonances By the 17th of the D string.	2 Resonances By the triple octave or 22nd of the G string.	

11726

The treatises of Duport, Dotzauer and Romberg contain clues as to this quest for resonance, each explaining the phenomenon of sympathetic vibrations as applied to the cello. Duport includes a table (Fig. 5.4) which plots the particularly resonant notes of the cello. He explains that an understanding of the 'coalition of vibrations' is of great value towards both the production of a pure tone and the regulation of intonation. Although he admits that it can only rarely be put into practice, Duport suggests an 'assisted' resonance for the two notes on the cello which are 'very harsh' – the e and f on the d string: 'If the lower octave of these notes is taken by another finger on the fourth string, as indicated below [Ex. 5.1], the second string will be found to vibrate very well, and will produce a sonorous and agreeable sound.'[11] Dotzauer also suggests a similar treatment for the e♭ and f♯ on the d string.

Ex. 5.1   Duport *Essai*, p. 143

Ex. 5.2a   Duport: *Essai*, Exercise 6, bars 42–3 (ed. Grützmacher)

(*cresc. poco a poco* -)

Ex. 5.2b   Duport: *Essai*, Exercise 6, bars 42–3

Ex. 5.3a   Duport: *Essai*, Exercise 20, bars 6–7

Ex. 5.3b   Duport: *Essai*, Exercise 20, bars 6–7 (ed Grützmacher)

(*cresc.*- - - - - - -) *f*

The high priority given to resonance is sometimes reflected in contemporary fingerings, notably those in the first edition (*c.* 1806) of Duport's *21 Exercices* (forming Part 2 of the *Essai*); Duport's prescriptions make an interesting comparison with later versions such as that of Friedrich Grützmacher (1832–1903), widely used nowadays. In Ex. 5.2a Grützmacher resolves the augmented fourth without shifting. Duport, who otherwise insists on resolving the *Quatre superflue* in one

11 Duport, *Essai*, p. 142: 'si l'on prend l'octave grave de ces tons avec un autre doigt sur la quatrième corde, comme je vais le marquer on trouvera que la seconde corde vibrera très-bien, et rendra un son agréable et sonore'.

position, allows the suspended g^1 to be taken by the same finger throughout its duration (see Ex. 5.2b). He was not averse to violating his own fingering rules in order to benefit from the resonance achieved by keeping one finger on a held note, even if it is not actually sustained by the bow. For example, the more resonant gamba-style cross-fingering of Ex. 5.3a, which allows the third finger to be held down until after the second finger has been depressed, is preferred to lifting the finger from the string to its parallel place on the adjacent string (Ex. 5.3b). Ex. 5.3a also illustrates Duport's preference for fingerings which follow the sequential patterns of the harmony, while Grützmacher generally gives convenience a higher priority. In Ex. 5.4a, Duport's colourful fingering, which emphasises each bar, is ironed out in Grützmacher's more logical version (Ex. 5.4b); similarly, Grützmacher uses a simple E♭ major scale fingering (Ex. 5.5b) as opposed to Duport's preference for the darker colour of the G string, using a typical late-eighteenth-century ploy of ascending with the usual scale fingering and remaining in thumb position for the descent[12] (Ex. 5.5a).

Ex. 5.4a   Duport: *Essai*, Exercise 20, bars 68–9

Ex. 5.4b   Duport: *Essai*, Exercise 20, bars 68–9 (ed. Grützmacher)

Ex. 5.5a   Duport: *Essai*, Exercise 18, bars 34–6

Ex. 5.5b   Duport: *Essai*, Exercise 18, bars 34–6 (ed. Grützmacher)

12 Duport, *Essai*, p. 22. See, for example, Haydn's D major Concerto Hob. VIIb: 2, 1/44–5 and 68–9.
    N.B. In the musical examples from Duport (1806) a = open string (a vide); o = thumb ('Q' nowadays).

Ex. 5.5a gives the lie to the assumption that Duport preferred to stay in the lower positions while his successor ventured rather more across the strings. Even without Romberg's grooved fingerboard, Duport was perfectly familiar with the problems of playing in the high positions on the lower strings, explaining the importance of regulating bow pressure according to each string thus:

In general, the force of the bow should be sparingly used on the first string; for which reason we should accustom ourselves to ascend on the second string as often as possible, if we wish to obtain great equality of sound . . . and it will assuredly be often found that an advantage will be gained in regard to equality of sound and quality of tone, by ascending on the second or even on the third string.[13]

In addition to the practice of scales on one string for all four strings, Duport recommends the preparation of conventional scales avoiding the use of open strings, but 'only for professors or very advanced amateurs'. (See, for example, Beethoven's Op. 69, 1/38–9). Duport gives the standard fingering for a scale of B♭ major played *détaché* but avoids open strings in slurred bowing in the interests of cultivating greater evenness of tone.[14]

Duport aimed to cultivate an expressive, singing style through the equalisation of all the sounds of the instrument in each part of the bow. By contrast, Dotzauer, like Baillot,[15] emphasises the different characteristics of each string:

The great capacity of the cello is that of producing a wide variety of characters. Serious and meaningful thoughts, which the composer gives to the deeper bass notes, never lose their effect when executed with strength. The notes of the a and d strings are very beguiling and in this, the region of the tenor, a performer gifted of feeling may speak to hearts. The upper and highest notes of the soprano [the French version has here 'produced by means of the thumb'] seem well suited to lively fancy and jokes.[16]

That Dotzauer mentioned the d string alongside the a suggests that he used it frequently, and his treatise includes examples of colourful exploitation of the d string (Exs. 5.6 and 5.7). Romberg advocates similar use of the d string (Ex. 5.8),

---

13 Duport, *Essai*, pp. 164–5: 'En général on doit ménager la force de l'archet sur la chanterelle, voilà pourquoi on doit s'habituer à monter le plus souvent possible par la seconde corde, si on veut obtenir une grande égalité de son . . . et sûrement on trouvera souvent de l'avantage à monter par la seconde, et même par la troisième, pour l'égalité et la qualité du son.'

14 *ibid.*, p. 19.

15 Pierre Baillot, *L'Art du violon* (Paris 1834), pp. 140–4; cited in Robin Stowell, *Violin Technique and Performance Practice in the Late Eighteenth and Early Nineteenth Centuries* (Cambridge 1985), pp. 131–6.

16 Dotzauer, *Violoncellschule*, p. 1: 'Der bedeutende Umfang des Violonzell's verstattet eine grosse Mannigfaltigkeit des Charakter's. Ernste und bedeutende Gedanken, welche der Componist den tiefern Basstönen giebt, verfehlen mit Kraft vorgetragen wie ihre Wirkung. Die Töne der A und D Saite haben viel einschmeichelndes, und in dieser Region des Tenor's ist dem empfindungsvollen Spieler möglich zum Herzen zu sprechen. Die obern und höchsten Töne des Sopran's scheinen sich mehr zu muntrer Laune und Scherz zu eignen.'

while Baudiot encourages the use of the combined colours of open string and its equivalent stopped note to disguise a string-change (Ex. 5.9).[17] (See Op. 69, 3/19–20)

Ex. 5.6   Dotzauer: *Violoncellschule*, p. 90

Ex. 5.7   Dotzauer: *Violoncellschule*, p. 46

Ex. 5.8   Romberg: *Violoncell Schule*, p. 99

Ex. 5.9   Baudiot: *Méthode de violoncelle*, Vol. II p. 37

The acceptance of the Tourte-model bow was perhaps the most significant development in string playing during Beethoven's lifetime. Duport's parting comment in his *Essai* leaves little doubt that its use was already widespread.[18] However, while a bow's design may make new types of stroke possible, the player's manner of using it remains the crucial factor in determining performing style. Duport, for example, discusses different types of slurring patterns and points to Tartini as the founder of them all.[19]

Most sources between 1768 and 1820 suggest that the bow was held further away from the frog than it is nowadays. Romberg, however, has his fourth finger 'covering the nut'[20] (see Figs. 5.3 and 5.5) and Baudiot has the hand 'very close to the frog'.[21] Dotzauer recommends having the thumb as near to the frog as possible but claims that 'Professors are scarcely in agreement over the manner of holding [the bow].

17   Charles-Nicolas Baudiot, *Méthode de violoncelle* 2 vols., (Paris 1826 and 1828), II, p. 37.

18   Duport, *Essai*, p. 175.

19   *ibid.*, p. 166.

20   Romberg, *Violoncell Schule*, trans. (London, 1840) p. 7.

21   Baudiot, *Méthode de violoncelle*, I, p. 8: 'tout près de la hausse'.

5.5   Romberg's manner of holding the bow: Bernhard Romberg, *Violoncell Schule* (Berlin 1840), facing p. 8

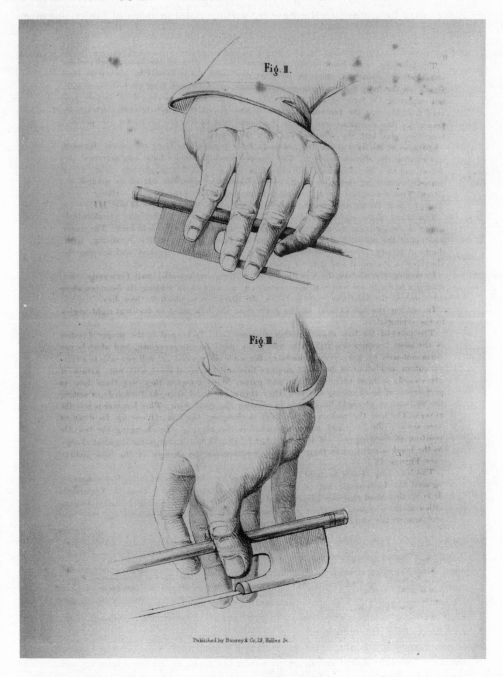

One finds that the best players hold the bow as near to the frog as possible, while the others leave a shorter [playing length of] bow. An excess of either way is harmful.'[22]

Power may be applied to the bow by various combinations of finger-pressure, forearm pronation and arm-weight. Duport describes a bow hold in which the first finger is allowed to move along the stick to give more 'support' to the bow as necessary, implying the use of pronation.[23] Although Leopold Mozart warns violinists against extending the first finger along the stick,[24] some cellists recommend this practice, perhaps because of the greater difficulty in setting thicker strings vibrating. Romberg and Dotzauer seem to advocate more arm-weight with a low right elbow, relaxed shoulders and the right-hand fingers 'neither too close to nor spread out from each other'.[25] However, Fig. 5.3 shows Romberg at the point of the bow with his right wrist dropped, allowing for little transference of arm-weight. Duport emphasises 'the mobility or play of the fingers, which is extremely useful',[26] while Romberg has the fingers about a quarter of an inch apart but suggests a less flexible bow-hold: 'all the fingers should be straight except the first finger . . . the thumb, between the second and third fingers, should hold the bow tightly . . . It is only by placing the hand firmly on the bow that a strong powerful tone can be drawn.'[27]

The 'ordinary' bowstroke of cellists during this period, like that of violinists, involved mainly the use of the forearm, with the shoulder and upper arm relaxed. Duport stipulated that 'the upper arm must remain in the same position' in order to avoid 'playing from the shoulder'.[28] Romberg observes: 'the great violinists in Paris have long perceived this [defect] and they therefore hold the elbow as low as possible when playing, as its elevation forces the shoulder out of its natural position. This can be avoided in cello playing by sitting up straight and never raising the shoulders.'[29]

22 Dotzauer, *Violoncellschule*, p. 6: 'Ueber die Haltung sind die Meister nicht einig, und man findet unter den besten Spielen solche, die ihn so nahe als möglich am Frosch, andere, die ihn bedeutend kürzer fassen. Von beyden ist das Extrem, wie überall so auch hier schädlich.'

23 Duport, *Essai*, p. 156.

24 L. Mozart, *Versuch einer gründlichen Violinschule* (Augsburg 1756), ch. 2 para. 5, pp. 54–5.

25 Dotzauer, *Violoncellschule*, p. 7: '[die Finger] ohne Zwang neben einander, weder zu weit noch zu nah zu halten'.

26 Duport, *Essai*, p. 156: 'la mobilité ou le jeu des doigts qui est très utile'.

27 Romberg, *Violoncell Schule*, p. 6: 'Der Daumen liegt auf der anderen Saite zwischen dem zweiten und dritten Finger, und hält mit dem Weichen des vorderen Gliedes den Bogen fest. Alle Finger, ausser dem ersten, liegen gerade. [Die Knöchel der Hand bilden eine gerade Linie mit der Strange des Bogens, welche Lage auch immer, so viel als möglich, beibehalten werden muss,] denn nur durch diese feste Lage der Hand am Bogen kann man einen starken, kräftigen Ton aus dem Instrumente ziehen, [ohne dass man die Kraft des Arms dazu nöthig hat].'

28 Duport, *Essai*, p. 159: 'le haut du bras doit rester dans la même position . . .'; 'jouer de l'épaule'.

29 Romberg, *Violoncell Schule*, p. 8. 'Die grossen Geiger in Paris haben dies schon lange erkannt, deshalb halten sie den Ellenbogen beim Spielen soviel als möglich gerade herunter, und nicht in die Höhe, weil dadurch die Schulter aus ihrer ungezwungenen Lage kommt. Beim Violoncell kann man dieses vermeiden, wenn man ganz gerade sitzt, und die Schultern nie in die Höhe hebt.'

Clive Brown claims that the springing bowstroke of the late eighteenth century 'was superseded under the impact of the Viotti school by a style which stressed sonority and expansiveness and largely rejected the springing bowstroke'.[30] He concludes that the main stroke of articulation was performed on the string towards the point. Romberg's bowing style was certainly broad and, with allowances for the nature of the instrument, many nineteenth-century cello sources seem to support such a conclusion.

Duport warns against using a bow that is too long 'as the upper part of the arm must necessarily move back in order to arrive at the point'. This part of the bow, he says, 'is very useful in a great many passages, especially in those where lightness is required'.[31] He qualifies this by describing two sorts of *détaché*: 'the first is pressed, which one uses when one desires a lot of sound, and the other a little jumping, which one uses in light passages. This latter is executed with the three quarters of the bow towards the point.'[32] Duport consistently emphasises the need for control and articulation at the point, and for equalising the attack or 'bite' at both ends of the bow. He advocates the 'hooked' bowing of dotted rhythms, which necessarily require strong articulation at the point, in preference to separate strokes (e.g. the Adagio of Op. 5 No. 2). While acknowledging the greater difficulty involved, he claims that 'it has the advantage that it can be performed with greater vivacity and with even greater force'.[33]

Froehlich's discussion of cello bowing is a digest of Duport's first six 'articles', with some passages quoted verbatim.[34] He refers the reader to his violin method, in which he describes two basic bowstrokes ('kräftig' and 'gelinden') and claims that 'with each the stroke must be made at the point of the bow with strength'.[35] He qualifies this by quoting from the Paris Conservatoire *Méthode* for cello of 1804: 'one performs faster passages not so sharply with the point, as with the violin, because it [the point] is not strong enough to set the thick cello strings vibrating'. The optimum contact-point, he continues, 'depends on the strength and weight of the bow, so one finds for oneself the place where the tone can be drawn out most

---

30 Clive Brown, 'Bowing Styles, Vibrato and Portamento in Nineteenth-century Violin Playing', *Journal of the Royal Musical Association*, 113 (1988), pp. 109–10.

31 Duport, *Essai*, p. 174: 's'il est trop long, il faut nécessairement tirer le haut du bras en arrière pour parvenir à la pointe, qui est très utile dans un grand nombre de passages, ceux surtout où il faut de la légèreté'.

32 *ibid.*, p. 170: '[Il y a deux sortes de détaché,] la première appuyé dont on se sert quand on veut tirer du son, et l'autre un peu sauté dont on se sert dans les choses de légèreté. Ce dernier s'exécute des trois quarts de l'archet vers la pointe.'

33 *ibid.*, p. 171: 'elle a l'avantage de pouvoir s'exécuter avec plus de vivacité et même plus de force'.

34 Froehlich, *Vollständige theoretisch-praktische Musikschule*, IV, pp. 57–91.

35 *ibid.*, p. 42: 'bei jenem muss der Strich mit der Spitze des Bogens gemacht und mit Festigkeit ausgeführt werden'.

strongly'.[36] Dotzauer likewise recommends the middle of the bow for fast passages: 'It is quite possible to execute fast strokes at the frog but as the sound only has little vibration this is rarely used. If these strokes demand strength they are performed in the middle of the bow, and if they require delicacy one does them at the point.[37] He continues by emphasising the benefits of a straight, broad and relaxed bowstroke in fast passages. Romberg has a different opinion from Duport regarding the execution of 'springing bowstrokes':

This mode of bowing may be introduced in light, easy passages and is peculiarly suited to those written in playful style, for example Rondos in $\frac{6}{8}$ [the English edition (1840) has 'or Solos for Chamber Music' here]. For music of a higher order it is not so well adapted and should not be used except in fast movements. This was formerly the solo stroke of all great virtuosos who used it in all passages. It is, however, quite incompatible with a firm broad style of playing . . . Now one expects more solidity, soul, and expression in music.[38]

Romberg's bow (of 30.25 inches) had nearly two inches more playing length than Duport's and was better suited to broad bowings on the string than to Duport's *détaché un peu sauté*. One of Romberg's exercises (Ex. 5.10) concludes with the following instruction: 'With very light bowing, and in proportion as they become more *piano* in tone the shorter should be the stroke of the bow . . . and the bow itself should be used gradually towards the point.'[39] A similar figuration occurs in Op. 5 No. 2 in bar 100 of the second movement.

In his *L'Art du violoncelle* (published in 1884 when he was ninety) Olive-Charlier Vaslin, a pupil of Baudiot, recalls Baillot's violin classes and acknowledges his influence. All of his examples regarding the relationship between bow-division and note-length focus on the middle of the bow, including the *martelé* and *détaché* strokes for which Baillot advocates using the point.[40] He quotes Variation 7 of Beethoven's

36 *ibid.*, p. 81: 'man schneller Passagen nicht so scharf mit der Spitze abstossen darf, wie bey der Violin, indem diese nicht stark genug ist, um die dicken Violoncell Saiten in die gehörige Schwingung zu setzen . . . Das es hierin viel auf die Stärke des Bezugs und Schwere des Bogens ankömmt, so such man den Platz auf demselben auszumitteln, wo die Töne mit gehörigen Kraft können herausgebracht werden, [und doch noch Klang genug haben].'

37 Dotzauer, *Violoncellschule*, p. 20: 'Geschwinde Passagen nahe bey'm Frosch zu machen, ist zwar möglich, aber wegen des kurzen Tones nicht gebräuchlich; man macht sie, sollen sie kräftig vorgetragen werden, in der Mitteschwächer, mit der Spitze.'

38 Romberg, *Violoncell Schule*, p. 109: 'Diese Strichart ist in leicht hinlaufenden Passagen anzubringen, und eignet sich nur für Stücke, in fröhlichen Stile geschrieben, wie Rondos im $\frac{6}{8}$ tel Takt; aber nicht zu ernsthaften Musik-Stücken, und kann auch nur in raschen Tempos angebracht werden. Ehemals war es der Solostrich sämmtlicher Virtuosen, aller Passagen wurden in dieser Strichart gemacht die jedoch ein grossartiges Spiel nie zulässt; [eben desshalb waren ihre Concerte von so geringem Gehalt in der Composition,] jetzt verlangt man mehr Gediegenheit, Seele und Ausdruck in der Musik.'

39 *ibid.*, p. 100: '[die Schluss Arpeggios werden] sehr leicht im Bogenstrich gemacht, und je mehr piano sie werden, desto kürzer muss der Bogenstrich werden, der sich dann immer mehr und mehr der Spitze nähert'.

40 Olive-Charlier Vaslin, *L'Art du violoncelle, conseils aux jeunes violoncellistes sur la conduite de l'archet* (Paris 1884), pp. 11–12; see Stowell, *Violin Technique and Performance Practice*, pp. 181–90.

Ex. 5.10   Romberg: *Violoncell Schule*, p. 108

Ex. 5.11 Beethoven: Variations on 'See the Conqu'ring Hero Comes' (*Judas Maccabeus*) Wo045, Variation 7, as played by Baillot according to Vaslin (*L'Art du violoncelle*, p. 14)

Variations on 'See the Conqu'ring Hero Comes' (*Judas Maccabeus*) WoO 45 for piano and cello and comments:

Playing this passage at the heel and doubling the speed of the movement is to betray the poverty of the bow and gives a bad example. I have heard Baillot perform this piece transcribed for the violin; the lesson was beautiful. He was not at all obliged to make one forget a gap in the passage with slides and exaggerated vibrato.[41]

The passage is given in Ex. 5.11 as played by Baillot, according to Vaslin. He also demonstrates the allocation of bow length (and hence speed) to accented notes, the first note having the most bow and the others successively less (Ex. 5.12). (See Op. 102 No. 2, 1/18)

Ex. 5.12   Vaslin: *L'Art du violoncelle*, p. 12

Ex. 5.13a   Beethoven: Cello Sonata Op. 69, first movement, bars 251–2 (arr. David)

Ex. 5.13b   Beethoven: Cello Sonata Op. 69, fourth movement, bars 42–3 (arr. David)

Both Duport and Baudiot admit to their inability to execute up- or down-bow staccato, Baudiot also adding that Rode found it embarrassing.[42] Romberg recommends cellists to abstain from its use,[43] while Dotzauer, describing a 'jumping staccato', claims that it is rarely required.[44] Grützmacher's bowing of an extract from Duport's *21 Exercices* (Ex. 5.5b) illustrates a late-nineteenth-century approach, its second bar demonstrating a bowing pattern typical of the violinist Ferdinand David (1810–73). David's adaptation for piano and violin of Beethoven's Cello Sonatas and Variations (1874) includes added slurs, such as those in Exs. 5.13a and b, which allow the semiquavers to be played nearer to the point of the bow. Such examples of 'convenience' bowings which demonstrate the use of broad strokes at the tip of the bow are more commonplace in violin playing; but, as the cellist's

41   Vaslin, *L'Art du violoncelle*, p. 14: 'Jouer ce trait du talon et en doublant de vitesse le mouvement, c'est trahir la pauvreté d'archet et donner un mauvais exemple. J'ai entendu Baillot exécuter ce morceau traduit pour le violon, la leçon était belle. Il n'avait point à faire oublier une lacune dans le trait par des glissades et des tremblements exagérés.'

42   Duport, *Essai*, p. 171; Baudiot, *Méthode*, p. 80.

43   Romberg, *Violoncell Schule*, p. 109.

44   Dotzauer, *Violoncellschule*, p. 28.

preferred part of the bow for a broad *détaché* was the middle, fewer obvious adjust-
ments to bow direction were required to arrive at the middle than the tip. The added
slur in Chopin's Cello Sonata Op. 65 (1/109) is a prime example.

Most treatises of the period encourage the cultivation of smooth and even bowing.
Romberg describes a *portato* stroke for dotted notes under a slur (as, for example, in
the opening of the Allegro of Op. 5 No. 1), articulating by means of a 'small stopping of the bow'.[45] By implication his legato was performed with a perfectly smooth
bow stroke. His bow-change was apparently executed without using movements
of the hand: 'the less the motion of the hand in changing the bow . . . the finer and
more connected the playing'.[46] Beethoven's prescription of very long slurs or phrase-
marks, for example in the opening melody of Op. 69 and in the opening of the
Adagio of Op. 102 No. 2, requires the cultivation of a smooth connected line. This
can be achieved using subtle bow changes described above, and, in the latter example,
by changing bow between the repeated notes. Dotzauer, however, expected many
notes to be slurred in one bow when required (Ex. 5.14). In Ex. 5.15, it seems
unlikely that Beethoven intended the cellist to ignore the pianist's legato (Ex. 5.16)
by stressing the slur in the middle of the bar each time throughout the movement.
Duport's comments on slurred notes seem to confirm this:

Ex. 5.14   Dotzauer: *Violoncellschule*, p. 20

Ex. 5.15   Beethoven: Cello Sonata Op. 5 No. 1, first movement, bars 49–50 (cello)

Ex. 5.16   Beethoven: Cello Sonata Op. 5 No. 1, first movement, bars 35–6 (piano)

[Bowing patterns] may be varied by the accent of the bow, but hitherto it has been
considered useless . . . to mark such accentuation in music; and I venture to say that these

---

45 Romberg, *Violoncell Schule*, p. 98: 'kleine Stillhaltung des Bogens'.
46 *ibid.*, p. 7: 'je weniger Bewegung in der Hand beim Umsatz des Bogens ist, desto schöner und zusammen-
    hängender ist das spiel'.

accents of the bow in passages are merely a matter of fashion, and subject to its changes. For example, when two notes are connected together, they will at one time be played perfectly equal, and, at another, with a slight pressure on the second, and so on. All this depends on the fancy of the player.[47]

Thus Beethoven's long slurs or phrase-marks countered the habits of instrumentalists who continued to some extent to stress the first note and release the last note of slurs, as Leopold Mozart and C. P. E. Bach had described.[48] It is evident, for example, that Dotzauer, in his edition (1827) of J. S. Bach's Solo Cello Suites, still considered the slur to be a means of shaping the contours of the music with stresses, notably in giving a cross-beat accent (Ex. 5.17), or stressing the note left out of the slur (Ex. 5.18). One aspect of Dotzauer's edition which illustrates the changes in the design and use of the bow since Bach's day is the addition of hooked bowings to the dotted rhythms in the French-style Prelude to the Fifth Suite. Similarly, he sometimes gives 𝅘𝅥𝅮𝅘𝅥𝅮𝅘𝅥𝅮 where a modern attempt at an *Urtext* (there being no autograph of the Cello Suites) might give 𝅘𝅥𝅮𝅘𝅥𝅮𝅘𝅥𝅮 or 𝅘𝅥𝅮𝅘𝅥𝅮𝅘𝅥𝅮. Despite the connected style associated with the Tourte bow, the gradual emergence of the phrase mark during Beethoven's lifetime and the adoption by string players of convenience bowings, the slur continued to some extent to be used for emphasis and remained a significant part of the performer's expressive vocabulary.

Ex. 5.17   J. S. Bach: Cello Suite in C BWV1009, Prelude, bars 21–2 (ed. Dotzauer)

Ex. 5.18   J. S. Bach: Cello Suite in C BWV1009, Prelude, bars 72–5 (ed. Dotzauer)

The bow, and the ability to control it, was considered the main expressive tool of the performer. 'Variety in the manner of playing', writes Duport, 'the gradations of sound, and consequently the expression, depend on the bow, and are matters of

---

47 Duport, *Essai*, p. 166: 'On peut les varier par l'accent de l'archet, mais jusqu'ici on a regardé comme inutile, [ou peut-être trop compliqué] de les marquer dans la musique. Ces différents accents de l'archet dans les passages sont, j'ose le dire, sujets à la mode et changent avec elle. Par exemple, quand on lie deux notes ensemble, une fois on les passera très égales; une autre fois on appuyera la première; une autre fois la seconde, etc.; cela dépend du caprice du joueur.'

48 L. Mozart, *Versuch*, ch. 7, sec. 1, para.20, p.135; C. P. E. Bach, *Versuch über die wahre Art das Clavier zu spielen,* 2 vols., (Berlin 1753; rpr. 1957 and 1762; rpr. 1957), trans. W. J. Mitchell (New York, 1949; rpr 1974), I, ch.3, sec. 1, para. 18, pp. 154–6.

taste and feeling.'[49] Re-emphasising the need for 'perfect command of the bow', he continues with the observation that 'the most celebrated singers have achieved the degree of perfection for which they have been or are acknowledged, only by labouring constantly to equalise the tones of their voice, although it may at first seem that it is only the modulation, the inflexions, the variety and agility which have constituted the charm of their singing'.[50]

Ex. 5.19   Beethoven: Cello Sonata Op. 5 No. 2, first movement, bars 27–9

Ex. 5.20   Beethoven: Cello Sonata Op. 5 No. 2, first movement, bars 5–6

49   Duport, *Essai*, p. 162: 'La variété du jeu, les nuances du son, et parconséquent l'expression, sont du resort de l'archet; et cela est l'affaire du sentiment et du goût.'
50   *ibid*., p. 165: 'les plus fameux chanteurs ne sont arrivés au point de perfection qu'on leur a reconnu, ou qu'on leur reconnoit, qu'en travaillant continuellement à égaliser les cordes de leur voix, quoiqu'il semble au premier abord, que ce ne soit que la modulation, les inflexions, la variété et l'agilité qui aient fait ou fassent tout le charme de leur chant'.

Ex. 5.21   Baillot, Levasseur, Catel and Baudiot: *Méthode de violoncelle*, p. 23

Ex. 5.22   Romberg: *Violoncell Schule*, p. 98

Ex. 5.23   Romberg: *Violoncell Schule*, p. 126

Ex. 5.24   Romberg: *Violoncell Schule*, p. 127

All cello methods of the period describe exercises for the bow similar to the *messa di voce* exercises of Leopold Mozart.[51] *Le son filé* or 'spun' sound, an indication of a sustained and connected style of playing, appears often in Beethoven's Op. 5 Cello Sonatas over long notes (see Ex. 5.19) and groups of slurred notes (Ex. 5.20). As well as an exercise in bow control, it was an expressive device often introduced by singers. The *Méthode* of the Paris Conservatoire (Ex. 5.21) and that of Dotzauer recommend a related expressive use of the bow called *ondulé*, a kind of bow-vibrato which Dotzauer describes as comprising many *sons filés*.[52] Romberg's chapter 'Of Light and Shade in Music' demonstrates the expressive role of the bow and includes passages annotated with expressive indications, a ploy which Duport had considered ridiculous.[53] One such example includes frequent use of the *messa di voce* (Ex. 5.22). Furthermore, Romberg uses words to illustrate the declamatory nature

51   L. Mozart, *Versuch*, ch. 5., pp. 101–8.

52   P. Baillot, J. H. Levasseur, C.–S. Catel and C.–N. Baudiot, *Méthode de violoncelle et de basse d'accompagnement* (Paris 1804; rpr 1974), pp. 22–3; Dotzauer, *Violoncellschule*, p. 47. See also n. 56.

53   Romberg, *Violoncell Schule*, p. 96; Duport, *Essai*, p. 162.

of the appoggiatura (Ex. 5.23) and includes a diagram to show the relative importance of a group of appoggiaturas according to tessitura (Ex. 5.24).

Harmonic awareness had long been considered especially important for cellists,
and many cello methods *c.* 1740–1850 devote large sections to the fundamentals of
harmony. Some, including those of Baillot et al., Baudiot and Dotzauer, provide
instruction for the realisation of figured bass on the cello, demonstrating that the
eighteenth-century notion of the cello as primarily a continuo or accompanying
instrument continued into the nineteenth century, despite its growing acceptance
in a solo capacity. Indeed, all of Beethoven's Sonatas for piano and cello incorporate
passages in which the cello has a distinctly accompanimental role, and an understanding of the underlying harmony of such passages will assist in shaping them
appropriately; for example, at the beginning of the Rondo of Op. 5 No. 2 the
subdominant (C) might with advantage receive more emphasis than the surrounding
notes (Ex. 5.25). Romberg explains the harmonic contours of several phrases (Exs.
5.26a and b) in order that they might be performed as expressively as possible. One
reviewer wrote of Romberg:

Ex. 5.25   Beethoven: Cello Sonata Op. 5 No. 2, second movement, bars 12–14 (cello)

Ex. 5.26a   Romberg: *Violoncell Schule*, p. 129

C♯ is the leading note, and therefore requires the strongest accent.

Ex. 5.26b   Romberg: *Violoncell Schule*, p. 129

E♭ is the most expressive note, and therefore requires to be emphasised [hervorgeholden]

It is impossible to express more deeply all the delicate shades of feeling, impossible to give
more variety of colour, especially by delicate shading, impossible to find the quite unique
tone, which goes straight to the heart and which Mr Romberg succeeds in producing in his
adagio . . . How he knows all the beauties of detail which lie in the nature and the given
sentiment of the piece, and for which the printer has no mark of expression! What effects
he produces by swelling his tone to the most powerful *fortissimo*, followed by the *diminuendo*
which dies out in a scarcely audible *pianissimo*![54]

54 Karl Ludwig Junker, cited in Edmond S. J. van der Straeten, *History of the Violoncello, the Viola da Gamba,
    Their Precursors and Collateral Instruments* (London 1915; rpr. 1971), pp. 223–4.

Closely associated with the expressive shading of the bow was the use of vibrato. Froehlich refers the cellist to his violin school for his views on this device, recommending only its sparing and appropriate use and relating vibrato speed to the tempo of the music.[55] Dotzauer's is the first cello method proper to mention vibrato; but although its predecessors, including Duport's treatise, are silent on this matter, we should not necessarily assume that vibrato was not part of the vocabulary of those times. It had certainly been in use among gambists. However, a continuous vibrato might have hindered the sympathetic resonances sought by Duport, and later Romberg and Dotzauer, in their quest for the 'coalition of vibrations'.

Dotzauer lists vibrato (tremolo which the French translation describes as 'used especially by Italian Professors') alongside *ondulé* and another similar expressive device: 'On long notes many make use where possible of *Pochens* (throbbings) which result from the coalition of vibrations.' [The French version explains that they are 'created by the resonance of the string which the finger beats [an octave] below to hinder the free vibration'.][56]

The fact that this effective ornament was rarely practicable – it was really suitable only for eb to f♯ on the d string – may give some indication of the frequency with which the actual vibrato was introduced, as these special effects appear side by side with equal significance. A rare possible application of *Pochens* in Beethoven's Cello Sonatas arises in Op. 69 (1/107–8) on the long held f♯. Romberg's discussion of vibrato suggests that, despite its absence from theoretical sources, its use had once been fashionable:

The close shake or *Tremolo* is produced by the rapid lateral motion of the finger when pressed on the string. When used in moderation and executed with great power of bow it gives fire and animation to the tone, but it should only be used at the beginning of the note and ought not to be continued through its whole duration. Formerly the close shake was in such repute that it was applied indiscriminately to every note of whatever duration. This produced a most disagreeable and whining effect, and we cannot be too thankful that an improved taste has at length exploded the abuse of this embellishment.[57]

Romberg gives Spohr's sign for vibrato ～～～ and claims that 'the second finger will be found best in making the close shake . . . the third finger is not well adapted . . .

55 Froehlich, *Vollständige Musikschule*, IV, p. 42.
56 Dotzauer, *Violoncellschule*, p. 47: 'Viele bedienen sich bey langen Tönen, wo es möglich ist des Pochens, welches vom Mitklingen der Töne herrührt'.

    The third finger repeatedly stops and releases the note an octave below that being played, creating an effect similar to vibrato. (See Ex. 5.1)
57 Romberg, *Violoncell Schule*, p. 85: 'Das Beben (Tremolo) wird hervorgebracht, indem man der finger, mit dem man einen Ton genommen hat, mehrere Male in sehr geschwinden Zeitmass vor und rückwärts biegt. Selten angebracht, und mit vieler Kraft des Bogens ausgeführt, giebt es dem Tone Feuer und Leben; es muss aber nur im Anfange der Note, und nicht durch die ganze Dauer derselben gemacht werden. In früherer Zeit konnte niemand einen Ton, wenn auch von noch so wenig Dauer, aushalten, ohne beständig mit dem Finger zu beben, und es wurde eine wahre Jammer-Musik daraus.'

The close shake must never be held on for the whole duration of the note otherwise it will fail in its effect, which is to add power to the tone; and should never exceed one third of the note's value.[58] Romberg's left-hand technique, however, would certainly have restricted the use of vibrato with the second finger. While most theorists cultivated a left-hand position in which each finger was perpendicular to the strings,[59] Romberg describes a sloping left hand like that of a violinist, with the third joint (i.e. that nearest the hand) of the first finger laid on the neck of the cello, the second finger describing three sides of a square, and the fourth finger kept straight[60] (see Fig. 5.3). Despite Romberg's great success and influence, this somewhat idiosyncratic left-hand technique proved to be a cul-de-sac.

Ex. 5.27   Kummer: *Violoncellschule*, p. 65, No. 68

Dotzauer's pupil Kummer (1797–1879) echoes Romberg's preference for expression through the varied use of the bow rather than vibrato.[61] Like Spohr and Romberg, he supplies 'exercises in style' containing detailed expressive indications. All twelve of Kummer's exercises contain frequent *messe di voce* and other expressive dynamics, but only four have indications for vibrato, annotated using Spohr's sign ∿∿∿ Ex. 5.27 shows the exercise most endowed with such indications, the majority of which occur at the high-point of a dynamic wave. Spohr further

---

58 *ibid.*, p. 89: 'Zu dem Beben ∿∿∿ (Tremolo) ist der zweite Finger oder geschickteste, weswegen ich ihn auch auf der ersten Note dieses Uebungsstück . . . Eigentlich sollte der dritte Finger zu Anfange genommen werden, allein dieser passt nicht so gut zum Beben. Das Beben muss nie die Dauer einer Note ausmachen sonst würde es seinen Zweck ganz verfehlen; es soll nur dem Tone mehr Kraft verleihen, und darf höchstens den dritten Theil davon ausfüllung.'

59 For example, Dotzauer and Kummer follow Berteau's principles as described by Duport in his *Essai*, p. 146.

60 Romberg, *Violoncell Schule*, p. 10.

61 Friedrich August Kummer, *Violoncello-Schule* Op. 60 (Leipzig 1839), Eng. trans. (London 1875), p. 28.

associates vibrato with dynamics, recommending the use of a fast vibrato for strong accentuation of all notes marked *fz* or >. [62] As to whether this would give 'fire and animation to the tone', or detract from the homogeneity of the piano and cello texture in Beethoven's Cello Sonatas (for instance, in imitative passages involving accents such as in the last movement of Op. 102 No. 2), is a matter for the performer to decide. Indeed, given the essentially different nature of the two instruments and their mutually supporting roles (as in Ex. 5.20 where the cello compensates for the piano's lack of sustaining power), it would be more appropriate to describe the texture of these sonatas as symbiotic rather than homogeneous.

Kummer also warns against overuse of portamento and rubato. Although earlier cello methods make no mention of rubato, Beethoven's pupil, the pianist and composer Carl Czerny (1791–1857), considered both tempo and the art of rubato to be of the utmost importance. He gave metronome marks for each movement of the five cello sonatas (see Table 5.1) and claims that, although each piece should be played 'from beginning to end . . . in the time prescribed by the author . . . there occurs in almost every line, some notes or passages, where a small and often imperceptible relaxation or acceleration of the movement is necessary, to embellish the expression and increase the interest'. He continues by describing rubato as 'the art of a good player . . . only to be acquired by highly cultivated taste, much attentive practice and by listening to great Artists on all instruments, particularly to distinguished singers'.[63]

The use of portamento among cellists was also subject to changes in taste. Bréval was the first cellist to advise that taking two consecutive notes with the same finger should be avoided as much as possible.[65] Duport agrees that 'it produces a bad effect . . . if the bow does not act on the string at the instant when the finger slides, a very disagreeable sound will be heard. It is true', he continues, 'that, in a rather slow time, two notes may be taken with the same finger; and even the interval of the third, a fourth, or a fifth, etc. may thus be played by a strong sliding of the same finger, which produces a very good effect, and is called *porter le son*. These slidings . . . are made more or less rapidly according to the expression the melody demands'[66] (see Ex. 5.28).

62 Louis Spohr, *Violinschule* (Vienna [1832]), pp. 175–6; cited in Stowell, *Violin Technique and Performance Practice*, p. 207.

63 Cited in P. G. le Huray, *Authenticity in Performance* (Cambridge 1991), p. 181.

64 Carl Czerny, *Vollständige theoretisch-praktische Pianoforteschule* Op. 500 (Vienna 1838–9), ed. Paul Badura-Skoda (Vienna 1963), p. 88. (See opposite page)

65 Bréval, *Traité*, p. 6.

66 Duport, *Essai*, pp. 17–18: 'elle produit un mauvais effet . . . car si l'archet ne saisit pas bien l'instant où le doigt a glissé, pour attaquer la corde, on entend quelque chose de très désagréable. On peut faire, il est vrai, deux notes du même doigt, un peu lentement; on passe même d'un intervalle de tierce, de quarte, de quinte, etc.: en glissant fortement le même doigt, et ceci produit un très bon effet, cela s'appelle porter le son. Ces glissades . . . se font plus ou moins rapidement, suivant l'expression qu'exige la mélodie.'

Table 5.1. *Czerny's recommended metronome markings for Beethoven's Cello Sonatas*[64]

Op 5 No. 1	I	♪ =	88	Adagio
		♩ =	160	Allegro
	II	♩. =	104	Allegro
Op. 5 No. 2	I	♩ =	50	Adagio
		♩. =	84	Presto
	II	♩ =	72	Allegro
Op. 69	I	♩ =	72	Allegro
	II	♩. =	108	Allegro molto
	III	♪ =	66	Adagio
		♩ =	88	Allegro vivace
Op. 102 No. 1	I	♪ =	66	Andante
		♩. =	76	Allegro vivace
	II	♪ =	56	Adagio
	III	♩ =	126	Allegro vivace
Op. 102 No. 2	I	♩ =	152	Allegro con brio
	II	♪ =	60	Adagio
	III	♩. =	63	Allegro

Ex. 5.28   Duport: *Essai*, p. 18

Baudiot includes *porte de voix* in his discussion of ornaments, explaining that 'the little note is often employed for *portamento*'.[67] (Ex. 5.29). Examples of such 'little notes' are few and far between in his *Méthode*, although Exs. 5.30 and 5.31 include fingerings which imply portamento. Romberg also describes *portamento di voce*, as an ornament, for it is 'applicable in the same manner to instrumental as to vocal music and signifies the gliding from one note to another by which means the most strongly accented notes of the melody are blended together with those which

67 Baudiot, *Méthode*, II, p. 50: 'souvent la petite note est employée comme porte de voix'.

precede them, and an agreeable effect is produced'.[68] Only one example of the 'little note' can be found in his *Violoncell Schule* (Ex. 5.32).[69]

Ex. 5.29   Baudiot: *Méthode*, p. 50

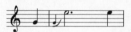

Ex. 5.30   Baudiot: *Méthode*, p. 248

Ex. 5.31   Baudiot *Méthode*, p. 18

Ex. 5.32   Romberg: *Violoncell Schule*, p. 87

Dotzauer, warning against inappropriate and excessive use of portamento agrees with Spohr's distinction between solo and orchestral playing, making the very pragmatic observation that it 'makes it easier for singers and instrumentalists surely to find the subsequent note, and the slide, when carried out in such a way as not to resemble a wail, can make a very agreeable effect. Naturally, this ornament, like all the others, belongs not in orchestral playing but in a Concerto or Solo context where the player may allow himself to submit to his own expression.'[70] He includes examples of sliding with one finger (Ex. 5.33) and where 'one finger obliges the other to give up its place' (Ex. 5.34).

68 Romberg, *Violoncell Schule*, p. 85: '[Die Benenung: das Tragen der Stimme (Portamento di voce) wird] bei der Instrumental-Musik eben so angewandt, als bei der Vokal-Musik, und bedeutet das Hinüberziehen eines Tones zu einem andern, durch welches die am stärksten betonte Note des Gesanges mit der vorhergegangenen zusammen gezogen wird, und dadurch mehr Anmuth erhalt.'
69 This convention may explain the 'little note' at the end of the Largo of Chopin's Cello Sonata Op 65.
70 Dotzauer, *Violoncellschule*, pp. 45–6: 'erleichtert dem Sänger und Instrumentisten in manchen Fällen den folgenden Ton sicher zu treffen, und gescheiht das Ziehen auf eine Art die nicht ins heulende fällt, so thut es eine sehr angenehme Wirkung. Natürlich gehört diese Verzierung so wie alle übringen, nicht ins Tutti-spiel, sondern in das Konzert oder Solo, welches dem Spieler gestattet sich seiner Empfindung hinzugeben.'

Ex. 5.33   Dotzauer: *Violoncellschule*, p. 46

Ex. 5.34   Dotzauer: *Violoncellschule*, p. 46

Portamento as an expressive device, along with the means of disguising unwanted glissandi by releasing bow pressure, had been described in cello methods since that of Duport. However, although some use of portamento and vibrato was characteristic of the expressive solo playing of many cellists during Beethoven's lifetime, the introduction of these devices did not necessarily follow the same criteria as they were to follow during the twentieth century. Perhaps Bernhard Romberg may best be regarded as an arbiter of taste for his time and for his instrument. By comparison with most cellists of the twentieth century he, like Spohr on the violin, used vibrato and portamento sparingly, the great depth and variety of expression evident by all accounts in his playing (and that of those he influenced) coming from the bow. The influence of the Viotti school was strongly felt by cellists during Beethoven's lifetime, but it was Romberg who inspired a school of cello playing which was characterised by a broad, resonant, on-the-string style of bowing that was both expressive and earnest, and included, in certain circumstances, the use of ornaments such as portamento and vibrato.

In addition to questions of playing style and technique, today's performers of Beethoven's cello sonatas are required to overcome problems presented by the instruments themselves. Although the cello has essentially changed little since Beethoven's day, the modern concert grand piano bears little resemblance to the 'Viennese' instrument for which Beethoven composed in 1796, and the fundamental change in balance between the two instruments in terms of their relative quantity and quality of sound dramatically affects the ensemble's overall textures. Early-nineteenth-century writers were already conscious of the effects of changing designs in piano construction, Hummel pointing out that the 'English' piano was louder than the 'Viennese', but made less impact on an ensemble because it had a more sustained and duller tone.[71] The argument that Beethoven would have preferred the sound and power of the modern piano may be admissible in the solo piano repertoire; however, when the modern piano is combined with another instrument

71 See le Huray, *Authenticity in Performance*, p. 186; also p. 165 for a comparison of English and Viennese pianos.

which has evolved differently, performers must acknowledge that they are to some extent making an 'arrangement' of the music and resign themselves to certain compromises in order best to serve the composer's intentions.

One such example is the modern pianist's dilemma when faced with Beethoven's pedal indications. We know from Czerny that Beethoven's playing was characterised by excessive use of the pedal.[72] Yet if the spirit of his playing is taken too literally, there is a danger of the modern piano drowning the cello in a wash of accumulating sound. Similarly, the dense left-hand textures in much of Beethoven's piano writing which is light enough for the cello to penetrate when performed on a 'Viennese' piano, can dominate the ensemble when played on a modern instrument.[73] A sensitive compromise is thus essential in order to achieve, using modern instruments, the balance between textual clarity and the intimacy sometimes required in the cello sonatas. Perhaps what detracts most often from their comprehensibility nowadays is the imbalance between the player's roles when these Sonatas for Piano and Cello are presented completely out of context as cello pieces with piano accompaniment.

72 See le Huray, *Authenticity in Performance*, p. 170.
73 For example those problems of balance consistently encountered in modern performances of the Triple Concerto Op. 56.

6

FERDINAND DAVID'S EDITIONS OF BEETHOVEN

CLIVE BROWN

Beethoven was ever alert to innovations in the construction and playing techniques of instruments[1] and he undoubtedly responded to the important developments in violin playing which took place during his lifetime. His notation alone, however, reveals little about the ways in which he might have expected specific styles or techniques to be employed. Rare occurrences of such instructions as *una corda, sul ponticello, punto d'arco* and an occasional isolated fingering provide very limited guidance; even his frequent bowing/phrasing slurs and staccato marks are open to a variety of interpretations. Nevertheless, consideration of the aesthetic and technical conventions with which Beethoven would have been familiar may help to clarify some of the implications behind his notation.

Little definite is known about Beethoven's own violin playing. He learned the instrument from an early age and was sufficiently competent to take part as a violist in performances of the Electoral Court Orchestra in Bonn, but string playing decidely took second place to keyboard playing. After moving to Vienna in 1792 he had violin lessons with Wenzel Krumpholz, with whom he remained on friendly terms until the latter's death in 1817. These did not, apparently, confer any lasting benefit. Beethoven's attempts to play the violin part of his own sonatas to his pupil Ferdinand Ries's accompaniment were far from successful; Ries recalled that 'it was really a dreadful sort of music; for in his enthusiastic ardour he did not hear if he began a passage in the wrong position'.[2] But Beethoven never entirely gave up playing the violin, even when he could scarcely hear what he was doing, and he was quite capable of making precise technical demands on the players. During a rehearsal of the String Quartet Op. 132 in 1825 Sir George Smart witnessed how

1 *Thayer's Life of Beethoven*, ed. Elliot Forbes (Princeton 1964).
2 Ferdinand Ries and Franz Gerhard Wegeler, *Biographische Notizen über Ludwig van Beethoven*, ed. Kalischer (Berlin 1906), p. 141: 'Das war aber wirklich eine schreckliche Musik; denn in seinem begeisterten Eifer hörte er nicht, wenn er in eine Passage falsch in die Applicatur einsetzte.' It has also been suggested that an entry in Beethoven's memorandum book in 1794 'Schupp. 3 times a W' refers to violin lessons with Ignaz Schuppanzigh; but since Ignaz Schuppanzigh was only 18 years old at the time, it is more likely to indicate lessons in cultural subjects with his father, a professor at the *Realschule*.

'A staccato passage not being expressed to the satisfaction of his eye, for alas, he could not hear, he [Beethoven] seized Holz's[3] violin and played the passage a quarter of a tone too flat.'[4]

Scanty surviving information about Beethoven's own violin playing throws no significant light on the technical and stylistic criteria which underlie his writing for the instrument, but his association with known string players of the period proffers an important clue to what he may have expected from performers. A list of the players with whom he came into close contact suggests that he was familiar with the major currents in late-eighteenth- and early-nineteenth-century string playing. During the latter part of his time in Bonn he worked with the violin- and cello-playing Romberg cousins Andreas and Bernhard, who joined the Bonn orchestra in 1790; while in Vienna, over a period of years, he was intimately involved with Wenzel Krumpholz, Anton Wranitzky, Ignaz Schuppanzigh, Franz Clement, Joseph Mayseder and Joseph Boehm; at various stages he also met and performed with other internationally acclaimed players who visited Vienna, chief among these being Rodolphe Kreutzer (1798), George Polgreen Bridgetower (1803), Pierre Rode (1812) and Louis Spohr (1812–15). Hearing and working with these and many other violinists, especially before his deafness became acute, will have contributed towards Beethoven's concept of violin playing and enlarged his repertoire of idiomatic writing for the instrument.

In certain works he seems to have been stimulated by the characteristics of particular players. The Op. 12 Violin Sonatas of 1799 may perhaps have been influenced by his intimacy with Rodolphe Kreutzer the previous year, for whose playing Beethoven's admiration is attested by the dedication of the 'Kreutzer' Sonata in 1804;[5] the Violin Concerto was written for Clement; the Violin Sonata Op. 96 was partly composed with Viotti's pupil Pierre Rode in mind and, as Beethoven's correspondence indicates,[6] certainly took account of his style of

---

3   Second violin in performances of Beethoven's later quartets.

4   *Leaves from the Journals of Sir George Smart*, ed. H. Bertram Cox and C. L. E. Cox (London 1907), p. 109. It is possible that Beethoven's intervention in that rehearsal concerned the indication *punto d'arco* in the Finale; *punto d'arco* is common in eighteenth- and early-nineteenth-century scores, particularly of Italian opera, but its meaning is not entirely clear. Johann Adam Hiller thought it indicated the up-bow staccato (*Anweisung zum Violinspielen* (Leipzig 1792), p. 41). Lichtenthal defined it in 1826 in the following terms: 'The notes marked with this expression require a special execution, which consists in beating gently on the string with the point of the bow, thus producing a light staccato.' ('Le Note marcate con tale espressione richiedono un'esecuzione particolare, la quale consiste ne battere dolcemente colla punta dell'arco sulla corda, producendo così uno staccato leggiero.') *Dizionario di musica* (Milan 1826), art. 'Punta d'arco'. Joachim was puzzled by Beethoven's use of the term, considering that the required effect could only be obtained by using an off-string stroke near the heel of the bow. *Violinschule* (Berlin 1904–5), III, p. 13.

5   Beethoven: letter of 4 October 1804.

6   Beethoven: letter of 29 December 1812.

playing to some extent. Many of the players with whom Beethoven was associated were disciples of the Viotti School. Bridgetower, with whom he first performed the 'Kreutzer' Sonata, though initially a pupil of Barthélemon and Giornovichi, had, according to Samuel Wesley, 'practised much with the celebrated Viotti, and imbibed largely of his bold and spirited style of execution'.[7] Schuppanzigh certainly performed Viotti concertos and it is likely that his style, too, derived much from the French school. The compositions and writings of the Rombergs suggest an orientation towards this style. Spohr and Boehm were both influenced by Viotti's pupil Rode. Subtle individual features in the playing of these violinists, which would have been evident to contemporaries, are, for the most part, lost beyond recall, but the principal stylistic characteristics which they shared are well documented. These included: frequent use of a broad *détaché* in fast movements,[8] contrasted from time to time with *martelé* bowstrokes (including the slurred staccato); extensively varied patterns of slurred and detached bowing; powerful tone; and a highly expressive cantabile often involving the use of prominent portamento.

Somewhat apart from these players stand Franz Clement (1780–1842) and Joseph Mayseder (1789–1863). Clement maintained his individual manner in defiance of changing fashion and consequently fell out of favour; almost alone of the celebrated players of his generation, he was not regarded as an adherent or close ally of the Viotti school. As the *Allgemeine musikalische Zeitung* observed in 1805, the hallmark of his style was 'not the marked, bold, powerful playing, the gripping, striking Adagio, the power of bow and tone which characterises the Rode/Viotti School: rather an indescribable delicacy, neatness and elegance; an extremely delightful tenderness and cleanness in playing which indisputably places Clement among the most perfect violinists'.[9] Eight years later, when the Viotti School's ascendancy was

---

7 In the British Library Department of Manuscripts Add. 27, 593, f.109.

8 Ernst Ludwig Gerber, *Neues Lexikon der Tonkünstlers* (1812–14) col. 118 referred, for instance, to the similarity between Viotti's and Kreutzer's style, saying of Kreutzer: 'Viotti's manner is also entirely his. The similarly strong tone and similarly long bowstroke characterise his allegro.' ('Die Manier des Viotti ist auch ganz die seinige. Eben der starke Ton und eben der lange Bogenstrich charakterisieren auch sein Allegro.') The same features among others were identified as being shared by Spohr and Kreutzer in a review of Spohr's playing in Prague in 1808 (*Allgemeine musikalische Zeitung*, 10 (1807/8), col. 313–14). A writer in 1825 remarked that the School of Viotti, Baillot and Rode was 'as everyone knows, distinguished by an individual use of the bow' adding that 'almost all celebrated modern virtuoso violinists have adopted it to a greater or lesser extent'. ('Sie unterscheidet sich bekanntlich durch einen eigenthumlichen Gebrauch des Bogens, und fast alle neue berühmte Violin-Virtuosen haben sie mehr oder weniger angenommen'). *Cäcilia*, 2 (1825), p. 267.

9 '[Es ist] nicht das markige, kühne, kräftige Spiel, das ergreifende, eindringliche Adagio, die Gewalt des Bogens und Tones, welche die Rodesche und Viottische Schule charakterisirt: aber eine unbeschreibliche Zierlichkeit, Nettigkeit und Elegance; eine äusserst lieblich Zartheit und Reinheit des Spiels, die Klement ausstreitig unter die vollendetsten Violinspieler stellt.' *Allgemeine musikalische Zeitung*, 7 (1805), col. 500.

virtually unchallenged, Clement's adherence to his own manner was seen as a serious drawback; after praising his technical command, a reviewer commented that 'his short bowstroke and overwhelming mannerisms, which certainly do not allow him to achieve an expressive cantabile, will always exclude him from the ranks of the *great* violinists'.[10] Despite such negative comments about Clement's style, however, it seems that some of his characteristics remained a strand in Viennese violin playing, for his 'indescribable delicacy, neatness and elegance' enjoyed a resurgence of popularity in the performance of Joseph Mayseder. Comparing Spohr and Mayseder in 1830, Mayseder's pupil Heinrich Panofka observed: 'While this master [Spohr] is great and original in serious performance, the second (Mayseder) comes to the fore in the Pollacca and Rondo with a wealth of charm and tenderness and the fullest and purest tone in Adagio.'[11]

None of the violinists directly connected with Beethoven, however, left any revealing information about the bowing style or fingering they would have regarded as appropriate in his violin music. Some violin parts in the Haslinger collected edition, supposedly overseen by Schuppanzigh and Holz, contain a few isolated fingerings, though these have little to reveal about style. Pierre Baillot cited a few passages from Beethoven's works with performance instructions in his *L'Art du violon* of 1834, including a couple of sections from the first movement of the Violin Concerto, but there is nothing to connect Baillot with traditions stemming from Beethoven himself. No other substantial examples of how violinists of Beethoven's generation might have treated his music seem to have survived. Ferdinand David's editions of Beethoven's violin sonatas, piano trios, string quartets and Violin Concerto, as well as his arrangement of the cello sonatas for violin and piano, therefore, are the earliest systematically bowed and fingered editions of these works. They are by far the most extensive body of information about what was regarded as an appropriate style of performance for them by an important German violinist whose training was already complete at the time of Beethoven's death.[12] However, while no other violinist born within Beethoven's lifetime produced similar editions of the chamber music, the Violin Concerto also exists in a fingered and bowed edition by

10 'sein kurzer Bogenstrich und seine überhäuften Kunsteleyen, die ihm gar nicht zu einem ausdrucks-vollen Gesang kommen lassen, werden ihn immer vom Range unter den *grossen* Violinspierlern abhalten'. *Allgemeine musikalische Zeitung*, 15 (1813), col. 400.

11 'Während nun dieser Meister gross und originell da steht im Vortrag des Ernsten, tritt der zweite (Maiseder) mit einer Fülle von Lieblichkeit und Zartheit hervor in der Pollacca, dem Rondo, und mit dem vollesten und reinsten Ton im Adagio.' *Berliner allgemeine musikalische Zeitung*, 7 (1830), pp. 65–6.

12 Ferdinand David (1810–73) studied with Spohr in Cassel between 1823 and 1825. After a successful debut at the Leipzig Gewandhaus in 1825, he spent several years touring and as leader of a private quartet in Dorpat before returning to Leipzig to lead the Gewandhaus orchestra at Mendelssohn's suggestion in 1836. He remained based in Leipzig, where he was appointed Professor of Violin at the newly founded Conservatoire in 1843, retaining that post until his death.

David's exact contemporary, the Viennese violinist Jacob Dont (1810–88), a pupil of Boehm and the elder Hellmesberger, who was a member of the orchestra of the Vienna Hofburgtheater from 1831 and of the Hofkapelle Orchestra from 1834. From 1873 he taught at the Vienna Konservatorium. His edition of the Violin Concerto was published by Schlesinger of Berlin in about 1880.

Though David's editions were all published around 1870[13] there is no reason to think that the style of performance suggested by his markings in these works, many of which he must first have performed during Beethoven's lifetime, would have been radically different from that which he might have employed forty years earlier. David's extensive manuscript markings in his copy of Mendelssohn's String Quartets Opp. 12–44, which seem clearly to derive from a much earlier period in his life,[14] reveal many of the same stylistic traits. In addition, the fingerings and bowings in David's editions of Beethoven are broadly consistent with those which Spohr marked in comparable passages in his own works, and can also be paralleled by markings in the music of other prominent violinists of Beethoven's generation. There is nothing to suggest that David's approach to performing Beethoven had any direct connection with the composer's own conception or even with traditions of performance stemming from Beethoven's circle; nor can it be assumed that Beethoven would have been uncritical of David's technical and aesthetic approach, but there can be little doubt that David's style of performance would not have seemed alien to him. David's position as a pupil of Spohr, who undoubtedly exerted a powerful, though not overwhelming influence on his style of playing, certainly establishes a link with Beethoven performance from the beginning of the nineteenth century. Spohr was one of the earliest violinists outside Vienna to champion

13 David's edition of the Violin Sonatas (Peters, pl. no. 4899) is listed in Hoffmeister/Wistling 1868–73. The plate numbers of his Peters editions of the Trios (4903) and Quartets (4908) suggest a similar publication date. A later edition of the Violin Sonatas by Peters with the plate number 6531, though re-engraved, is textually identical except for a few amplifications of fingering in parallel passages where the earlier edition seems to have omitted them in error (for example, in the fourth bar from the end of the theme of the Andante of Op. 47). The plate number of his edition of the Violin Concerto for Breitkopf and Härtel suggests a similar date of publication. Reference will also be made in this article to Joseph Joachim's edition of Beethoven's Violin Sonatas for Peters (pl. no. 8762) which replaced David's edition in 1901. Though there are many differences of detail between David's and Joachim's editions, which sometimes reveal the influence of the *Gesamtausgabe* and sometimes a difference of technique, a considerable number of David's modifications were taken over by Joachim. Comparison of the two versions of the Violin Sonatas reveals both similarities and differences of approach between the two violinists; some of the differences may simply have resulted from artistic temperament, but others may represent a newer phase in German violin playing.

14 The evidence of date is circumstantial. These first editions of the quartets were evidently bound into a single volume when David used them, for the fly-leaf contains his signature in the same blue crayon with which the markings are made; the absence of Op. 80 suggests that they were already bound, and presumably in use, before 1848 when Op. 80 was posthumously published.

Beethoven's Op. 18 Quartets and violin sonatas (playing them frequently, as his diaries and reminiscences indicate, during the first five years of the century).[15] Throughout his life, Spohr performed Beethoven's chamber music regularly in his own private music parties,[16] and his sense of the style appropriate to different composers' music is attested by a number of contemporaries.[17] David's approach to performing Beethoven can hardly fail to have been influenced by Spohr's. Yet in some respects David's playing represented a more modern phase in German violin playing; Ferdinand Hiller observed that it: 'combined the sterling qualities of Spohr's style with the greater facility and piquancy of a later school'.[18] Nevertheless, Hermann Mendel, writing at about the time of David's death, commented that David's violin playing had 'a Classical, truly German accent'.[19] Other opinions of David's playing were not so favourable; he was criticised among other things for lapses of taste such as embellishing Haydn quartets, a practice common enough in Haydn's day but, by then, an unfashionable habit.[20]

David's Beethoven editions are far removed from the critical editions of the twentieth century or even from the *Gesamtausgabe* of Beethoven's works which was being produced by Breitkopf and Härtel at about the time they were issued. For the most part David's editions are accurate with respect to the note lengths and pitches, though there are a couple of instances of deliberately altered notes. In Ex. 6.1a the correct version is given in David's piano part; in Ex. 6.4a David has sharpened the c^3 on the third beat of bar 463 (Ex. 6.4b gives the original). In one or two places dynamics are incorrectly placed or an appoggiatura rendered as a grace note (Ex. 6.1b: bar 19, first beat), but this was almost certainly a result of oversight or the imperfect state of textual research at that time. There are many places, however, where phrasing and articulation differ from the most reliable textual sources. These differences sometimes occur in both the score and the separate violin part, suggesting that they are not so much a deliberate departure from Beethoven's text as a misreading or an alternative interpretation of the sources; frequently this is simply a matter of a slur extended or shortened by a single note, especially over a bar-line or on to a strong beat. In many cases, though, the score contains one version (usually identical or almost identical with that of the *Gesamtausgabe*)

15 Clive Brown, *Louis Spohr: A Critical Biography* (Cambridge 1984), pp. 11, 20–2, 30–1.

16 Despite his recorded misgivings about the style of Beethoven's late quartets, Spohr also performed these in his soirées. There is a reference to his playing Op. 131 in an article by Spohr's pupil H. Wichmann, 'Spohr über eine mögliche Reform des Streichquartetts', *Deutsche Revue*, 12 (1887), p. 355.

17 Johann Friedrich Rochlitz *Allgemeine musikalische Zeitung* VII (1804/5), 201ff. (quoted in Brown, *Louis Spohr*, p. 31) and Alexander Malibran, *Louis Spohr* (Frankfurt 1860).

18 *Dictionary of Music and Musicians*, ed. G. Grove (London 1879–89), art. 'David, Ferdinand'.

19 Hermann Mendel and August F.W.Reissman, *Musikalisches Conversations-Lexikon* (Berlin 187?–80), art. 'David, Ferdinand' ['ein classisches, ächt deutsches Gepräge'].

20 See Edmond van der Straeten, *The History of the Violin* (London 1933; rpr. New York 1968), II, pp. 225–6.

Ex. 6.1a   Beethoven: Violin Sonata in A Op. 47, first movement, bar 495 (ed. David)

Ex.6.1b   Beethoven: Violin Sonata in A Op. 30 No. 1, third movement bars 18–19 (ed. David)

while the violin part has another. These modifications seem to have been introduced for the sake of technical convenience, a more idiomatic bowing, or occasionally (as in bar 26 of Op. 12 No. 1, where David indicated separately-bowed semiquavers instead of Beethoven's slurred ones) a particular effect. In some instances alterations or additions to the *Urtext*[21] were inevitable because of the impracticability of what Beethoven wrote. Like subsequent editors, David was obliged to divide the impossibly long slurs which Beethoven, following earlier practice, seems often to have employed as an indication of legato rather than specific bowing. In these cases David sometimes retained Beethoven's long slurs and indicated the bowing with up- and down-bow symbols; at other times he simply replaced the long slur with a succession of shorter ones (though mostly retaining the original in the piano part). Occasionally, most notably in the case of the first movement of the 'Kreutzer' sonata (bars 210–26) Beethoven indicated bowing that is very awkward, if not impossible, to execute effectively; here David substituted a more idiomatic version. In the Violin Concerto alteration and amplification of Beethoven's bowing marks is much more frequent than in the chamber music, for reasons which are considered below. Another respect in which David altered and obscured the *Urtext* (especially in the quartets where he provided no score from which to identify his changes) was the addition of dots under slurs as an indication for staccato and the alteration of some of Beethoven's dots under slurs to horizontal lines, blurring the import of Beethoven's own *portato* notation.

All these infidelities to the letter of the *Urtext* reveal a disinclination, typical of David's and of Beethoven's period, to regard it as a binding indication of the composer's wishes. To some extent this standpoint is legitimised by accounts of Beethoven's own attitude; he is said, for example, to have been delighted by an impromptu addition by Bridgetower in the first movement of the 'Kreutzer'

21 The somewhat ambiguous term *Urtext* is used throughout to mean the *Fassung letzter Hand*, the composer's latest approved text, as far as that can be ascertained.

Sonata,[22] and Ries testifies that Beethoven occasionally added impromptu embellishment into his performance.[23] But the evidence is equivocal: in characteristically inconsistent manner, Beethoven improvised a long, unmarked cadenza in a performance of his Quintet Op. 16, but was incensed by Czerny's embellishment of the piano part of the same work (though this may have been related to the nature of Czerny's additions). In the case of the Violin Concerto, however, there are particular circumstances for believing that while Beethoven may have been precise in his markings for the orchestral parts, he did not regard the text of the solo part in the autograph or first edition as definitive, especially with respect to bowing; in this instance the currently fashionable notion, that the nearer we get to a slavish observance of Beethoven's *Urtext* the nearer we get to his intentions for the performance of the work, may be very much mistaken.

THE VIOLIN CONCERTO

David's and Dont's editions of the Violin Concerto contain not only an abundance of fingerings and bowing marks, but also, in contrast to David's editions of the chamber music, very many radical deviations from the *Urtext* in the matter of slurring and articulation. Yet either of these versions, greatly as they differ from one another, almost certainly provides a better guide to how a violinist of Beethoven's day might have played the work than does the *Urtext*; indeed, it is highly unlikely that, particularly in the matter of bowing, Beethoven would have been content with an interpretation of the concerto in which the soloist adhered literally to the *Urtext*.

Dont's edition is of particular interest on account of its editor's close connections with the Viennese tradition; his credentials are best summed up by quoting the preface to his edition which, apart from suggesting that the Concerto was more frequently performed during Beethoven's lifetime than is usually thought, provides valuable clues about the composer's attitude towards the text. The complete preface reads:

Several deviations from older editions will not escape the attentive player of this edition of Beethoven's Violin Concerto. On the basis of reliable tradition Professor Jac. Dont in Vienna is in a position to write down much of the generally accepted version which differs especially in the tone-shadings. His father, first cellist in the Imperial and Royal Court Opera in Vienna in Beethoven's time, heard and accompanied the Violin Concerto, written for the then violin virtuoso Fr Clement, from the first performance on, very often, again also in Beethoven's presence. Solicitous for the education of his son, to whom he taught the violin at that time, he noted and marked very precisely the version wished for by Beethoven. What the youth learned then, the experienced teacher has now reproduced in the

22 Bridgetower's account is cited in F.G.Edwards, 'George P. Bridgetower and the Kreutzer Sonata', *The Musical Times*, 49 (1908), p. 302.

23 Ries and Wegeler, *Biographische Notizen über Ludwig van Beethoven* (ed. Kalischer), p. 127. It is attested in a way which implies that others did this more often. Ries wrote: 'he very rarely added notes or an ornament' ('äußerst selten setzte er Noten oder eine Verzierung zu').

present edition with critical discrimination. All dynamic signs, fingerings and such like are, however, the independent contribution of the editor.[24]

Ex. 6.2a   Beethoven: Violin Concerto in D Op. 61, first movement, bar 132 (ed. Dont)

Ex. 6.2b   Beethoven: Violin Concerto in D, Op. 61, first movement, bars 204–5 (ed. Dont)

Ex. 6.2c   Beethoven: Violin Concerto in D Op. 61, second movement, bars 62–3 (ed. Dont)

Ex. 6.2d   Beethoven: Violin Concerto in D Op. 61, first movement, bars 423–5 (ed. Dont)

Ex. 6.2e   Beethoven: Violin Concerto in D Op. 61, third movement, bars 356–60 (ed. Dont)

24 'Dem aufmerksamen Spieler dieser Ausgabe des Beethoven'schen Violinconcerts werden einige Abweichungen von älteren Ausgaben nicht entgehen. Professor Jac. Dont in Wien durfte auf Grund zuverlässiger Tradition Manches von der landläufigen Auffassung namentlich in den Tonschattirungen [the German word 'Tonschattirungen' (tone-shadings) is unspecific] abweichend vorschreiben. Sein Vater, zu Beethovens Zeit erster Violoncellist in der K.K. Hofoper in Wien hat das für den damaligen Violin-Virtuosen Fr Clement componirte Violinconcert von der ersten Aufführung an sehr oft noch auch in Beethovens Anwesenheit gehört und accompagnirt. Vorsorglich für die Ausbildung seines Sohnes, den er damals im Geigenspiel unterrichtete, notirte und merkte er auf das Genauste die von Beethoven gewünschte Auffasung. Was der Jüngling damals erlernte, hat der erfahrene Lehrer heute in vorleigender Ausgabe mit kritischer Sichtung wiedergegeben. Alle dynamischen Zeichen, Fingersatz und dergl. sind dagegen selbständige Zuthat des Herausgebers.' Preface to Jacob Dont's edition of Beethoven's Violin Concerto (Berlin, Schlesinger (pl. no. S.7367), c.1880)

As well as a few small, but apparently deliberate, differences from the notes of the autograph and first editions in Dont's version,[25] (Exs. 6.2a–e) there are a large number of passages where Beethoven's slurring and articulation is modified or amplified. In the light of Dont's preface, these additions may be important in two significant respects. First, they may offer clues about the sort of slurring which Clement, with Beethoven's concurrence, introduced into the Concerto. Secondly (whether or not they reliably reflect Clement's practice or Beethoven's specific wishes) they support the hypothesis that the composer himself, possibly recognising the limitations of his knowledge of the intricacies of soloistic bowing technique, sanctioned additions to or alteration of the slurring in his original text. Andreas Moser's account of 'Viennese traditions' in his *Geschichte des Violinspiels* also suggests that Beethoven, even at the earliest stage in the performance history of the Concerto, did not intend his bowings and articulations to be more than a rough guide for the soloist.

Discussing the so-called 'Paganini' bowing, Moser wrote:

Certainly Joachim told me that already during his time of study with Joseph Böhm [sic][26] the opinion was widespread among the Viennese violinists that Franz Clement, at the first performance of the Beethoven Violin Concerto which was written for him in 1806, had already used the aforesaid bowing at the following place in the first movement [Ex. 6.3a].[27]

This bowing is almost exactly that employed by David for the same passage (Ex. 6.3b); Dont, however, slurred it differently (Ex. 6.3c). Assuming that Moser's 'traditions' and Dont's preface can be relied on, this raises the possibility that Clement (presumably with Beethoven's concurrence) later changed his treatment of the passage. But whatever patterns of bowing Beethoven may directly have sanctioned, the implication that he expected some of the passages of separate notes to receive this kind of treatment seems irresistible.

In fact, the differences between David's and Dont's versions of the solo part, though considerable, are perhaps less profound than their points of similarity. This is not altogether surprising since, although they represent rather different strands in

25 The most significant of these are, in the first movement, bar 132 (Ex. 6.3a) and bar 204 (Ex. 6.3b) and, in the second movement, bar 63 (Ex. 6.3c). In the Finale there is one slight difference which may be a misprint at bar 355 (Ex. 6.3e; the upbeat to bar 356 is missing, though the f$\sharp^1$ appears as the last note of the violin 1 cue, whereas that note should actually be an a^1). In addition to these changes there are two *ossia* passages: first movement bars 423–5 (Ex. 6.3d) and Finale bars 356–60 (Ex. 6.3e).

26 Joseph Boehm (1795–1876) rehearsed Beethoven's A minor Quartet Op. 132 under the composer's guidance at about the time Dont was his pupil. Joseph Joachim studied with him in Vienna about 1841–2, at which time Clement still lived there.

27 'Freilich erzählte mir Joachim, schon während seiner Studienzeit mit Joseph Böhm wäre unter den Wiener Geigern die Meinung allgemein verbreitet gewesen, daß sich bereits Franz Clement bei der Uraufführung des für ihn geschriebenen Violinkonzerts von Beethoven 1806 an der folgenden Stelle des ersten Satzes der besagten Strichart bedient hätte.' Andreas Moser, *Geschichte des Violinspiels*, rev. H. J. Nösselt (Tutzing 1967), II, p. 148.

Ex. 6.3a   Beethoven: Violin Concerto in D Op. 61, first movement, bars 139–41 (Clement – according to Moser)

Ex. 6.3b   Beethoven: Violin Concerto in D Op. 61, first movement, bars 139–41 (ed. David)

Ex. 6.3c   Beethoven: Violin Concerto in D Op. 61, first movement, bars 139–41 (ed. Dont)

nineteenth-century German violin playing, they evidently drew heavily on common roots.[28] David added slurring rather more frequently than Dont to figures left unbowed by Beethoven (for example, bars 151–64 of the first movement), but there is little difference in the overall extent of the editorial intervention and there are many places where their additions are very similar; where, for instance, both David and Dont added bowings to a passage left entirely unslurred by Beethoven.

In general David's approach to bowing, with its tendency towards more varied and intricate patterns, seems closer than Dont's to that of the Viotti School as reflected in Spohr's practice (Exs. 6.4a and b; the semiquavers are all separate in Beethoven's text). Dont's, while often similar to David's, is generally 'squarer' – more on the beat than across the beat. In view of Dont's preface, this aspect of his bowing may possibly reflect something of the difference between Clement's style and that of the Viotti School. With respect to specific bowing patterns, however, it is not easy to determine the extent to which David's and Dont's editions reflect one style or another. At first sight it might seem as if Dont's bowing of bar 428 of the first movement (Ex. 6.4c), which Beethoven left unmarked, is more likely to represent a style associated with Clement than does David's bowing (Ex. 6.4d), which is typical of violinists of the Viotti School; but a glance at Clement's own D major Concerto (first performed on 7 April 1805, some twelve months before Beethoven's)

---

28 Dont is likely to have received some of the same influences from Boehm as David did from Spohr, though the direct influence of the Viotti School waned considerably between David's and Dont's student years.

Ex. 6.4a   Beethoven: Violin Concerto in D Op. 61, first movement, bars 463–5 (ed. David)

Ex. 6.4b   Beethoven: Violin Concerto in D Op. 61, first movement, bars 463–5 (ed. Dont)

Ex. 6.4c   Beethoven: Violin Concerto in D Op. 61, first movement, bars 428–9 (ed. Dont)

Ex. 6.4d   Beethoven: Violin Concerto in D Op. 61, first movement, bars 428–9 (ed. David)

Ex. 6.4e   Clement: Violin Concerto in D, first movement, bars 276 and 278

shows a similar passage using first one bowing scheme and then the other (Ex. 6.4e).[29] Similarly, in the first movement passage cited above, where David used the Paganini bowing, Dont's different bowing is equally, if not more, convoluted (Ex. 6.3c).

Both David and Dont freely employed fingering patterns which invite portamento; for instance at bar 150 of the first movement, where they used the same fingering (Ex. 6.5a). David was on the whole rather more liberal with such fingerings than Dont. In the Larghetto he used them, presumably for expressive purposes, where

29 The similarity of the passagework and melodic material to Beethoven's here and throughout Clement's Concerto is also striking; this relationship between the two concertos, which I discussed and illustrated in a BBC Music Weekly broadcast on 7 May 1989, will be examined in greater detail in an article which I am presently preparing.

Ex. 6.5a   Beethoven: Violin Concerto in D Op. 61, first movement, bars 150–1 (ed. Dont)

Ex. 6.5b   Beethoven: Violin Concerto in D Op. 61, second movement, bars 15–17 (ed. David)

Ex. 6.5c   Beethoven: Violin Concerto in D Op. 61, second movement, bars 15–17 (ed. Dont)

Dont's fingering clearly indicates a 'clean' execution (Exs. 6.5b and c). (Neither editor observed Beethoven's bowing here.) Elsewhere, on the other hand, Dont's fingering implies a portamento where David's does not. Both editors frequently marked harmonics and open strings, the implications of which are considered below, though again David did so more often than Dont.

The technical and stylistic trends implied by David's and Dont's editions of the Violin Concerto are confirmed and elucidated by the much more wide-ranging evidence of David's chamber music editions. The rest of this chapter will explore the extent to which David's performance markings may reflect some of the general characteristics of violin playing in Beethoven's time.

LEFT-HAND TECHNIQUE

David's fingerings illustrate many traits that are quite uncharacteristic of modern violin playing. They yield information on two levels: the purely mechanical matter of getting the hand into a convenient position to play the notes; and the employment of particular fingerings or shifts for expressive ends.

Before looking more closely at David's choice of fingering for aesthetic purposes, it may be helpful briefly to consider a few mechanical aspects of his fingering which are primarily indicative of his own technical proclivities or those of the period.

David frequently employs the technique, characteristic of nineteenth-century violin playing in general, of playing notes which go above or below the hand's current position by means of a repetition of the previous finger (i.e. the use of 1–1–1 or 4–4–4), which may sometimes have portamento implications, but often does not. On the other hand, David shows a greater reluctance than his older and younger contemporaries Spohr and Joachim to use the even-numbered positions where such an approach would seem logical; this often leads to awkward position changes. Joachim sometimes preserved these fingerings in his edition of the violin sonatas (Ex. 6.6a), but often adopted a more 'modern' approach (Exs. 6.6b–e). At times it seems as if David doubted whether it were safe to shift from a distance to one of the even-numbered positions; in the Adagio cantabile of the Quartet Op. 18 No. 2, for instance, he marked a shift from first to third and then to fourth position (Ex. 6.6f). Sometimes David's avoidance of these positions seems particularly perverse. In the recapitulation of the first movement of the 'Kreutzer' Sonata the second subject lies comfortably in first position, and David marked no fingering, but in the exposition, where it would easily have been playable in second position without shifts, David gave the fingering in Ex. 6.6g (Joachim used second position throughout for this passage). Not all David's avoidance of second position may be attributable to the same motives, and in Ex. 6.6h, for instance, where a shift to second position for the c^2, d^2, $e\flat^2$ and f^2 would seem logical, David's fingering may have been deliberately chosen to achieve a portamento between the c^2 and d^2.

Many of David's fingerings have a potential for portamento and it seems likely that he and his contemporaries would have allowed these shifts to be heard quite prominently in performance. Leading violinists of the period, including Joachim, warned strongly against abusing portamento and cautioned that in many cases the shifts should 'not impinge on the consciousness' of the listener;[30] but we know from Joachim's own recordings that this did not exclude frequent, perceptible, sometimes very obtrusive shifts. To what extent this type of portamento was a feature of violin playing approved of, let alone envisaged, by Beethoven is an entirely different matter. Towards the end of the eighteenth century solo violinists certainly began to employ portamento with much greater frequency and prominence as an expressive colouring to their playing. It became an especially prominent aspect of the playing of Viotti's disciples; in his *L'Art du violon*, Baillot (b. 1771) gave specific examples of its use in his own music and that of Kreutzer (b. 1766) and Rode (b. 1774)[31] and it

30 'Gar nicht zum Bewußtsein kommt': Joseph Joachim and Andreas Moser, *Violinschule* (Berlin 1902–5), II, p. 94.

31 Pierre Baillot, *L'Art du violon* (Paris 1834), p. 149. These examples are reproduced in Robin Stowell, *Violin Technique and Performance Practice in the Late Eighteenth and Early Nineteenth Centuries* (Cambridge 1985), pp. 95–6.

Ex. 6.6a   Beethoven: Violin Sonata in E♭ Op. 12 No. 3, first movement, bar 15 (ed. David)

Ex. 6.6b   Beethoven: Violin Sonata in C minor, Op. 30 No. 2, fourth movement, bars 31–4 (ed. David)

Ex. 6.6c   Beethoven: Violin Sonata in C minor, Op. 30 No. 2, fourth movement, bars 31–4 (ed. Joachim)

Ex. 6.6d   Beethoven: Violin Sonata in G Op. 96, first movement, bars 63–5 (ed. David)

Ex. 6.6e   Beethoven: Violin Sonata in G Op. 96, first movement, bars 63–5 (ed. Joachim)

Ex. 6.6f   Beethoven: String Quartet in G Op. 18 No. 2, second movement, bars 14–18 (ed. David)

Ex. 6.6g   Beethoven: Violin Sonata in A Op. 47, first movement, bars 91–101 (ed. David)

Ex. 6.6h   Beethoven: String Quartet in E♭ Op. 74, first movement, bars 189–92 (ed. David)

is well known from many other contemporary sources that these violinists used the device liberally. The extent to which Viotti (b. 1755) himself employed it is less clear, but it was certainly much used by other, older Italian violinists such as Antonio Lolli (b. 1725) (sometimes credited with being the first to make a speciality of it),[32] and Nicola Mestrino (b. 1748) became so notable an exponent of the device that Woldemar used the term 'couler à Mestrino' to designate a prominent portamento.[33] In this context it is interesting to note that Haydn, who marked fingerings suggestive of portamento in some of his quartets,[34] counted Mestrino among his musicians at Eszterháza between 1780 and 1785. The extent to which this technique was already well established by the end of the eighteenth century is suggested by the remarkable introduction to Woldemar's *Grande méthode* of c. 1799.[35] In singing it was already well established as an important means of expression, as Corri's somewhat earlier *A Select Collection* testifies. There were many types of portamento,[36] however, and some authorities made a sharp distinction between the subtle connection between notes, which was a hallmark of fine singing, and the more pronounced portamento which could be likened to the effect made by a violinist 'if the player, with one finger on one string, draws two different notes into one another and at the same time melts them into each other'.[37] This latter effect could nevertheless be described as 'a real beauty in singing if it is well performed and used in the right place'.[38]

No record of Beethoven's views on the matter of portamento seems to have been preserved, but an isolated fingering in his own quintet arrangement of his Piano Trio Op. 1 No. 2 suggests that he may sometimes have felt the effect to be appropriate (Ex. 6.7a). He also, apparently, intended it in the Finale of Op. 96.[39] David curiously provided no guidance at this point, though Beethoven's slurring implies a portamento from sixth position on the a^1 string to first on the d^1; Joachim made the portamento explicit by giving the appropriate fingering.[40] (Ex. 6.7b).

32 Salieri, in *Allgemeine musikalische Zeitung* 13 (1811), col. 209.
33 Michel Woldemar's edition of Leopold Mozart's *Violinschule*. P. Barbieri's assertion (*Early Music*, 19/1 (1991), p. 81) that a literal, audible use of quarter tones is indicated by Woldemar's notation seems highly dubious.
34 For further detail see W. Drabkin 'Fingering in Haydn's String Quartets', *Early Music*, 16/1 (1988) pp. 50–7.
35 Michel Woldemar, *Grande méthode* (Paris (1799?)), pp. 1–2.
36 For various types of portamento in violin playing, see Baillot *L'Art du violon*, pp. 76–8 and Spohr, *Violinschule*, pp. 120–1. These, together with other aspects of portamento, are discussed in Stowell, *Violin Technique*, pp. 98–103 and 315–18.
37 Johann Friedrich Schubert, *Neue Singschule* (Leipzig 1804), p. 57: 'wenn der Spieler mit einem Finger auf einer Saite zwei verschiedene Töne aneinander zieht, und gleichsam in einander schmelzt.'
38 *ibid.*, p. 57. 'eine wesentliche Schönheit des Gesanges, wenn es gut executirt und am rechten Ort angebracht wird'.
39 He wrote the sonata for Rode, whose prominent portamento was already commented on by Reichardt in 1805.
40 See Clive Brown, 'Bowing Styles, Portamento and Vibrato in Nineteenth-century Violin Playing', *Journal of the Royal Musical Association*, 113/1 (1988), pp. 123–4.

Ex. 6.7a   Beethoven: arrangement of Op. 1 No. 3 for string quintet, second movement, Variation V, bars 34–5 (ed. David)

Ex. 6.7b   Beethoven: Violin Sonata in G Op. 96, fourth movement, bars 157–9 (ed. Joachim)

David's fingerings, as a whole, make it clear that he regarded portamento as an extremely important aesthetic resource, and he frequently indicated inessential position changes to allow for the introduction of portamento. In addition, there are many places where, when a particular phrase or passage necessitates a change of position, David chose a fingering which would have been likely to give rise to a noticeable slide rather than a clean position change; in many such instances the potential portamento appears to have no particular aesthetic motivation and probably reveals more about the prevailing tolerance of audible shifting than about any deliberate expressive intention.

A number of different types of portamento effect are revealed in Exs. 6.8a–e. It is interesting to note that Joachim avoided the portamento in Ex. 6.8b, but retained David's fingering in Ex. 6.8c; he changed the fingering in Ex. 6.8d but kept the portamento in the second and fourth bars (descending from sixth rather than fifth position). In Ex. 6.8e David seems to have chosen a fall from fifth to first position to produce a particularly expressive portamento; it would have been consistent with his normal practice to have shifted to a first finger on the second half of the second beat, with a 1–1–1 fingering for the following g^1–$f\sharp^1$–g^1. David seems frequently to have used fingerings with a potential for portamento which were dictated primarily by the need to change position and secondarily by the musical appropriateness of the effect. Though, with few exceptions, he seems to have introduced shifts in places where he felt that a portamento would be musically apt, the effect often seems inconsequential (e.g. Exs. 6.9a–c). Sometimes the inevitable portamento (however slight) seems entirely unmotivated; for instance in Ex. 6.9d, where in the immediate repetition of the phrase David indicated no shift of position at the same place. Joachim seems to have been conscious of the incongruity here and introduced an inessential shift at the same place in the second phrase (Ex. 6.9e).

Ex. 6.8a   Beethoven: Piano Trio in D Op. 70 No. 1, second movement, bars 30–1
(ed. David)

Ex. 6.8b   Beethoven: Violin Sonata in A Op. 12 No. 2, first movement, bars 172–4
(ed. David)

Ex. 6.8c   Beethoven: Violin Sonata in A Op. 12 No. 2, first movement, bars 76–81
(ed. David)

Ex. 6.8d   Beethoven: Violin Sonata in A Op. 12 No. 2, second movement, bars 33–9
(ed. David)

Ex. 6.8e   Beethoven: String Quartet in G Op. 18 No. 2, second movement, bars 13–14
(ed. David)

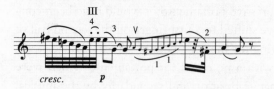

David often employed semitone shifts to change position. Sometimes this type of
shift may imply a portamento effect (Ex. 6.10a–c). Such effects had been specifically
asked for by Rameau[41] and were indicated in the nineteenth century by, among
others, Meyerbeer[42] and Wagner.[43] In these cases and in many instances in David's

41 Jean-Philippe Rameau, *Platée* (Paris 1749) p. 99.
42 In the full scores of *L'Étoil du nord*, p. 184 (with the instruction 'glissez . . . avec le même doigt') and
    Les Huguenots, I, bar 104 (with the instruction 'con molto portamento').
43 In *Der fliegende Holländer*. See Clive Brown, 'Performing Practice in Wagner', in *Wagner in Performance*
    (Yale 1992).

Ex. 6.9a Beethoven: Piano Trio in C minor Op. 1 No. 3, second movement, bars 28–32 (ed. David)

Ex. 6.9b Beethoven: Piano Trio in D Op. 70 No. 1, first movement, bars 29–32 (ed David)

Ex. 6.9c Beethoven: Piano Trio in D Op. 70 No. 1, third movement, bars 340–4 (ed. David)

Ex. 6.9d Beethoven: Violin Sonata in A minor Op. 23, third movement, bars 25–32 (ed. David)

Ex. 6.9e Beethoven: Violin Sonata in A minor Op. 23, third movement, bars 25–32 (ed. Joachim)

editions it seems identical with the *mesa di voce crescente* and *decrescente* described by Lasser[44] and with one of Fröhlich's recommended types of *Cercar della nota*.[45]

Related to portamento, since it often involves large shifts, is the use of *una corda*. But *una corda* was also employed simply for tonal effect. It is occasionally marked by Beethoven himself (for instance, in the cello part in the Finale of the Piano Trio Op. 1 No. 3) and it was certainly used by violinists in his circle. A striking example of phrases played across the strings contrasted with the same phrases played on one string can be found in the Minuetto of his violin teacher Wenzel Krumpholz's *Eine*

44 Johann Baptist Lasser, *Vollständige Anleitung zur Singkunst* (Munich 1798).
45 Franz Joseph Fröhlich, *Vollständige theoretisch-praktische Musikschule* (Bonn 1810–11), I, p. 59.

Ex. 6.10a   Beethoven: String Quartet in E♭ Op. 74, second movement, bars 62–4 (ed. David)

Ex. 6.10b   Beethoven: Trio in B♭ Op. 11, first movement, bars 135–9 (ed. David)

Ex. 6.10c   Beethoven: String Quartet in A minor Op. 132, third movement, bars 80–2 (ed. David)

viertel Stunde für eine Violin. There are many instances where David marked fingerings, particularly in cantabile melodies, which retain the colour of a single string for short phrases, changing with the natural phrase divisions of the melody (Exs. 6.11a–b). Sometimes he used *una corda* to contrast with a similar phrase played across the strings (Ex. 6.11c).

As well as including many fingerings that suggest portamento, David's Beethoven editions have a strikingly large number of indications of open strings and natural harmonics, both of which occur not only on short notes, but also, frequently, on notes of considerable duration. David's use of open strings and harmonics, which is very much in line with that of his teacher Spohr and probably also of the Viotti School, is sharply at odds with the conventional eighteenth-century attitude articulated by Leopold Mozart, Reichardt and many other authorities (though not by Loehlein) that open strings should be avoided wherever possible, unless required for a special effect, and should in any case only occur on short notes. David's editions contain many examples of open strings and harmonics on long or melodically important notes. Sometimes, particularly in the case of harmonics, these may be introduced for the sake of a particular tone colour, but often they seem to be there simply for convenience. David's lack of inhibition in the use of them is evidently related to the prevailing vibrato aesthetic of the period. Nineteenth-century methods are unanimous in recommending a sparing use of vibrato. David's editions are consistent with this attitude, for if anything like a continuous or even frequent

Ex. 6.11a   Beethoven: String Quartet in C Op. 59 No. 3, second movement, bars 1–5 (ed. David)

Ex. 6.11b   Beethoven: String Quartet in F minor Op. 95, second movement, bars 1–12 (ed. David)

Ex. 6.11c   Beethoven: Piano Trio in C minor Op. 1 No. 3, fourth movement, bars 300–13 (ed. David)

vibrato had been expected, his harmonics and open strings would often have sounded unpleasantly incongruous. It is possible that the leading violinists of Beethoven's time may have made even more sparing use of vibrato than their immediate predecessors; one writer in 1811 went so far as to state that vibrato ('Tremolo or Close Shake') 'is become obsolete',[46] though he admitted that it could, for the sake of variety, be occasionally introduced on a long note in a melody. Viotti was once accused of having a 'somewhat too strong vibrato',[47] though he was not charged with using it too often.

Exs. 6.12a–q are illuminating. Exs. 6.12a–b show the use of open strings on relatively long notes for position changing. Exs. 6.12c–g show various situations in which the open string seems to have been chosen so that a phrase or section retains the colour of a single string. In Ex. 6.12h the open string appears to have been chosen for its particular tonal quality. Exs. 6.12i–k are instances of the harmonic being apparently used simply for tonal effect, while Exs. 6.12l–m also have an element of portamento (as does Ex. 6.8c). In Exs. 6.12n–p the harmonics seem largely to have been chosen for technical convenience. All these examples argue for a basically non-vibrato sound – in the case of the harmonics, reflecting Spohr's observation that these notes could be used wherever convenient because they were not substantially different in sound from the ordinary stopped notes.

46 John Jousse, *The Theory and Practice of the Violin* (London 1811).
47 *Allgemeine musikalische Zeitung*, 1 (1798/9), 762.

Ex. 6.12a   Beethoven: String Quartet in D Op. 18 No. 3, first movement, bars 76–8 (ed. David)

Ex. 6.12b   Beethoven: String Quartet in C♯ minor Op. 131, fifth movement, bars 69–73 (ed. David)

Ex. 6.12c   Beethoven: String Quartet in D Op. 18 No. 3, first movement, bars 1–4 (ed. David)

Ex. 6.12d   Beethoven: Violin Sonata in A Op. 30 No. 1, first movement, bars 195–6 (ed. David)

Ex. 6.12e   Beethoven: Quartet in A minor Op. 132, third movement, bars 21–5 (ed. David)

Ex. 6.12f   Beethoven: String Quartet in E♭ Op. 74, first movement, bars 18–19 (ed. David)

Ex. 6.12g   Beethoven: String Quartet in A Op. 18 No. 5, fourth movement, bars 12–15 (ed. David)

Ex. 6.12h   Beethoven: String Quartet in A minor Op. 132, fifth movement, bars 1–4 (ed. David)

Ex. 6.12i   Beethoven: Violin Sonata in A Op. 30 No. 1, second movement, bars 1–4 (ed. David)

Ex. 6.12j   Beethoven: String Quartet in A Op. 18 No. 5, second movement, bars 1–12 (ed. David)

Ex. 6.12k   Beethoven: Violin Sonata in A Op. 47, first movement, bars 116–18 (ed. David)

Ex. 6.12l   Beethoven: String Quartet in C Op. 59 No. 3, second movement, bars 93–7 (ed. David)

Ex. 6.12m   Beethoven: String Quartet in F minor Op. 95, second movement, bars 170–3 (ed. David)

E. 6.12n   Beethoven: Piano Trio in E♭ Op. 70 No. 2, first movement, bars 112–16 (ed. David)

Ex. 6.12o   Beethoven: Violin Sonata in A Op. 12 No. 2, third movement, bars 120–3
(ed. David)

Ex. 6.12p   Beethoven: String Quartet in D Op. 18 No. 3, fourth movement, bars 76–80
(ed. David)

Ex. 6.12q   Beethoven: Violin Sonata in A minor Op. 23, third movement, bars 327–32
(ed. David)

In certain circumstances, where no harmonic is marked, it is likely that David expected the player, in the absence of fingering to the contrary, to use a harmonic rather than shifting the hand into a new position or using an ordinary extension (as specified in the second bar of Ex. 6.12p). In Ex. 6.12q David did not indicate a fingering for the top e^3, but probably expected a harmonic; Joachim marked a harmonic as shown in square brackets. There seem to be many similar places where David tacitly expected this use of a harmonic, though in slower passages, especially where the preceding note is $d\#^3$, an ordinary extension might have been employed.

BOWING TECHNIQUE

Among the most noticeable features of David's bowing indications is his employment of dots and, occasionally, horizontal lines under slurs. The range of meaning of these marks was a problem in David's day and still presents difficulties for editors and performers.[48] Where Beethoven himself used dots under slurs there is little doubt that he invariably intended it to indicate *portato* (i.e. with a slight articulation between notes); for this type of performance David seems to have employed lines under slurs. David's dots under slurs appear mostly to have the implication, common in violinists' compositions at that time, of sharp separation by means of a succession of very short up- or, more rarely, down-bows produced towards the

---

48 See Clive Brown, 'Dots and Strokes in Late-Eighteenth- and Nineteenth-Century Music', *Early Music* 21/4 (1993), pp. 593–610.

point of the bow by a series of pressures of the hand (usually referred to as up-bow or down-bow staccato). David appears not always to have understood Beethoven's dots under slurs as *portato*, for he sometimes retained Beethoven's notation and sometimes changed it to lines under slurs, a method of indicating *portato* that was just beginning to be widely accepted by violinists at that time.[49] Continuing confusion over this matter in the middle of the nineteenth century is attested by a correspondence between Brahms and Joachim on the subject.[50] A good example of this confusion is shown in Ex. 6.13a: in the first bar David added dots under the slur indicating up-bow staccato and, apparently taking Beethoven's *portato* notation in the third bar to indicate the same type of staccato bowing, modified it so that it too would be played in a single up-bow; Joachim who, as his correspondence with Brahms shows, was aware of Beethoven's meaning, reverted to the original notation for this passage (Ex. 6.13b).

Ex. 6.13a   Beethoven: Violin Sonata in E♭ Op. 12 No. 3, first movement, bars 29–31 (ed. David)

Ex. 6.13b   Beethoven: Violin Sonata in E♭ Op. 12 No. 3, first movement, bars 29–31 (ed. Joachim)

David seems sometimes to have employed slurred staccato to achieve an especially sharply-detached execution, where violinists of a later school would most probably have used lifted or bounced separate bows in the lower half (Exs. 6.14a–b); but his indication of a succession of staccato up-bows frequently appears to arise less from his desire for a particular effect than from his need to bring the bow back from the point towards the middle for the following note or notes. In some of these cases the staccato may perhaps have been executed in a less percussive manner. Sometimes, as in Exs. 6.14c–e, the bow will have arrived at the point because of a long down-bow; sometimes, however, it will have been near the point because a succession of relatively fast-moving notes was apparently played with short on-string strokes in the upper half of the bow (Exs. 6.14f–g). Sometimes a pair of short staccato down-bows were used to keep the bow at the point after a series of short notes to allow for a long up-bow or chord (Exs. 6.14h–i, also Ex. 6.16c).

49 Franz Berwald, however, used the horizontal line under a slur as early as his String Quartet in G minor of 1818.

50 *Johannes Brahms; Briefwechsel* (Berlin, 1907–22), VI pp. 146–53.

Ex. 6.14a   Beethoven: String Quartet in C minor Op. 18 No. 4, fourth movement, bars 204–8 (ed. David)

Ex. 6.14b   Beethoven: String Quartet in B♭ Op. 18 No. 6, first movement, bars 2–5 (ed. David)

Ex. 6.14c   Beethoven: String Quartet in D Op. 18 No. 3, first movement, bars 28–31 (ed. David)

Ex. 6.14d   Beethoven: Piano Trio in E♭ Op. 1 No. 1 fourth movement, bars 54–64 (ed. David)

Ex. 6.14e   Beethoven: String Quartet in B♭ Op. 130, sixth movement, bars 48–56 (ed. David)

Ex. 6.14f   Beethoven: String Quartet in F Op. 59 No. 1, first movement, bars 259–62 (ed. David)

Ex. 6.14g   Beethoven: String Quartet in F Op. 59 No. 1, second movement, bars 463–8 (ed. David)

Ex. 6.14h   Beethoven: String Quartet in B♭ Op. 18 No. 6, first movement, bars 74–80 (ed. David)

Ex. 6.14i   Beethoven: String Quartet in E minor Op. 59 No. 2, first movement, bars 207–11 (ed. David)

The preceding examples illustrate a striking feature of David's editions: that many passages which would now be performed with a lifted or springing bow in the middle or lower half of the bow were intended by him to be performed with an apparently on-string stroke in the upper half. In this David seems to be characteristic of the majority of early-nineteenth-century German violinists.

A short-lived vogue for springing bowstrokes among certain players around the end of the eighteenth century, the rare use of these strokes by string players of the Viotti School, and their subsequent employment later in the nineteenth century for figures which would earlier have been performed on the string in the upper half of the bow, have been considered in detail elsewhere.[51] A few supplementary points may be added here. The late-eighteenth-century springing bowstroke, popularised by Wilhelm Cramer, was associated particularly with sections of continuously running passagework in concertos and in pieces of a lighter character. Bernhard Romberg commented in his retrospective *Méthode de violoncelle* of 1840 that the springing bowstroke might be 'introduced in light, easy passages, and is particularly suited to those pieces which are written in a playful style such as Rondos in $\frac{6}{8}$ time, or solos for chamber music. For music of a higher order it is not so well adapted, and should never be used except in quick movements.' Then, after explaining how it should be executed, he commented rather dismissively: 'This bowing was formerly in great repute with all Artists, who introduced it in passages of every

51 Brown, 'Bowing Styles', pp. 97–128.

description. It is, however, quite incompatible with a fine broad style of playing, which fully accounts for the inferiority of their compositions.'[52]

A strong tradition that springing bowstrokes, except in a few rare circumstances, were inappropriate and unauthentic in the music of Classical German composers existed among violinists of the first half of the nineteenth century. Alexander Malibran, a pupil of Spohr, gave the following interesting account of a conversation with his master in the 1840s (when springing bowings were becoming common, especially among French-trained violinists) about the correct performance styles for Haydn, Mozart and Beethoven:

To his horror he noticed how violinists played the *detachés* in a springing manner, and that they did this even in the earliest masters, who, more than all others wish to have a free, well-nourished tone. He was absolutely adamant that one should not play all composers in the same way; on the contrary, he wished the artist to adhere to the true tradition; so to say, to deny himself and reproduce the composition himself, just as it is. 'There, however,' he exclaimed, 'they do not bother either about the style of the man nor about the instrument, which in the time of the composer was a wholly different one than now; they depict Frederick the Great with a haircut *à la Titus*, in a black coat and trousers!' – Only in certain passages, in certain scherzos of Beethoven, Onslow and Mendelssohn did he allow that one could let the bow spring.[53]

Joachim seems to have been among the earliest German violinists to employ and advocate, after a certain amount of soul searching,[54] various kinds of springing strokes (whose effect he described as snow, rain and hail) in Classical compositions; David, though briefly explaining in his *Violinschule* how springing bowings should be executed, appears, on the evidence of his editions, largely to have eschewed them in his performance of the Classical repertoire.

In many instances the markings in David's editions provide insufficient information to be positive whether the bow was intended to be used in the upper or lower half, or whether the bowing was to be on or off the string; but in numerous passages there can be little doubt about the type of bowing envisaged. The overall

---

52 Bernhard Romberg, *Méthode de violoncelle*, English edition, (London, 1840), p. 109.

53 'Zu seinen Schrecken nahm er es wahr, wie die Violinisten die *Detachés* springend spielen, und dies selbst bei den ältesten Meistern Thun, die, mehr als alle andere, einen freien, wohlgenährten Ton haben wollen. Er wollte es durchaus nicht zugeben, daß man alle Authoren auf dieselbste Weise spielen; er wollte im Gegentheile, daß der Künstler sich an die wahre Tradition halte; daß er sich so zu sagen selbst verläugne und den Composition, so, wie er ist, selbst wieder gebe. "Da kümmert man sich aber," rief er aus, "weder um den Styl des Mannes, noch um das Instrument, das in der Zeit der Componist ein ganz anderes war, als jetzt; man stellt Friedrich den Großen dar, mit Harschnitt *à la Titus*, im Rock und in Hosen von schwarzer Farbe!' – Nur in einigen Passagen, in einigen Scherzos von Beethoven, Onslow und Mendelssohn ließ er es zu, daß man den Bogen springen lassen.' Malibran, *Spohr*, pp. 207–8.

54 Andreas Moser, *Joseph Joachim*, trans. Lilla Durham (London 1902), p. 46. The relevant passage is quoted in Brown, 'Bowing Styles', pp. 107–8.

impression is that in the vast majority of cases an on-string stroke, sometimes at the point, sometimes in the middle and occasionally near the heel, was intended for moderately fast-moving staccato notes. Like his master, Spohr, David expected the player to be able to play short notes with the same effect at any part of the bow. Though a sharply detached *martelé* stroke (up to a certain speed) is normally executed near the point of the bow, both context and circumstantial evidence suggest that this would only rarely have been the intended stroke; it seems likely that David more often intended *détaché* strokes, ranging from short and distinctly separated to broad and connected. The overall impression is of a more legato, singing style than that produced by the much shorter lifted and springing strokes in the lower half which are widely employed today in the performance of this repertoire.

Many instances of David's use of the upper half of the bow in contexts where it would seldom be employed in modern violin playing may be found in his *Violinschule*. Several of his exercises shed light on the bowing marks in his Beethoven editions (Exs. 6.15a–b).

Ex. 6.15a   David: *Violinschule*, p. 38 No. 59
Sp = Spitze (point); M = Mitte (middle); HB = halbe Bogen (half bow)

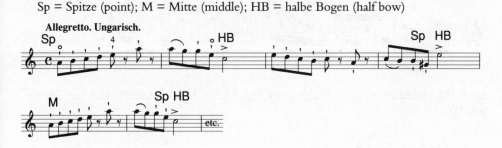

Ex. 6.15b   David: *Violinschule*, p. 41 No. 61
Sp = Spitze (point)

These passages, in conjunction with the bowing marks in the editions, suggest a style of performance very different from the modern approach for movements such as the Andante scherzoso quasi allegretto of Op. 18 No. 4 (Beethoven's metronome marking: ♩. = 56) and the Allegretto vivace e sempre scherzando of Op. 59 No. 1 (♩. = 56). Exs. 6.16a–c (and 6.14g) indicate that in Op. 59 No. 1 David intended an on-string stroke in the middle or upper part of the bow for the performance of the semiquavers. Much the same approach is implied by his bowings in Op. 18 No. 4. Most of the quavers in these two movements were evidently also meant to be played in a similar manner. There are many other

Ex. 6.16a   Beethoven: String Quartet in F Op. 59 No. 1, second movement, bars 78–84 (ed. David)

Ex. 6.16b   Beethoven: String Quartet in F Op. 59 No. 1, second movement, bars 177–201 (ed. David)

Ex. 6.16c   Beethoven: String Quartet in F Op. 59 No. 1, second movement, bars 251–4 (ed. David)

Ex. 6.16d   Beethoven: String Quartet in A minor Op. 132, second movement, bars 144–54 (ed. David)

Ex. 6.16e   Beethoven: Violin Sonata in A minor Op. 23, second movement, bars 43–51 (ed. David)

Ex. 6.16f   Beethoven: Violin Sonata in A minor Op. 23, second movement, bars 166–71 (ed. David)

Ex. 6.17a   Beethoven: Violin Sonata in F Op. 24, third movement, bars 18–19 (ed. David)

Ex. 6.17b   Beethoven: String Quartet in A minor Op. 132, third movement, bars 122–6 (ed. David)

Ex. 6.17c   Beethoven: Violin Sonata in C minor Op. 30 No. 2, third movement, bars 41–8 (ed. David)

Ex. 6.17d   Beethoven: Violin Sonata in A Op. 12 No. 2, first movement, bars 119–27 (ed. David)

examples of moderately rapid notes, now generally performed off the string, that seem to have been intended to be played near the point (Ex. 6.16d).

Elsewhere in David's Beethoven editions, short strokes on the string seem intended to be played alternately in the upper and lower half (or middle) of the bow (Exs. 6.16e–f): these examples show the passage played with exactly the opposite bowing in the recapitulation. David, again recalling Spohr's practice, also liked scale and arpeggio passages to be played so that the final note receives an up-bow. Passages such as Exs. 6.17a–b are quite frequent. David often used the point of the bow for the execution of sforzando notes. In Ex. 6.17c the sforzandos on up-bows only make sense if performed right at the point. A rare instance where David definitely seems to have envisaged a sprung stroke in the lower half of the bow is the violin's accompaniment figure at the beginning of the first movement of Op. 12 No. 2: when this figure occurs in the recapitulation it comes at the end of a very long up-bow (Ex. 6.17d).

Ex. 6.18a   Beethoven: String Quartet in F Op. 59 No. 1, third movement, bars 125–32 (ed. David)

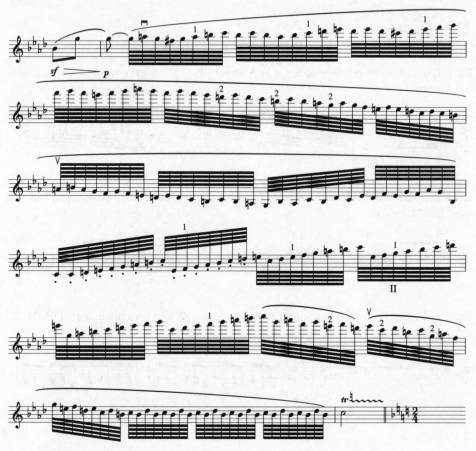

Finally, some of David's bowing marks also have implications for speed and/or volume. Though he often broke up Beethoven's long slurrings/phrasings – sometimes because they are impossibly long, sometimes because he wants to produce more volume or tone, sometimes for technical reasons, i.e. string crossing and avoidance of awkward position changing – there are also many places where he retained bowings of very considerable length which require enormous control and suggest a very low dynamic (Exs. 6.18a–c). Even at a considerably faster tempo than is normal today these bowings are long.[55] In the Sonata Op. 12 No. 3 Joachim divided the slurs in both these places.

Ex. 6.18b   Beethoven: Violin Sonata in E♭ Op. 12 No. 3, second movement, bars 22–32 (ed. David)

Ex. 6.18c   Beethoven: Violin Sonata in E♭ Op. 12 No. 3, second movement, bars 64–8 (ed. David)

David's and Dont's editions yield much more information about where and how these and other techniques (for instance, such things as *bariolage* and the use of the *contre coup d'archet*) were employed. Many of their bowings and fingerings are open to a variety of interpretations but the violinist who lives and works with these editions for long enough will find that in observing the editor's markings he must discard many of the preconceptions of modern violin playing and will gain valuable insights into a treatment of the instrument that would undoubtedly have been familiar to Beethoven.

55 See W. Malloch, 'Carl Czerny's Metronome Marks for Haydn and Mozart Symphonies' (appendix), *Early Music*, 16/1 (1988), p. 82 for discussion of the tempo of the Adagio from Op. 12 No. 3.

7

THE VIOLIN CONCERTO OP. 61: TEXT AND EDITIONS

ROBIN STOWELL

It was after abandoning an early attempt at a concerto for the instrument[1] and completing his two Romances Opp. 40 and 50 (for violin and orchestra)[2] and the celebrated 'Kreutzer' Sonata (for violin and piano) 'written in a concertante style, rather like a concerto',[3] that Beethoven embarked upon the composition of his Violin Concerto in D major Op. 61. He finished the work in December 1806. The original manuscript[4] bears the amusing inscription 'Concerto par Clemenza pour Clement, primo Violino e Direttore al Theatro a Vienne, dal L.v.Bthvn. 1806'[5] and the work was premiered in Vienna on 23 December 1806, by the aforementioned Franz Clement (1780–1842), an esteemed friend of Beethoven who had conducted the first performance of the 'Eroica' Symphony Op. 55 in the previous year. The concerto gained a mixed reception. While admiring its originality and many beauties, one critic complained that 'its continuity frequently appears broken, and that the ceaseless repetition of some commonplace passages is apt to become tiresome'.[6] A second performance (1807) is reported by Schindler to have been somewhat better received. Nevertheless, almost forty years elapsed before the work gained a regular

---

1 The manuscript of this Concerto in C (WoO 5) comprises only nineteen pages/259 bars of the first movement and appears to date from Beethoven's last years in Bonn (1790–2). The first published version of this work (1875) was edited and completed by Joseph Hellmesberger (1828–93), who added trumpets and drums to the score and treated it in a somewhat inflated manner. A later version by Juan Manén (1883–1971) retains the composer's original scoring and adopts a more Beethovenian harmonic style. See Rosemary Hughes, *Beethoven* (London 1970), p. 79.

2 Written in 1802, but published respectively in 1803 and 1805.

3 'Scritta in un stilo molto concertante, quasi come d'un concerto'.

4 Housed in the Nationalbibliothek in Vienna. Reference has here been made to the '*Vollständige Faksimile-Ausgabe im Originalformat der Handschrift aus dem Besitz der Österreichischen Nationalbibliothek (Mus. Hs. 17.538). Herausgegeben und kommentiert von Franz Grasberger. Mit einem Vorwort von Wolfgang Schneiderhan*' (2 vols., Graz, Akademische Druck-u. Verlagsanstalt 1979).

5 'Concerto written by clemency for Clement [lit.], First Violin and Director of the Vienna Court Theatre, by Ludwig van Beethoven, 1806.'

6 Johann Nepomuk Möser, in *Wiener Zeitung für Theater Musik und Poesie* (8 Jan. 1807): '[bekennt aber, daß] der Zusammenhang oft ganz zerrissen scheine, und daß die unendlichen Wiederholungen einiger gemeinen Stellen leicht ermüden könnten'.

place in the violin repertory, thanks partly to isolated performances by a few well-known violinists[7] but largely to Joseph Joachim (1831–1907), who played it under Mendelssohn's baton for the first time in London on 27 May 1844, and gave further significant performances, notably in Berlin (1852) and Düsseldorf (1853) with Schumann at the helm.

Czerny reports that Beethoven composed the concerto in some haste.[8] While stories that Clement premiered the work at sight without a single rehearsal must be considered highly dubious, the numerous crossings-out and emendations contained in Beethoven's autograph lend much credibility to Czerny's statement. Alan Tyson concludes that haste and uncertainty probably account 'for the impression that Beethoven was partly still composing the work while he was writing it out', and he considers the autograph 'a confusing document' which 'represents something short of the composer's final intentions'.[9] Certainly, much confusion has been caused by the numerous alternative versions for the solo violin incorporated in the autograph and, to compound the chaos, 'there are many places in which the solo violin part of the first edition is quite different from any of them'.[10] Tyson also refers to other textual problems such as the cello response to the bassoon in bars 525–6 of the first movement. He tells us too about the missing bar (3/217) and how it was omitted and then reinstated; and he informs us how the two pizzicato notes in the Finale (3/218)[11] were apparently an afterthought of the composer and how an *espressivo* was misread by the engraver as *sempre fsimo* (*sempre fortissimo*). Furthermore, Norman Del Mar points out inconsistencies of note-lengths in various parallel passages, and numerous discrepancies between editions in respect of rhythm, slurring, ornaments, dynamic markings and other effects.[12]

Beethoven's Violin Concerto was first published (Vienna, August 1808) with a dedication not to Clement but to the composer's childhood friend Stephan von Breuning, appearing simultaneously with its adaptation for solo piano (dedicated to von Breuning's wife, Julie). Clementi's editions of both forms of the work were

---

7 The performances given by Luigi Tomasini jr. in 1812 (Berlin), Pierre Baillot in 1828 (Paris, during the inaugural season of the *Société des concerts du conservatoire*), Henri Vieuxtemps in 1834 (Vienna) and Karl Wilhelm Uhlrich in the Leipzig Gewandhaus in 1836 stand out during the long period of its comparative neglect; but as Clive Brown points out elsewhere in this volume (p. 124), Dont implies in the preface to his edition that the Concerto was more frequently performed in Beethoven's lifetime than is generally acknowledged.

8 Carl Czerny, *Vollständige theoretisch-praktische Pianoforte-Schule* Op. 500 (Vienna 1846), IV, p. 117.

9 Alan Tyson, 'The Text of Beethoven's Op. 61', *Music and Letters*, 43 (1962), p. 109.

10 *ibid.*, p. 107. See also Alan Tyson, 'The Textual Problems of Beethoven's Violin Concerto', *Musical Quarterly*, 53 (1967), pp. 482–502.

11 Specifically prescribed for the right hand by Szigeti; Hubay, on the other hand, specifies a left-hand pizzicato here.

12 Norman Del Mar, 'Confusion and Error III', *The Score*, 20 (1958), pp. 38–40.

published without dedications in London in the summer of 1810. Joachim's championing of the Concerto towards the middle of the nineteenth century gradually spawned several editions by various violinists, which together provide us with a wide and sometimes bewildering range of proposed solutions to the many details and inconsistencies that Beethoven left unresolved, as well as offering editorial suggestions regarding matters of technique, interpretation and performance practice. As Alberto Bachmann has remarked:

There are not two violinists in the world who interpret this work in the same manner, and it may be said with entire frankness, that many are guilty of crimes against art in allowing themselves liberties in its interpretation which would have shocked Beethoven himself . . . The various editions of this work also display a tendency to improve upon it which may truly be deplored, for, from the moment when editors allow themselves to "correct" Beethoven, one cannot take them seriously.[13]

Bachmann illustrates from memory just a few of the liberties taken in respect of the opening three solo bars of the concerto by Joachim, Wilhelmj, Sarasate, Ysaÿe, Thomson, Kreisler and Kubelík (Ex. 7.1), examples ranging from the somewhat insensitive version ascribed to Wilhelmj through the more articulated and accented interpretations of Thomson and Kreisler to the more faithful (to the original sources) versions of Joachim and Ysaÿe.[14]

The aims of this essay are to review briefly the Concerto's various textual corruptions, which date right back to the first edition of 1808, and to give a flavour of how subsequent editions of (or commentaries on) the solo violin part have reflected the technical and interpretative practices of their respective eras. Although there is no single definitive text of this concerto, it is essential for us to have a reliable point of reference – a scholarly critical edition whose sources are fully documented – in order to analyse and make useful conclusions regarding different performers' and editors' interpretations of the work. Alan Tyson's score[15] has been selected as this aide on account of the sources on which it is founded, its editor's established reputation for work with autographs, particularly with those of Beethoven, and also its ready availability. Tyson's score is based on four main sources: the autograph, in which the orchestral parts are more or less in their final form but the solo violin part is not;[16] a full score, currently housed in the British Library, in the hand of a copyist, with the orchestral parts copied from the autograph and the solo part

13 Alberto Bachmann, *An Encyclopedia of the Violin* (New York 1925), p. 224.
14 *ibid.*, p. 163.
15 'Concerto. D major. For violin and orchestra . . . Op. 61. Revised edition by Alan Tyson' (London, Ernst Eulenberg, [1968]).
16 There are two (or even more) alternatives for a number of bars written on staves left blank at the bottom of the score.

Ex. 7.1   Beethoven: Violin Concerto Op. 61, first movement, bars 89–91 (Bachmann)

appearing here for the first time in the form in which we know it today. Tyson tells us that this latter source, which also contains the solo piano part, 'served as the *Stichvorlage* (the score from which the separate parts were copied by the engraver) of the first edition, and it contains corrections and additions by Beethoven in pencil and red crayon, which were duly incorporated into the first edition';[17] the first edition of the parts, published by the Bureau des Arts et d'Industrie, Vienna, in August 1808; and the London edition of the parts published by Clementi and Co. in 1810. The British Library score and the 1808 edition form the basis of the solo

17 Alan Tyson, Preface to 1968 edition of the Violin Concerto, p. II.

part of Tyson's edition,[18] but the versions of the solo part to be found in the autograph have naturally been 'of high corroborative value'.[19]

Except for the one significant aspect of stringing, the violinist's tools-in-trade have remained fairly consistent throughout the performance history of Beethoven's Concerto and have thus influenced editorial decisions somewhat less than previously. By the early nineteenth century the violin and bow had each achieved essentially its modern form. The Tourte-model bow, developed in the 1780s, gradually displaced earlier types and has, apart from some minor modifications, remained standard to the present day;[20] the modern neck fitting was prevalent from about 1800; the chin rest was introduced c. 1820, by which time most bass bars in old instruments had been replaced by ones of more substantial 'modern' dimensions. Apart from the silver- or copper-wound gut g, nineteenth-century strings were generally of pure gut, and their thicknesses varied considerably according to the taste and tonal requirements of the performer.[21] The metal e^2 string did not gain widespread acceptance until about 1920, and the gut a^1 and d^1 strings were commonly employed for some time after that by many violinists, although Flesch recommends aluminium-covered steel for the a^1, and a d^1 of gut covered with aluminium.[22] But it was not until c. 1950 and the development of more flexible metal windings that full stringing with all-metal strings gained some measure of universal acceptance.

The principles governing the editing of music have changed considerably in recent years, advancing from those late-nineteenth- and early-twentieth-century publications which 'contain purely subjective annotations with a profusion of dynamic and agogic markings that frequently have nothing to do with the composer's original text'[23] to those which display more reverence towards primary sources, in many cases with an identifiable apparatus for editorial suggestions about interpretation. Some editions provide a first-hand record of the approach to playing the Concerto in the distant past of a fêted virtuoso (for example, those of Joachim himself, Ferdinand David, August Wilhelmj, Jenö Hubay and Joseph Szigeti) or teacher (notably those of Jakob Dont, Leopold Auer, and Carl Flesch), Dont's edition (Berlin, c. 1880) probably most closely approximating early-nineteenth-century Viennese practice. Others, like that of Heinrich Dessauer, which incorporates 'explanatory remarks

---

18 They are nearly identical, but neither is copied directly from the other.

19 Tyson, Preface to 1968 edition, p. III.

20 The manner of holding the bow was also standardised to a great extent, although some minor national differences have persisted.

21 Spohr, for example, preferred thick strings strung at maximum tension in order to achieve his characteristically strong tone, while Paganini favoured thin strings and an unusually low bridge to assist in the cultivation of his own unique performing style.

22 Carl Flesch, *The Art of Violin Playing*, trans. Frederick H. Martens (2 vols., New York 1924–30), I, p. 11.

23 Max Rostal, *Beethoven: The Sonatas for Piano and Violin. Thoughts on Their Interpretation*, trans. H. and A. Rosenberg (London 1985), p. 17.

for concert performance with special reference to the artistic conception of Joseph Joachim', offer information second-hand. Furthermore, extracts from standard texts about violin technique and interpretation[24] provide excellent source material for this investigation; and, of course, the increasing availability nowadays of historical recordings sometimes enables us to verify whether or not some of our editors actually practised what they preached![25]

On the other side of the coin, the so-called '*Urtext*' (whatever that means!) of Hess (1969), for example, concentrates on the provision of the text, with little in the way of editorial apparatus.[26] However, few editors over the years have been as faithful to what Beethoven wrote, or evidently sanctioned, as Max Rostal, who allows the player to study and, if necessary, modify or reject the performing suggestions that lack the composer's authority. He thus steers a middle course between 'an original text which, as it stands, provides only a bare outline of the composer's ideas of instrumental execution, and . . . an edition, which fails to indicate where important additions or modifications have ben made'.[27] Beethoven's corrections and variations (clearly distinguished and without any editorial modification) are incorporated in the violin part of Rostal's piano score, 'to give violinists the opportunity to follow Beethoven's trend of thoughts and development';[28] however, following for the most part the first printed edition, Rostal also suggests his own fingerings and bowings as well as some additional dynamic markings (in brackets) in the separate solo violin part.[29]

Many editors throughout the years have been fairly faithful to what Beethoven wrote or evidently sanctioned. A few, however, have attempted to 'improve' musically on Beethoven's text(s) by adding or changing notes. Wilhelmj, for example, performed the very opening bars of the first solo entry of the opening movement in octaves (see Ex. 7.1), adds a d^2 (and in his 1896 edition a d^1 and a a^1

---

24 For example, Flesch, *The Art of Violin Playing*; Carl Flesch, *Violin Fingering, Its Theory and Practice*, trans. Boris Schwarz (London 1966); Sol Babitz, *The Violin: Views and Reviews* (2nd edn, Urbana, Illinois 1959); Ivan Galamian, *Principles of Violin Playing and Teaching* (London 1964); Joseph Szigeti, *Szigeti on the Violin* (London 1969).

25 For example, two recordings of the work by Fritz Kreisler 'remastered and presented in state-of-art digital transfers from original material' by Biddulph Recordings. It should be noted, however, that historical recordings are liable to offer less accurate and precise information about many aspects which form the basis of this study, especially fingering and precise details of bowing.

26 'Konzert für Violine und Orchester D dur . . . Mit beiden autographen Fassungen des Solostimme erstmals herausgegeben und mit Nachwort versehen von Willy Hess' (Wiesbaden, Breitkopf and Härtel [1969]). Hess includes Beethoven's variants as well as a few editorial slurs in his edition.

27 Max Rostal, Preface to his edition (Mainz, B. Schott's Söhne 1971).

28 *ibid.*

29 As well as providing, like Jacobsen (Vienna, Universal Edition, n.d.), a detailed explanation of the signs employed in his edition. What a pity that Hubay (Budapest, R. Károly 1918) does not appear to have contemplated including a key to the various annotations (arrows; golf flags; etc.) he himself employs!

instead) below the written f$\sharp^3$ (1/365), and emphasises the sf in 1/286 and 287 by means of a triple-stopped ornament (g–d^1–f^2). David gives a c$\sharp^3$ (instead of a c$\natural^3$) on the third beat of 1/46. Dont suggests a couple of passages that might be played an octave higher than written (1/423–5, and the last two chords of the Finale)[30], while ornaments are added by, for example, Dont at 1/204 and Szigeti at 2/25. Furthermore, Tyson's version differs from most other editions at 3/83, Tyson opting for the more plausible change of register in line with the previous pair of bars (3/81 and 82). Apart from these instances and the addition of unison notes for greater sonority,[31] most discrepancies involving notes in the editions examined would appear to be misprints (e.g. Dont at 2/63 and 2/77; Szigeti at 3/58; Hubay at 1/203).

Editorial modifications of rhythm focus largely on whether the latter part of 1/341 is given as three quavers or as a triplet. Szigeti, Hubay and Joachim are among those who specify a triplet figure as in the autograph, while Flesch, Wilhelmj and Rostal, among others, opt for a version in quavers. Curiously, Wilhelmj is alone in subscribing to triplets in the latter half of 1/106, and he is also responsible for substituting a dotted rhythm for the two quavers in the *ad libitum* passage in 2/24. Dont's edition, meanwhile, adds a tie between the two a^{3}s in 1/132, while Hubay's omits the customary tie over the bar-line at 1/490–1, a place where the tie is in any case often 'abused' through the addition of a termination to the trill.

Addition of expressive terminology foreign to our various primary sources is characteristic of the more 'historic' editions, notably those of Holle and Schultze-Biesantz, Joachim and Moser, Hubay and Wilhelmj. Joachim and Moser add terms such as *con suono* (1/92), *leggiero ma non troppo spiccato* (1/315), *sciolto* (1/395), *soave* (1/199 and 1/525), and *tranquillo* (2/77), Hubay includes numerous annotations like *espressivo ma teneramente* (1/331) or *dolce con suono* (3/136), and Wilhelmj prescribes *molto equale* (1/116), *largamente* (1/328), *molto semplice* (1/511) and other similar directions. Holle and Schultze-Biesantz, meanwhile, use both German and Italian terminology, augmenting conventional Italian terms such as *poco stringendo* (1/531) with expressions like *mit vollem Ton* (1/92), *Durchweg zart und ruhig aber gesangvoll* (at the head of the second movement) and *mit keckem Humor* (at the head of the Finale). Few of these additions are distinguished as editorial. Rostal and Jacobsen, however, place some of their additions in brackets, and Rostal takes pains to point out his relocation of *dolce* at 3/127.

While numerous editors are quick to add dynamic markings to their editions, in order to help and inspire performers towards more musical and stylish performances in keeping with the taste of their times, many again fail to distinguish between their

---

30 See Clive Brown's Exs. [6.3d and e], p. 125.

31 For example, Emile Sauret (London, Augener 1915) and August Wilhelmj (London, St Cecilia Music Publishing Co. [1896]) specify a unison d^1 for the soloist on the final 'chord' of the first movement, as does the edition by Paul Dukas (Paris, A. Durand and fils [1916]) for 1/452.

own and Beethoven's markings. Rostal and to a certain extent Szigeti (although his additions are not always acknowledged) have close regard for Classical style and expression while others (e.g. Wilhelmj, Sauret, Hubay, Auer and, perhaps surprisingly, Dont and Dessauer) adorn their editions with a heavy overlay of dynamic and expressive indications. The addition of echo effects through contrast in dynamic or string timbre is a particular device employed – 2/12 is a case in point, where, for example, Bachmann indicates the contrast through dynamic 'yet without exaggeration'[32] and Dessauer, Hubay, Szigeti and Rostal, among others, opt for a change of string timbre (Ex. 7.2). Bars 21–2 of the second movement come into the same category, and Szigeti and Auer opt for a similar play of timbre in 3/158–61.

Ex. 7.2   Beethoven: Violin Concerto Op. 61, second movement, bars 11–12

The practical application of dynamic markings, whether editorial or not, presents other notable problems. Dessauer warns the prospective soloist that the observance of *piano* dynamics should be kept in proportion, and that the *piano* indication in 1/93 should 'not be followed too closely, as too weak a tonal production in this particular place would not be of special advantage'.[33] He stresses both the symphonic conception of the work and the equal parity of soloist and orchestra, 'owing to which conspicuous *piano* and *pianissimo* effects, which are of such wondrous efficacy in chamber-music, are only serviceable in rare instances, for the performance of this Concerto'. Bachmann, too, indicates that some of the prescribed dynamics are impracticable for the soloist;[34] accordingly, he frequently prescribes higher dynamic levels than our Beethovenian sources. However, he recommends the avoidance of any crescendo in 1/97ff. Szigeti is at pains to point out that the crescendo before the tutti at 1/365 is misplaced in many editions, while Flesch bemoans the fate in most performances of the *sempre perdendosi* passage of the Larghetto (2/58ff.); he claims that this term means 'not alone softly, but losing itself, dreaming itself away, forgetting surroundings and self' and that Beethoven 'has indicated by a continuous uninterrupted *p*, that he wished to express this mood during the entire first period'.[35]

32 Bachmann, *An Encyclopedia*, p. 230.
33 Heinrich Dessauer, edition of solo violin part, p. 1.
34 Bachmann, *An Encyclopedia*, p. 229.
35 Flesch, *The Art of Violin Playing*, II, p. 47.

'Most violinists,' he continues, ' . . . play this sublime, mystic inspiration rather in the style of the currently familiar violin cantilenas, and thus deprive it of its character of a revelation of profoundest, yet *repressed* passion. Expressional ability in the long continued p presupposes a high degree of violinistic, musical and psychic culture, one which is very rarely encountered.' Of our other editors, Hubay, Sauret, Auer and Wilhelmj are notable for numerous unacknowledged additions, gradations and modifications of dynamic, some of the more ostentatious examples being Wilhelmj's (1896) prescription of *forte* both at 2/57 and at the very beginning of the Finale.

Ex. 7.3   Beethoven: Violin Concerto Op. 61, first movement, bars 195–6 (Durand edn.)

Ex. 7.4   Beethoven: Violin Concerto Op. 61, first movement, bars 400–6

Editorial assistance regarding phrasing is only rarely included; this is perhaps not surprising, as it is naturally each editor's aim to make his version of the solo part practicable, a task which may involve the breaking up of some of Beethoven's long 'phrasing slurs' into more manageable lengths with factors in mind such as the balance between the soloist and orchestra – for example the Durand edition's bowing recommendations for 1/195–6 (Ex. 7.3). Joachim and Moser, Szigeti and Jacobsen, however, occasionally mark off one phrase from another with a caesura, and Bachmann indicates the phrasing in 1/97–8 by means of square brackets;[36] but apart from these examples (or perhaps the annotation of a sudden dynamic or string change), there is little help for the performer. In fact some editors suggest fingerings and bowings which prove contrary to the interests of the musical phrase. Szigeti, for example, deplores the 'bow phrasings' of some who disregard Beethoven's text entirely, for example at 1/400–6 (see Ex. 7.4). David and Auer, among others, prescribe an identical slurring (although David commences down-bow), which

---

36 Bachmann, *An Encyclopedia*, p. 225. It may be argued that some editors make an attempt at indicating phrasing at 1/97. Joachim, Wilhelmj and Holle/Schultze-Biesantz, for example, suggest taking the first five pairs of semiquavers in one bow. However, since other editors (e.g. Auer; Flesch; Schirmer edn; Sauret) take only the first three pairs in the one bow, such annotations are probably more of a convenience measure for getting to the right part of the bow than any indication of phrasing. David, incidentally, bows the pairs out as they come.

ignores 'the "breathing" cesura[sic]' between the dotted minim and the crotchet.[37] Prescriptions for the bowing and fingering of 1/101–9 also provide a useful test-case regarding editorial respect for the musical phrase.

This lack of agreement amongst editors over bowings and articulations is perfectly understandable, especially considering the incomplete and chaotic state of Beethoven's autograph. Furthermore, such additions inevitably varied according to the performing styles in vogue. Szigeti admits, 'we neglect many bowing subtleties . . . we articulate with less character than even a few decades ago',[38] while Bachmann suggests that some violinists articulate too harshly, often resulting in a false adaptation of the rhythm (Exs. 7.5a and b); Rostal makes a similar point in his footnote about 1/322 (Ex. 7.5c). There is no better example of a passage on whose bowing editors almost always beg to differ than 1/134–41, where, as Bachmann confirms, 'every violinist uses a different bowing' (Ex. 7.6).[39] Some versions of this passage include slurring patterns which give variety and comfort (one slur counteracting another to enable the performer to preserve a contact-point in the middle of the bow), while many seem designed more for the purpose of bravura display; interestingly though, Bachmann stresses the need 'to maintain the interpretation on a level of simple grandeur, and to avoid all buffoonery'.[40]

Ex. 7.5a   Beethoven: Violin Concerto Op. 61, first movement, bar 322

Ex. 7.5b   Beethoven: Violin Concerto Op. 61, first movement, bar 322 (Bachmann)

Ex. 7.5c   Beethoven: Violin Concerto Op. 61, first movement, bar 322 (Rostal)

The principal theme of the Finale is central to a burning editorial issue in respect of articulation. Many editors (e.g. Flesch, Szigeti, Hess, Rostal and, perhaps surprisingly, Hubay) claim, incorrectly, that the articulation dot on the d^1 that follows the a in 3/1 and 2 is faithful to the original manuscript. However, most nineteenth-

---

37 Joseph Szigeti, Preface to his edition (1963).
38 Joseph Szigeti, *A Violinist's Notebook* (London 1964), p. 134.
39 Bachmann, *An Encyclopedia*, p. 225.
40 *ibid.*, p. 226.

Ex. 7.6   Beethoven: Violin Concerto Op. 61, first movement, bars 134–41

century editions (notably those of Dont, Baillot[41], David, Sauret, or even Jacobsen in the current century) omit the offending dot, as does Bachmann, who is particularly concerned with the elimination of false accents in the execution of this theme (Ex. 7.7a). He recommends that 3/3 should be well articulated (Ex. 7.7b) and advises: 'Use the same accentuation when the theme is repeated in the higher position, and use the shading *mezzo forte* for the initial appearance of the theme, and the shading *mezzo piano* for its repetition.'[42]

41 Pierre Baillot, *L'Art du violon: nouvelle méthode* (Paris 1835), pp. 44 and 143.
42 Bachmann, *An Encyclopedia*, p. 231.

Ex. 7.7a   Beethoven: Violin Concerto Op. 61, third movement, bars 1–4 (Bachmann)

Ex. 7.7b   Beethoven: Violin Concerto Op. 61, third movement, bars 3–4 (Bachmann)

Two particular developments in nineteenth-century interpretation were the increased prominence given to the cultivation of an expressive singing style, with the strong tone and broad or *martelé* bowstrokes characteristic of the Parisian violin school of Viotti and his contemporaries, and a greater virtuoso element. Dessauer, for example, consistently emphasises the need for cultivation of the singing qualities of the instrument, recommending that 1/126ff should be 'performed more in a *cantabile* than *bravura* style. The lower notes of the broken octaves must not be treated slightingly nor be played with too weak a tone, in order that the melody may be heard very prominently and to good advantage.'[43] Dessauer further suggests re 1/314: 'While very clear and distinct, the *staccati* therein are not to be detached too sharply; with more smoothness and singing quality than brilliancy', while in 1/151 'The . . . triplets must be played with broad *legato* and *cantabile* bowing, with good tone and with intimate tonal-blending with the orchestral volume';[44] and even at 1/185 the semiquavers 'should be executed with distinct and individual attack' but 'should not be played abruptly or in too hammered a style; the passage should create rather a singing effect'.[45]

Dessauer's cantabile emphasis is mirrored in other editions by the addition of slurs (particularly the so-called 'overlapping slur'), the increased use of *portato*, broad *détaché* and 'hooked' strokes, as well as in attitudes towards fingering (e.g. the use of portamento). Overlapping slurs – slurs which traverse the beat for reasons of greater cantabile or phrasing – feature prominently at 1/93ff. (Ex. 7.8a) and its parallel passage at 1/288 where the idea of the seamless phrase is especially prominent.[46]

43 Dessauer, edition of solo violin part, p. 2.

44 Baillot, for a similar passage (1/425), suggests 'très légèrement et du milieu de l'archet' (*L'Art du violon*, p. 116).

45 Dessauer, edition of solo violin part, p. 3.

46 See, for example, the editions of Hubay, Sauret, Dukas, David (1875), Wilhelmj (1883), Auer (1917), Flesch [1938] and Jacobsen. Joachim and Moser, however, recommend a bow change on the strong beats of the bar.

Ex. 7.8a   Beethoven: Violin Concerto Op. 61, first movement, bars 93–101

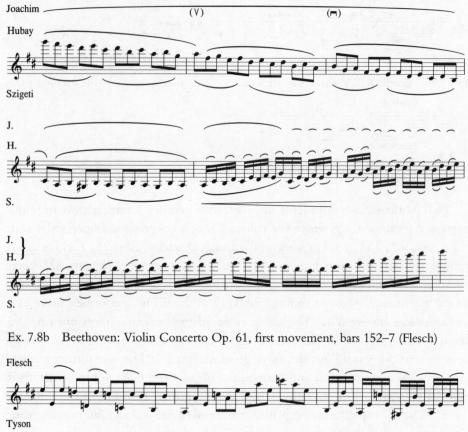

Ex. 7.8b   Beethoven: Violin Concerto Op. 61, first movement, bars 152–7 (Flesch)

Ex. 7.8c   Beethoven: Violin Concerto Op. 61, first movement, bars 181–5 (Flesch)

Ex. 7.8d   Beethoven: Violin Concerto Op. 61, first movement, bars 216–24 (Flesch)

Ex. 7.9   Beethoven: Violin Concerto Op. 61, first movement, bars 126–30 (Flesch)

The passages at 1/152,[47] 1/181 and 1/216 (Exs. 7.8b–d) provide other instances where overlapping slurs are commonly, but by no means universally, employed. The increased incidence of *portato* bowing is admirably illustrated in the slow movement, where 'lines' consistently replace Beethoven's 'dots'[48] and the broad *détaché* stroke is consistently preferred for passages which suggest a more staccato rendering. 'Hooked' bowings came into fashion with the Tourte-model bow, when, largely on account of that model's greater length and weight, they proved more comfortable and convenient (but, some would argue, less articulate) for certain passages and at the same time helped to eliminate the undesirable up-bow accents which might result from the use of a separate bowstroke. The very beginning of the Finale (Ex. 7.7a) is a case in point in most editions, as is also, for example, 1/126 (Ex. 7.9) and 1/386.

47 e.g. Hubay, Schirmer edition (1950), Dukas, Wilhelmj (1896), and Jacobsen; however, Auer and Rostal each come up with different solutions.
48 e.g. Dessauer, Szigeti, Hubay, Dukas, Wilhelmj. See also Clive Brown's essay in this volume, p. 140ff.

The sonorous, expansive style of the Viotti school which greatly influenced Beethoven[49] was succeeded by a trend towards greater virtuosity. This virtuoso element led to freer exploitation of the various left-hand positions, especially half and second positions, greater consideration for expressive fingerings and timbre, and increased use of effects such as portamento, harmonics and pizzicato. It was reflected in right-hand technique by the use of the wider range of bowstrokes afforded by the Tourte bow. Many of these strokes exploited the greater strength, elasticity, hair tension, legato, expressive potential, and the more immediate attack of Tourte's model, leading to the development of a range of accented bowings including *martelé* and sforzando effects.[50] As Clive Brown remarks:

One of the most important conflicts of opinion occurred over the question of whether, particularly in passages of successive detached notes in a moderate to fast tempo, the bow should bounce or should remain firmly on the string . . . the notation is not, in most cases, precise enough to indicate whether any particular interpretation was intended by the composer, but there is sufficient evidence to suggest that a nineteenth-century violinist's choice of bowstroke would have been dictated largely by when and where he lived, or to what school he belonged.[51]

Ex. 7.10a   Beethoven: Violin Concerto Op. 61, third movement, bars 75–8 (Dessauer)

Ex. 7.10b   Beethoven: Violin Concerto Op. 61, first movement, bar 151 (Dessauer)

Ex. 7.10c   Beethoven: Violin Concerto Op. 61, first movement, bar 189 (Dessauer)

---

49 See Boris Schwarz, 'Beethoven and the French Violin School', *Musical Quarterly*, 44 (1958), pp. 431–47.

50 See Robin Stowell, *Violin Technique and Performance Practice in the Late Eighteenth and Early Nineteenth Centuries* (Cambridge 1985).

51 Clive Brown, 'Bowing Styles, Vibrato and Portamento in Nineteenth-century Violin Playing', *Journal of the Royal Musical Association*, 113 (1988), p. 99.

Indeed, although one would surmise that a broad, on-the-string stroke would be most appropriate to the character of passages of detached notes in Beethoven's Concerto, some editors think otherwise, suggesting the use of slurred staccato or lighter springing bowings. Dessauer, for example, suggests that the *piano* semiquavers in 3/75–6 be played with 'jumping bow', with these 'jumping strokes' being 'exchanged for the usual decided bowing' for the ensuing crescendo and *forte* (Ex. 7.10a). He also indicates that 1/151 (and 1/425) should be taken in one stroke, incorporating slurred staccato (Ex. 7.10b),[52] and remarks: 'Not infrequently this *staccato* is executed by many artists with springing (*spiccato*) bowing; at any rate it is to be performed lightly and elegantly.' The slurred staccato stroke appears again at 1/189 (Ex. 7.10c; and 1/463f.)[53] with the performing instruction 'very light', while the 'dotted' semiquavers in the following bar should be played 'with jumping bow'. Dessauer exploits the same stroke in varying formations in 1/314, 1/316, 1/319–20 and 1/321–3,[54] generally with an expressive rather than bravura goal; among other notable examples of slurred staccato in the up-bow should be mentioned the suggestions of David and Szigeti at 1/463, Auer at 1/160 and 1/434, the Durand edition at 1/183, and David at 2/85–6 (Exs. 7.11a–e). Instances of down-bow staccato are not as prevalent, but Hubay suggests the use of both up- and down-bow varieties in 1/319 (Ex. 7.11f).

Most editors opt to give similar bowing and interpretative treatment to parallel passages within a movement. Dessauer, for instance, favours playing the passage at 1/426 'exactly as the first time', but he records that, 'for the sake of variety . . . some players prefer to omit the slurs the second time, so that every note is slightly detached', a modification which, he claims, 'endangers a well-rounded rendition of this passage'.

Fingering is an individual matter dependent largely on the conformation of the player's hand and the structure, size and strength of his fingers, as well as his musical intentions. Although common ground is almost inevitable regarding accepted fingerings of certain passages, many editorial additions are widely divergent, especially when musical and expressive intentions hold sway. Szigeti acknowledges Flesch's valuable role in improving approaches to fingering but complains 'how conservative and "tradition" ridden' violinists are as a whole, adding Mahler's celebrated exclamation: 'What you take for tradition is nothing but slovenliness!' to his argument for re-examining and re-evaluating fingerings. Not all the fingerings and bowings annotated are of Szigeti's own recommendation, for some are included 'to give "two sides" to the question, as documentary evidence of what *can* be done – if it is done supremely well!'.[55]

52 The Schirmer edition and those of Sauret and David suggest a similar bowing. Interestingly, Rostal mirrors a more modern approach here by specifying a fairly short, separated, on-the-string stroke.

53 Similarly in the Schirmer edition and those of Sauret, David and Durand.

54 A bowing mirrored in the Schirmer edition and those of Sauret, Durand, David, Auer and Jacobsen.

55 Szigeti, Preface to his edition; e.g. 1/101 three different fingerings are given. He occasionally states a preference, e.g. of bowing on p. 5 of solo violin part – see his footnote.

Ex. 7.11a   Beethoven: Violin Concerto Op. 61, first movement, bar 463 (David and Szigeti)

Ex. 7.11b   Beethoven: Violin Concerto Op. 61, first movement, bar 160 (Auer)

Ex. 7.11c   Beethoven: Violin Concerto Op. 61, first movement, bar 434 (Auer)

Ex. 7.11d   Beethoven: Violin Concerto Op. 61, first movement, bar 183 (Durand edn.)

Ex. 7.11e   Beethoven: Violin Concerto Op. 61, second movement, bars 85–7 (David)

Ex. 7.11f   Beethoven: Violin Concerto Op. 61, first movement, bars 318–19 (Hubay)

With the cultivation of tonal uniformity in mind, many late-nineteenth- and early-twentieth-century editions favour fingerings which exploit the high positions (see Exs. 7.12a–d). Among the other most common passages taken *una corda* should be mentioned 1/333–4 (Dont; Dessauer; Hubay; Auer; Rostal; and Schirmer edn), 1/348–51 (Dont; Szigeti), 1/399 (Dessauer; Hubay; Auer; Szigeti; Rostal; Sauret; Schirmer and Durand edns), and 1/511ff. (Dessauer; Schirmer and Durand edns; Sauret; Auer; Szigeti). Dessauer provides us with an insight into Joachim's timbral preferences in 3/11ff:

Ex. 7.12a   Beethoven: Violin Concerto Op. 61, first movement, bars 396–8 (Dont)

Ex. 7.12b   Beethoven: Violin Concerto Op. 61, second movement, bars 63–9 (Dont)

Ex. 7.12c   Beethoven: Violin Concerto Op. 61, second movement, bars 45–51

Ex. 7.12d   Beethoven: Violin Concerto Op. 61, third movement, bars 332–5 (Szigeti)

In order that this passage may sound exactly as bright and harmonious as before in the lower position, many violinists, among them Joachim, play it entirely upon the E-string. For playing it in this way the fingering marked *above* the notes is to be taken (Ex. 7.13). Other violinists again use the fingering marked *below* the notes, through which the disagreeable sliding from the third to the sixth position is avoided, once at least. In my opinion a fine performance may be brought about with either of the two fingerings.[56]

Ex. 7.13   Beethoven: Violin Concerto Op. 61, third movement, bars 10–18 (Dessauer)

Ex. 7.14a   Beethoven: Violin Concerto Op. 61, first movement, bars 309–10 and 311–12 (Flesch)

Ex. 7.14b   Beethoven: Violin Concerto Op. 61, third movement, bars 151–4 (Dont)

While most seventeenth- and eighteenth-century composers probably intended broken thirds such as those at 1/97–9 (Ex. 7.8a) for execution on two strings, Flesch claims that Beethoven unquestionably meant them to be played on one string for reasons of tonal uniformity, thereby necessitating more frequent shifts.[57] He further demonstrates how the optimum fingering of thirds may depend on the bowing indicated, for bowing articulations can assist in camouflaging shifts,[58] and he advocates a 'primitive yet all the more secure alternation of the first and third positions' as the simplest approach to this passage.[59] Curiously, Flesch takes a contrary view of a passage like 1/309–14 (Ex. 7.14a), which, he claims, sounds more expressive when played on two strings and also better supports the theme in the orchestra.[60]

56 Dessauer edition, solo violin part, p. 13.
57 Flesch, *The Art of Violin Playing*, I, pp. 132–3.
58 *ibid.*, p. 133.
59 *ibid.*, pp. 170–1.
60 *ibid.*, p. 132; Flesch, *Violin Fingering*, p. 174.

Many recognise the value of open strings to facilitate shifts, and timbre and phrasing are given appropriate consideration, especially by Rostal and Jacobsen. One particular oddity worthy of exposure is Dont's weird fingering for the broken thirds in 3/151 and 153 (Ex. 7.14b).

Ex. 7.15a   Beethoven: Violin Concerto Op. 61, first movement, bars 386–7

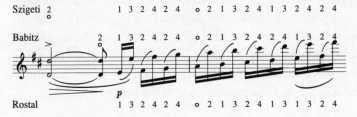

Ex. 7.15b   Beethoven: Violin Concerto Op. 61, first movement, bars 435–7

Hubay	II	3		4		4		4					3
Flesch	II	3		4	4								3
Wilhelmj (?1880)	II	3		4	4		4		4		4		4	3
Szigeti		3			3					3 1 3 4 2 4			3

Ex. 7.15c   Beethoven: Violin Concerto Op. 61, third movement, bars 173–4

Joachim, Wilhelmj,
Hubay & Flesch

Szigeti 1 3 2 4 2 4

The prominent profile of octave passagework in this concerto has occasioned much debate among more recent editors as to the employment of fingered (or 'extended'[61]) octaves. Flesch prefers fingered octaves 'because by using them the constant change of position is partly suppressed', avoiding audible glissandi and 'the leap into the uncertain'.[62] Babitz and Rostal opt for a compromise between octave-fingerings (Ex. 7.15a), while Szigeti expresses surprise that his edition (1963) is the first to recommend a fingered-octave solution to those redoubtable D minor and D major octave runs in the first movement;[63] he extols the virtues of fingered octaves

61 Babitz, *The Violin*, p. 4.
62 Flesch, *The Art of Violin Playing*, I, p. 139.
63 Szigeti, *Szigeti on the Violin*, p. 81.

for 1/435f and 3/173 as compared with the fingerings of Joachim, Hubay, Flesch and Wilhelmj (Ex. 7.15b and c). Szigeti also recommends quasi-fingered octaves in 1/90f., 1/114f., 1/126f., 1/386f and 3/172f.

The traditional fingering for passages in sixths often leaves the performer open to problems of intonation if he fails to recognise accurately the changes in the distances between the fingers according to the intervals of the scale. Szigeti chastises Flesch (and Dont) for adhering to the traditional fingering[64] for 3/68ff. (Ex. 7.16a), suggesting 'a less "bumpy"' one as an alternative (Ex. 7.16b),[65] and Babitz offers a fingering which adjusts the position shifts to suit the intervals (Ex. 7.16c).[66] Jacobsen, too, comes up with a practicable alternative (Ex. 7.16d). Of the more 'historical' editions, Dessauer offers a different fingering for each of the two parallel phrases in 3/243.

Ex. 7.16   Beethoven: Violin Concerto Op. 61, third movement, bars 68–72

The so-called artistic shift, 'which is used most often in singing passages where the sound of gliding fingers is sometimes deliberately emphasised in order to intensify the emotional expression',[67] was known and occasionally employed by eighteenth-century violinists,[68] but it seems to have come into its own as an essential expressive device in the early nineteenth century.[69] It was commonly exploited in solo and orchestral spheres well into the current century when, broadly speaking, its execution became less frequent and more refined and discreet with a faster left-hand movement and less bow-pressure in line with a general trend towards 'cleaner' shifting.[70] Flesch distinguishes two distinct types of 'gliding ornaments' –

64 Used also by, among others, Sauret, David, Hubay and Wilhelmj.

65 Szigeti, Preface to his edition.

66 Babitz, The Violin, pp. 12–13.

67 ibid., p. 8.

68 See, for example, Johann Friedrich Reichardt, Ueber die Pflichten des Ripien-violinisten (Berlin and Leipzig 1776), p. 35; Charles Burney, A General History of Music (4 vols., London 1776–89), II, p. 992; Baillot, L'Art du violon, pp. 146–9; Michel Woldemar, Grande méthode (Paris 1800), pp. 33–4.

69 The device is considered in detail by, for example, Spohr, Joachim, Baillot and de Bériot in their treatises, and its application and effect were paralleled in vocal methods of the period, notably Nicola Vaccai's Metodo pratico (London 1832) and Manuel García's Traité complet de l'art du chant (Paris 1840).

70 Brown, 'Bowing Styles', p. 121.

the glissando, involving a continuous glide up or down the fingerboard as inaudibly as possible, and the portamento, a gliding ornament employed intentionally as an '*emotional* connection' of two notes.[71] He provides examples from Beethoven's Concerto to illustrate their differences:

Ex. 7.17a   Beethoven: Violin Concerto Op. 61, second movement, bars 45–6 (Flesch)

Ex. 7.17b   Beethoven: Violin Concerto Op. 61, first movement, bar 93 (Flesch)

In Ex. [7.17a] the movement of the same finger strives to express heightened emotion, and is intentional; in Ex. [7.17b] it is compulsory, since otherwise it is impossible to reach the lower position. The first type of gliding, according to individual taste and feeling, may be carried out more slowly or more rapidly; the more unobtrusively, however, the second type of gliding occurs, the better.

Flesch further differentiates between two kinds of portamento, the 'B–' and the 'L–', whose characteristics depend on whether the player slides into position and then leaps to the finger required for the subsequent note (B–) or leaps to the finger required and then slides to the required pitch (L–). He records that the straightforward slide and the B–portamento were commonly employed in the early years of the twentieth century, but that the L–portamento was rarely used until the 1930s, when, however, it was still the least common of the three.

   Portamentos were generally employed to shape melodies by emphasising important expressive notes, with ascending portamentos normally applied before those notes and descending portamentos added afterwards. As Finson explains, the placement of the portamento is not arbitrary, 'but involves a conscious effort on the part of the string player to shape the melodic line and accentuate structurally important pitches'.[72] With sparing use, portamento was considered, in the words of Leopold Auer, 'one of the great violin effects, which lends animation and expression to singing phrases'.[73] Auer is quick to point out, however, that the device 'becomes objectionable and inartistic – resembling more than anything else . . . the mewing of a cat – when it is executed in a languishing manner, and used continually. The

71 Flesch, *The Art of Violin Playing*, I, p. 28.

72 Jon W. Finson, 'Performing Practice in the Late Nineteenth Century, with Special Reference to the Music of Brahms', *Musical Quarterly*, 70 (1984), p. 465.

73 Leopold Auer, *Violin Playing As I Teach It* (New York 1921), pp. 24–5.

portamento should be employed only when the melody is descending, save for certain very exceptional cases of ascending melody'. Flesch also criticises the excessive use of portamento by late-nineteenth- and early-twentieth-century violinists, the false accents it creates and the fact that it was usually employed too slowly and merely for the player's convenience in shifting rather than for expressive ends. He found Joachim's crescendo during a portamento particularly 'offensive'.[74]

Ex. 7.18a   Beethoven: Violin Concerto Op. 61, first movement, bars 331–3

Ex. 7.18b   Beethoven: Violin Concerto Op. 61, second movement, bar 27

Ex. 7.18c   Beethoven: Violin Concerto Op. 61, third movement, bars 311–14

Ex. 7.18d   Beethoven: Violin Concerto Op. 61, first movement, bars 392–3

So common is the incidence of fingering patterns which invite portamento in most available nineteenth- and early-twentieth-century editions that it is possible here to give only a small selection of examples.[75] These are sub-divided for convenience into two of the categories employed by Flesch:[76] '*portamenti* based on an increased need of expression' (Exs. 7.18a–d) and 'unmotived *portamenti*', i.e. non-expressive slides occasioned by technical needs (Exs. 7.19a–c). Comparison of the fingering approaches of selected violinists/editors to the interpretation of what is perhaps the

74 Flesch, *Violin Fingering*, p. 365.
75 See also the examples from Dont's and David's editions cited by Clive Brown elsewhere in this volume, p. 130f.
76 Flesch, *The Art of Violin Playing*, I, p. 144.

emotional core of the work (2/45–52) also helps to create a picture of portamento usage, although this picture is arguably distorted somewhat by the uncharacterful omission of the device in bar 45 by Hubay, Dont, Sauret, David and Wilhelmj (see Hubay's fingering in Ex. 7.12c). Bachmann, while providing no fingering, describes this as 'the sublime phrase which veritably seems to have been set down "by the hand of God". To do justice to it the violinist should seek inspiration in the principle of *bel canto* song, and carry the note with distinction.'[77]

Ex. 7.19a   Beethoven: Violin Concerto Op. 61, third movement, bar 139 (Flesch)

Ex. 7.19b   Beethoven: Violin Concerto Op. 61, first movement, bars 195–6

Ex. 7.19c   Beethoven: Violin Concerto Op. 61, third movement, bars 131–5 (David)

The expressive potential of glissandos and portamentos, milked unflinchingly by most late-nineteenth-century editors and performers, has not entered so readily into the vocabulary of modern violinists, many of whom advocate the use of extensions to eliminate shifts and avoid 'slides'. As Galamian confirms, 'extensions outside the frame have always been a part of the violinistic equipment, but in recent times many novel types of extensions have been added, and, in general, their use has become more frequent as well as more varied'.[78] He isolates for special comment 'the *creeping* fingering', a technique of changing position based on extensions or contractions with the extended/contracted finger acting as a pivot for a caterpillar-like readjustment of the hand. Such a technique enables one 'to cover a substantial section of any one string without audible shifting' and normally results in cleaner and clearer articulation (Exs. 7.20a and b). Szigeti also supports the trend away from a

77 Bachmann, *An Encyclopedia*, p. 230.   78 Galamian, *Principles*, pp. 33–5.

Ex. 7.20a   Beethoven: Violin Concerto Op. 61, first movement, bars 90–2

Ex. 7.20b   Beethoven: Violin Concerto Op. 61, first movement, bars 304–6

Ex. 7.20c   Beethoven: Violin Concerto Op. 61, third movement, bars 1–3

Ex. 7.20d   Beethoven: Violin Concerto Op. 61, first movement, bars 406–8

Ex. 7.20e   Beethoven: Violin Concerto Op. 61, first movement, bars 515–18

strict notion of positions, recommending the use of extended positions for legato phrases and contracted positions for clear articulation in bravura passages. He criticises Flesch for disregarding the simple 'natural' falling of the fingers in a motive like Ex. 7.20c and using instead the fourth finger.[79] The advantages of such 'unorthodox contracted fingerings' (Exs. 7.20d–e), he claims, 'are obvious'.[80] Flesch, furthermore, gives a useful example of an extension which occasions a '*portamento* in half-tones', (Ex. 7.21a) a ploy which offers the significant technical advantage of a firmly set preparatory finger.[81] In similar fashion, Rostal's suggested fingering for 1/363 facilitates the formation of the hand ready for the tenths in the following bar (Ex. 7.21b).

79 Szigeti, Preface to his edition.
80 Szigeti, edition of solo violin part, p. 13 n4.
81 Flesch, *The Art of Violin Playing*, I, p. 146.

Ex. 7.21a   Beethoven: Violin Concerto Op. 61, first movement, bars 525–6 (Flesch)

Ex. 7.21b   Beethoven: Violin Concerto Op. 61, first movement, bars 363–5 (Rostal)

Ex. 7.22a   Beethoven: Violin Concerto Op. 61, first movement, bars 130–1 (Rostal)

Ex. 7.22b   Beethoven: Violin Concerto Op. 61, first movement, bars 396–8 (Rostal)

Ex. 7.22c   Beethoven: Violin Concerto Op. 61, first movement, bars 103–5 (Dont)

Ex. 7.22d   Beethoven: Violin Concerto Op. 61, first movement, bar 106 (Dont)

Ex. 7.22e   Beethoven: Violin Concerto Op. 61, first movement, bars 108–9 (Dont)

Ex. 7.22f   Beethoven: Violin Concerto Op. 61, first movement, bars 148–9 (Dont)

Ex. 7.23a   Beethoven: Violin Concerto Op. 61, first movement, bars 421–3 (Hubay)

Ex. 7.23b   Beethoven: Violin Concerto Op. 61, third movement, bars 311–15 (Rostal)

Ex. 7.24a   Beethoven: Violin Concerto Op. 61, first movement, bars 181–3 (Flesch)

Ex. 7.24b   Beethoven: Violin Concerto Op. 61, first movement, bar 297 (Szigeti)

Ex. 7.24c   Beethoven: Violin Concerto Op. 61, first movement, bar 297 (Rostal)

Some of the more recent editions look towards cultivating 'cleaner' left-hand articulation and tend to favour, where practicable, the lower, more fundamental left-hand positions. Rostal's is a case in point, profiting particularly from the use of second (e.g. at 3/153–4) and half (e.g. at 1/197 and 1/218) positions as well as semitone shifts (Exs. 7.22a and b). This is not to say that the semitone shift was at all foreign to the thinking of, for example, Dont or Hubay, both of whom include some notable examples (Exs. 7.22c–e and 7.12c); nor does it mean that the kind of shift over a tone more common in Dont's or Hubay's era (Exs. 7.22f and 7.23a) is not occasionally emulated by the likes of, say, Rostal (Ex. 7.23b). It is simply a matter of proportional use determined by differences in taste. Some of the more recent publications also address the very different problems encountered in playing semitones in the higher positions, Flesch, Szigeti and Rostal, for example, suggesting fingerings (Ex. 7.24a–c) which take into account the lateral or oblique inclination, or very simply, the close proximity of the fingers.[82]

Surprisingly few editors seem to share Szigeti's view regarding the benefits of playing identical repeated notes with different fingers.[83] Szigeti emphasises the 'expressive enhancement' thus gained, notably the natural changes in timbre and vibrato, and the 'infinitesimally changed intonation', especially in passages such as Ex. 7.25. He dislikes Joachim's use of a harmonic for the second g^1 and claims that 'hardly any interpreter today would follow him in this'.

Ex. 7.25   Beethoven: Violin Concerto Op. 61, second movement, bars 45–7 (Szigeti)

There have long been two schools of thought regarding chromatic fingerings, but the so-called 'slide' fingering seems to have been far more common than the use of one finger for each note, even though the latter offered greater evenness, artic-ulation and clarity. Hubay, Dessauer and Baillot endorse the above observation,[84] although Dessauer bows towards the rarer approach at 1/200 (312121) and Dont seems fairly progressive for his time at 2/23 (1231212).

Many recognise the value of open strings to assist in routine shifting (Ex. 7.26a) or in overcoming certain difficulties such as the formation of tenths (Ex. 7.26b). Open strings can also play a role in artistic phrasing, 'often serving', according to Yampolsky, 'as a means of strengthening the expressive contrast in a musical phrase. Thus the juxtaposition of stopped and open strings for a single note in a repeated melodic phrase throws it into relief and gives it a variety of tone colour.'[85] Comparison of Yampolsky's recommendations with those of other editors (e.g. Hubay), however, reveals some disparity of thought regarding Ex. 7.26c. Changes in string materials also directly affected tonal considerations, especially the use of open strings. Szigeti directs Ex. 7.26d to be played legato and exploits the e^2 string's propensity to sound an octave higher when the first finger is released from

82 ibid., I, p. 119.   83 Szigeti, Szigeti on the Violin, p. 58.

84 Dessauer – (112233) at 1/167, (1122334) at 1/441; Hubay (1122334) at 1/167; Baillot L'Art du violon, p. 116: annotations for 1/441 and 443 suggest that slide fingerings should be used.

85 Izrail' Markovich Yampolsky, The Principles of Violin Fingering, trans. Alan Lumsden (London 1967), p. 98.

Ex. 7.26a   Beethoven: Violin Concerto Op. 61, first movement, bars 164–5

Ex. 7.26b   Beethoven: Violin Concerto Op. 61, first movement, bars 364–5

Ex. 7.26c   Beethoven: Violin Concerto Op. 61, first movement, bars 140–2

Ex. 7.26d   Beethoven: Violin Concerto Op. 61, first movement, bars 183–4 (Szigeti)

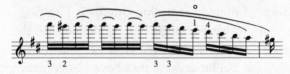

Ex. 7.26e   Beethoven: Violin Concerto Op. 61, first movement, bars 394–6 (Flesch)

Ex. 7.26f   Beethoven: Violin Concerto Op. 61, third movement, bars 53–9 (Dessauer)

the f♯³ in order to effect this. He admits that 'it is characteristic of our present-day "line of least resistance" attitudes that some brilliant soloists evade the issue by playing the downward scale *détaché* or *sautillé* instead of *legato*'.[86] Flesch, meanwhile, warns that the 'steel string' often produces an undesirable whistling noise in an ascending legato passage such as Ex. 7.26e. While this may be avoided by bringing the bow nearer the bridge at the critical moment, such enforced changes in the bow-position can have a detrimental effect on tone-production; thus, a fourth finger should be substituted for the open string.[87] Dessauer's recommendations in,

Ex. 7.27a   Beethoven: Violin Concerto Op. 61, first movement, bars 167–8 (Flesch)

Ex. 7.27b   Beethoven: Violin Concerto Op. 61, first movement, bars 159–60 (Dessauer)

Ex. 7.27c   Beethoven: Violin Concerto Op. 61, second movement, bar 20 (Flesch)

Ex. 7.27d   Beethoven: Violin Concerto Op. 61, third movement, bars 10–12 (Flesch)

Ex. 7.27e   Beethoven: Violin Concerto Op. 61, first movement, bars 511–14 (Flesch)

Ex. 7.27f   Beethoven: Violin Concerto Op. 61, first movement, bars 159–60 (Yampolsky)

86 Szigeti, *A Violinist's Notebook*, pp. 58–9.   87 Flesch, *Violin Fingering*, p. 10.

Ex. 7.27g   Beethoven: Violin Concerto Op. 61, first movement, bars 101–3 (Flesch)

for example, Ex. 7.26f, serve to illustrate how much freer some earlier violinists were with the use of open strings.

Although harmonics are not specified either in the autograph or in the other principal primary sources, their use is recommended in varying quantities by many editors for technical or expressive reasons, whether to avoid formal shifts (Ex. 7.27a), to assist in making a shift (Ex. 7.27b), to complement the use of open strings (Ex. 7.27c), to facilitate accuracy of intonation (Ex. 7.27d), or to avoid either portamento (Ex. 7.27e) or awkward string crossings (Ex. 7.27f). The unanimous acceptance of harmonics into the violinist's technical vocabulary had been slow to materialise in the seventeenth and eighteenth centuries due to their inferior tone quality, Leopold Mozart, for example, particularly disapproving of any juxtaposition of harmonics and normally-stopped notes within the same piece or movement.[88] The nineteenth century witnessed a more liberal approach to their use. Even Spohr, who was reserved about the employment of all harmonics because of their lack of tonal affinity with stopped notes, allows their limited introduction, 'chiefly in order to make one single note stand out more clearly than the others, for example the final note of ascending scales or broken chords'.[89] Flesch, too, seems concerned about matters of timbre when considering a fingering for 1/101 (Ex. 7.27g), 'one of the most precarious passages in violin literature'.[90] He admits that every violinist uses his own individual fingering but claims that the tonal result is all-important. He gives four fingerings and discusses the merits of each; he favours fingering (b) and, contrary to, for example, Dessauer, is adamant that a harmonic should not be employed for the b[3]:

Fingering (a) has the disadvantage of a glissando; (d) that of an unprepared entrance on the A-string; (c) has hardly anything to recommend it. One good thing, however, all these fingerings have in common: they eliminate the harmonic on the high b, and that is very important.[91]

Dessauer, Hubay and others prescribed harmonics freely in their editions (Exs. 7.28a–g), sometimes following an implicit portamento, and Flesch appreciates the

88 Leopold Mozart, *Versuch einer gründlichen Violinschule* (Augsburg 1756), ch. 5, para. 13, pp. 106–7.
89 Louis Spohr, *Violinschule* (Vienna [1832]), p. 108.
90 Flesch, *Violin Fingering*, p. 314.   91 *ibid.*, p. 314.

Ex. 7.28a   Beethoven: Violin Concerto Op. 61, first movement, bars 142–3 (Dessauer)

Ex. 7.28b   Beethoven: Violin Concerto Op. 61, second movement, bar 30 (David)

Ex. 7.28c   Beethoven: Violin Concerto Op. 61, first movement, bars 391–3 (Hubay)

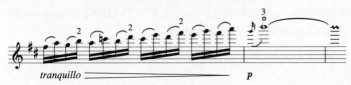

Ex. 7.28d   Beethoven: Violin Concerto Op. 61, first movement, bars 155–6 (Hubay)

Ex. 7.28e   Beethoven: Violin Concerto Op. 61, first movement, bar 429 (Wilhelmj, 1896)

Ex. 7.28f   Beethoven: Violin Concerto Op. 61, first movement, bars 165–6 (Rostal)

Ex. 7.28g   Beethoven: Violin Concerto Op. 61, second movement, bar 15 (Dessauer)

gracefulness with which they can adorn slow passages, especially in works of the Classical period, when 'violinists were in the habit of avoiding the fourth position and of reaching for the harmonic from the third position'.[92] Editors have also favoured harmonics for their soft, expressive sound quality and especially, in keeping with Spohr's preference, for 'top-notes of a passage, provided a fleeting effect rather than an intense expression is desired'[93] (see Exs. 7.28a and g). Szigeti, however, mirrors a more modern attitude, claiming that the bad old days of Exs. 7.29a and b, advocated by, among others Dont, Dessauer, Wilhelmj, Joachim/Moser and Flesch, 'seem to be over, happily!'.[94] Nevertheless, harmonics still play a fairly prominent role in his fingering aesthetic, notably an artificial harmonic at 1/142 for technical facility, or natural harmonics to facilitate fingering (the adjacent fifths at 1/158 and 2/20 or the extension into second position at 3/61) and emphasise phrasing at 1/151 (and 1/424). Most of Szigeti's recommendations on harmonics are endorsed by Rostal, who, however, employs an artificial harmonic for the a^3 at 1/312 but prefers a more orthodox fingering without harmonic for the e^3 at 1/142.

Ex. 7.29a   Beethoven: Violin Concerto Op. 61, first movement, bars 150–1 (Dont)

Ex. 7.29b   Beethoven: Violin Concerto Op. 61, first movement, bars 521–3

Many writers and performers extol the expressive virtues of flexibility of tempo while others encourage either a precise literal interpretation of the text or a compromise. Flesch relates the two interpretative extremes by contrasting Ysaÿe's imaginative rubato and style of 'the impulsive romantic, who was concerned not so much with the printed note-values, the dead letter, as with the spirit that cannot be reproduced graphically',[95] with Hugo Heermann's faithful, distinctly German approach to the work on his Parisian debut (1893).[96] Ysaÿe's rubato appears to have been frequently misplaced in Classical compositions, because 'he could not avoid

---

92 *ibid.*, p. 310.

93 *ibid.*, p. 312. See also, for example, Wilhelmj (1896) 2/15 and 16. The acceptance of natural harmonics in this way is partly explained by the fact that the prevalent performing trend was to use vibrato sparingly. See pp. 192–4.

94 Szigeti, Preface to his edition.

95 Hans Keller and C.F. Flesch, eds., *The Memoirs of Carl Flesch*, trans. Hans Keller (London 1957), p. 79.

96 *ibid.*, p. 84.

putting his own personality before that of the composer'.[97] In his hands, therefore, Beethoven's Concerto 'suffered an imaginative remodelling of the original into a personal experience, which did not leave much of the unadulterated Beethoven spirit'.[98] Ysaÿe's approach may well have been exceptional. Nevertheless, it is common knowledge that tempo in late-nineteenth and early-twentieth-century performance was treated more flexibly than it is today, this freedom appearing on the level of both the musical phrase and the musical paragraph and often taking on a structural function.

Ex. 7.30a   Beethoven: Violin Concerto Op. 61, first movement, bars 307–8 (Dessauer, Bachmann, Rostal)

Ex. 7.30b   Beethoven: Violin Concerto Op. 61, first movement, bars 333–5 (Bachmann)

The chief means of freedom for expressive melodic effect within the 'outlines' of the pulse was *tempo rubato*, which involved a natural flexibility of the prescribed rhythm within a constant tempo, after which the ensemble was restored. As Finson has pointed out, rubato 'was a device applied to the motivic and melodic structure of a piece in order to outline that structure for the audience. It was not merely a sentimental device applied haphazardly.'[99] Faithful accentuation and, in some cases, prolongation (the so-called agogic accent) of important notes within the phrase are vital for the listener's comprehension of the performer's, and hence the composer's, intentions. Thus, many editors highlight notes particularly appropriate for such treatment by adding certain symbols of poetic meter and other indications to suggest articulations or notes of emphasis,[100] notably Dessauer, Bachmann[101] and Rostal (Ex. 7.30a). Flesch claims that such a melodic counterpoint in the form of a frame for a theme presented by the orchestra 'calls for agogic accents in increased number on such notes which have been borrowed from the theme or which are closely related to it. When these agogic accents are not employed the places in question

97 *ibid.*, p. 80.

98 *ibid.*, p. 80.

99 Finson, 'Performing Practice', p. 473.

100 For example, the greater significance of the *note buone* ('good notes') in the bar implicit in the rule of the down-bow.

101 Bachmann, *An Encyclopedia*, p. 227.

easily assume a certain stiff, lifeless etude-like character.'[102] Some editors (e.g. Dont at 1/134, 1/136, 1/407, 1/408 and 1/410; Hubay at 1/211f.(trills), 1/307 and 1/485–6; and sometimes Szigeti, e.g. at 3/301) go to extreme lengths by using accent signs to indicate notes of emphasis when the attack implicit in this sign might be considered inappropriate nowadays. Bachmann, who is a prime example, isolates the passage around 1/330[103] as one of the most moving in the work, in which 'accent plays a large and extremely important part . . . and the whole question is one of making a correct use of accentuation' (Ex. 7.30b).[104] Despite the availability of the Tourte-model bow, with its greater strength (particularly at the point), broader ribbon of hair, quicker take-up of hair and increased potential for a more immediate attack, few accents or true sforzandos appear in the solo part of our four original Beethoven sources.[105]

Ex. 7.31a   Beethoven: Violin Concerto Op. 61, first movement, bars 114–16

Ex. 7.31b   Beethoven: Violin Concerto Op. 61, third movement, bars 68–9

Ex. 7.31c   Beethoven: Violin Concerto Op. 61, first movement, bars 130–2

Ex. 7.31d   Beethoven: Violin Concerto Op. 61, third movement, bars 45–6 (Wilhelmj)

Ex. 7.31e   Beethoven: Violin Concerto Op. 61, third movement, bars 218–19 (Wilhelmj)

102 Flesch, *The Art of Violin Playing*, II, p. 59.   103 See Ex. 7.18a.

104 Bachmann, *An Encyclopedia*, p. 228.

105 Accents appear in the solo part only in 2/43 and 44, while sforzandi appear only in 1/91 and 92; 1/107 (second beat) and 1/286 and 287.

While careful to warn against roughness and harshness of accent on notes of emphasis in order to avoid 'falsifying' the ensuing rhythm (1/322), Bachmann requires that the first note of the first and third beats in 1/114 and 115 be 'underlined' and claims that 'too marked a dwelling' on the first note of the lower octave 'results in an incorrect accent'.[106] This particular passage is one in which the traditional rule of the down-bow, which accommodated notes of rhythmic stress (for example, the first note of each bar or various accented beats of the bar) in the stronger down stroke, is often not observed, most editors (Dont and Joachim included, although Dessauer and Wilhelmj are notable exceptions) opting for Ex. 7.31a as the optimum execution. Another passage in which the use of 'counterclockwise' bowing contrary to the rule of the down-bow is generally preferred is 3/68ff. (and its parallel at 3/243ff.), because it facilitates dexterity in string-changing (Ex. 7.31b).[107] Galamian here recommends the use of the *fouetté* bowstroke in the upper half of the bow, the required up-bow accent being provided by 'quickly (and barely) lifting the bow off the string and striking it down again with suddenness and energy'.[108] Many versions of 1/131 also involve the player in some unexpected 'topsy-turvy' bowing (Ex. 7.31c). There are also some unusual up-bow starts to savour from, among others, Hubay, Wilhelmj, Rostal, David and Auer in instances (like 1/111 and 1/457) where a down-bow would be more customary and 'weighty'; furthermore, there are some puzzling down-bow starts when an up-bow would, nowadays at least, be more conventional and comfortable (Exs. 7.31d and e). Finally, Flesch emphasises the importance of cultivating changes of position on strong beats in order to avoid false (weak-beat) accentuation (Ex. 7.32a).[109]

Ex. 7.32a   Beethoven: Violin Concerto Op. 61, third movement, bars 322–4 (Flesch)

Ex. 7.32b   Beethoven: Violin Concerto Op. 61, second movement, bar 77 (Bachmann and Auer)

106 Bachmann, *An Encyclopedia*, p. 226.
107 Wilhelmj is one of the few editors to prescribe 'clockwise' bowing here.
108 Galamian, *Principles*, pp. 69–70.
109 Flesch, *Violin Fingering*, p. 155.

There is a wealth of evidence regarding Beethoven's own use of rubato in his performances[110] and many editors have attempted to indicate their preferences for such rhythmic freedom in their texts. Bachmann suggests that the first four notes of 1/174 should be 'lightly stressed' rather than the bar being played rigidly as written;[111] and in 1/91 he prescribes 'a slight holding back on the first triplets, with a very brief stop' on the f^3.[112] An improvisatory approach is encouraged for 2/18ff., and Bachmann requires 2/77 to be played as in Ex. 7.32b, *forte* and in declamatory style, equally divided, but stressing the last seven notes of the passage.[113] With a similar aim of rhythmic flexibility in mind, Dessauer recommends that 2/43 and 44 should be given 'broad and very free treatment' and should not be 'treated as an unimportant transitional passage, as [it] might seem at first glance'.[114] Although he prescribes even playing of the triplets in 1/111 and 113, he encourages rhythmic freedom at one particularly significant structural point in the first movement (1/331ff.) to produce a 'warm and deeply-felt interpretation'. After the last quaver of 1/332, he recommends the player to 'indulge in an imaginary pause', just as if he needs 'to breathe once more . . . to express his innermost feelings'.[115]

There are, of course, a number of brief passages in the slow movement which lie outside its rhythmic structure and for which an 'improvisatory' *ad libitum* interpretation is either prescribed or implied.[116] Curiously, some nineteenth-century editors (e.g. Auer and, in some passages, Joachim/Moser and Holle/Schultze-Biesantz) have felt the need to write out some of these passages painstakingly in a rhythmic form, implying an interpretation contrary to the composer's intentions (Exs. 7.33a and b). Wilhelmj has even gone so far as to alter Beethoven's prescribed rhythm in 2/24, adding, at the same time, a termination to the trill! (Ex. 7.33c). Joachim and Moser adopt a compromise solution for 2/40ff.:

In order to give full effect to the peaceful mood which should undoubtedly reign here, the semiquavers printed in small notes that throw themselves, like tendrils, from one crotchet to another, must not be played too quickly. One must endeavour to obtain the time necessary for their quiet and unhurried performance by diminishing the value of the preceding crotchet by almost one half as indicated in [Ex. 7.33d].[117]

110 See, for example, Bernhard Bartels, *Beethoven* (Hildesheim 1927), p. 345; Anton F. Schindler, *Beethoven As I Knew Him*, trans. C. Jolly and ed. Donald W. MacArdle (London 1966), p. 412; Franz Gerhard Wegeler and Ferdinand Ries, *Biographische Notizen über Beethoven* (Coblenz 1838), p. 106.

111 Bachmann, *An Encyclopedia*, p. 226.

112 *ibid.*, p. 225.

113 *ibid.*, p. 230.

114 Dessauer, edition of solo violin part, p. 12.

115 *ibid.*, p. 7.

116 Bars 14, 24, 40–2, 73–4, 77 and 91.

117 Joseph Joachim and Andreas Moser, *Violinschule* (Berlin 1902–5), III, p. 183.

Ex. 7.33a   Beethoven: Violin Concerto Op. 61, second movement, bars 40–3 (Auer)

Ex. 7.33b   Beethoven: Violin Concerto Op. 61, second movement, bars 40–3 (Holle and Schultze-Biesantz)

Ex. 7.33c   Beethoven: Violin Concerto Op. 61, second movement, bar 24 (Wilhelmj)

Ex. 7.33d   Beethoven: Violin Concerto Op. 61, second movement, bars 40–1 (Joachim and Moser)

Flexibility of tempo and rhythm – or 'tempo modification' as Wagner called it[118] – was also applied on a much larger scale to articulate the structure of whole movements. Since every theme had its own optimum tempo which, in theory, was retained consistently throughout the movement, tempo differentiations tended to highlight significant structural landmarks. Thus, as Finson puts it, 'differing stable tempos were matched to stable thematic and harmonic areas in a movement, while tonally unstable areas were marked by changing tempos. Large unstable areas, like the development and coda, often featured accelerating tempos to heighten tension and drama when appropriate.'[119] Robert Philip, in his fascinating study of early

118 See Richard Wagner 'Ueber das Dirigieren', *Gesammelte Schriften und Dichtungen*, 3rd edn (Leipzig n.d.), VIII, pp. 287–308.

119 Finson, 'Performing Practice', p. 473.

recordings, confirms that it was usual in the 1920s and 1930s for performers to underline contrasts of mood and tension by changes of tempo, lyrical and reflective passages being played more slowly and energetic passages more quickly. He provides an interesting and revealing table of tempo differences in the opening fifty bars of selected recordings of Beethoven's Violin Concerto to illustrate his point[120] (see Table 7.1). He concludes that performances 'from the 1920s and (to a decreasing extent) 1930s very often show substantially greater fluctuations of tempo within movements than late-twentieth-century recordings' and that 'the most striking differences are in the speeding up of energetic passages'. This characteristic helps to underline the more relaxed passages (e.g. 1/331ff.) in the older recordings, espe-cially the contrast between

Table 7.1. *Beethoven, Violin Concerto, first movement*

	bars	1–9	28–41	43–50
Kreisler, cond. L. Blech (rec. 1926)	♩ =	108	128	112
Szigeti, cond. Walter (rec. 1932)		96	132	112
Huberman, cond. Szell (rec. 1936)		108	120	116
Kreisler, cond. Barbirolli (rec. 1936)		108	120	116
Kulenkampff, cond. Schmidt-Isserstedt (rec. 1936)		108	120	116
Heifetz, cond. Toscanini (rec. 1940)		116	124	124
Menuhin, cond. Klemperer (rec. 1966)		104	108	104
I. Oistrakh, cond. D. Oistrakh (rec. *c.* 1971)		100	104	108
Szeryng, cond. Haitink (rec. 1973)		108	112	110
Grumiaux, cond. C. Davis (rec. 1974)		96	112	110
Zukerman, cond. Barenboim (rec. *c.* 1977)		104	112	112

the generally reflective nature of the solo sections and the more march-like character of the orchestral sections, so that a firm sense of forward motion is renewed whenever an orches-tral tutti is reached. In modern performances the tempos of the orchestral sections are closer to the slower speeds of the solo passages, so that contrasts in character between solo and tutti are less clearly defined than in the old recordings.[121]

Bachmann's (1925) recommendation for 1/511 appears to be contrary to the underlying trend of his times – 'The sublime phrase which follows the cadenza should be played with simplicity, piano, *and in the actual tempo of the beginning of the Concerto.*'[122] Philip's conclusions confirm that the tradition of flexible tempo has been refined in more recent years rather than abolished.

120 Robert Philip, *Early Recordings and Musical Style* (Cambridge 1992), p. 16. See also the present volume
    pp. 196–8.
121 *ibid.*, p. 17.   122 Bachmann, *An Encyclopedia*, p. 229 (my italics).

A few editors, among them Hubay, have added tempo indications such as *poco allargando* (1/96; 1/142), *a tempo* (1/97), *largamente* (1/152) and *poco meno* (3/293) to Beethoven's text in order better to realise the expressive potential of the work in the style of their time; some others, notably Holle and Schultze-Biesantz and Joachim, prescribe metronome markings for individual movements.[123] By comparison, some of Rudolf Kolisch's views on tempo seem somewhat extreme, at least in respect of the opening movement. He classifies it as an example of 'the *alla breve* form of the slow *Allegro*' which 'exhibits the typical "*Allegro* melody", in quarter-notes, conceived in long phrases in singing style without separation into small motives', and he prescribes ♩ = 84–88 for its optimum execution.[124] The central movement is also considered in terms of alla breve character (♩ = 30),[125] while the Finale is characterised by 'a theme of gently rocking nature with dotted-eighth formations and passage-work in sixteenths'; a tempo of ♩. = 104 is recommended,[126] somewhat faster than the more usual ♩. = *c.* 80. Of our editors, Dessauer emphasises the *ma non troppo* of the first movement and suggests that the tempo should not be chosen 'at too rapid a gait but still not rob the movement of the real character of a flowing Allegro'.[127] Meanwhile, Flesch recalls that he once heard Enesco play the last movement at ♩. = 48 instead of the generally accepted 69, 'which for a musician of his rank was an inexplicable blunder'.[128] Such a surprisingly wide range of recorded tempi (from ♩. = 48–104) for the Finale begs an equally diverse range of interpretations.

Taste, contextual requirements and musical instinct have consistently been the deciding factors in the interpretation of specific ornaments. Although written trills tended to be modified by the addition of preparations and/or terminations or by varying the number, rhythm, speed and nuances of their constituent notes, editors of this concerto have provided performers on the whole with minimal help towards the formulation of an appropriate interpretation. In the early years of the nineteenth century trills were generally well accented and commenced on the beat on the note a semitone or tone above the written note, depending on the position of that written note in the scale, but other designs co-existed with the upper auxiliary preparation and most of Beethoven's designated trills in the Violin Concerto would appear to be better suited to a principal-note start for reasons of

123 Holle and Schultze-Biesantz: first movement: ♩ = 132; second movement: ♩ = 58; third movement: ♩. = 96–104. Joachim: first movement: ♩ = *c.* 116; second movement: ♩ = *c.* 54; third movement: ♩. = *c.* 92.

124 Rudolf Kolisch, trans. Arthur Mendel, 'Tempo and Character in Beethoven's Music', *Musical Quarterly*, 29 (1943), p. 187.

125 *ibid.*, p. 306.

126 *ibid.*, p. 299. Kolisch's opinion is confirmed in Rudolf Kolisch and René Leibowitz, 'Aufführungsprobleme im Violinkonzert von Beethoven', *Musica*, 33 (1979), p. 153.

127 Dessauer, edition of solo violin part, p. 1.

128 Keller and Flesch, eds., *The Memoirs of Carl Flesch*, p. 179.

taste, technique or melodic fluidity.[129] In keeping with this observation, there is thus little annotation of trill preparation in published editions of the work. The indication of trill terminations is a very different matter, Exs. 7.34a–k demonstrating some of the more common editorial additions.

Ex. 7.34a   Beethoven: Violin Concerto Op. 61, first movement, bar 47

Ex. 7.34b   Beethoven: Violin Concerto Op. 61, first movement, bars 216–17

Ex. 7.34c   Beethoven: Violin Concerto Op. 61, first movement, bars 329–31

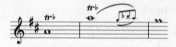

Ex. 7.34d   Beethoven: Violin Concerto Op. 61, first movement, bars 419–20

Ex. 7.34e   Beethoven: Violin Concerto Op. 61, first movement, bars 490–1

Ex. 7.34f   Beethoven: Violin Concerto Op. 61, second movement, bar 24

129 Furthermore, from about the second quarter of the nineteenth century onwards most German sources (for example, Johann Nepomuk Hummel's *Ausführliche theoretisch-practische Anweisung zum Pianofortespiel* (Vienna 1828) and Spohr's *Violinschule*, which quotes Hummel's work as its authority but incorrectly states that the main-note start was first advanced by Hummel) argue on melodic grounds or for brilliance of effect in favour of a main-note 'preparation' as the norm, but such an interpretation is not without exception.

Ex. 7.34g   Beethoven: Violin Concerto Op. 61, second movement, bars 51–4

Ex. 7.34h   Beethoven: Violin Concerto Op. 61, third movement, bars 91–2

Ex. 7.34i   Beethoven: Violin Concerto Op. 61, third movement, bar 4

Ex. 7.34j   Beethoven: Violin Concerto Op. 61, third movement, bar 9

Ex. 7.34k   Beethoven: Violin Concerto Op. 61, third movement, bars 292–3

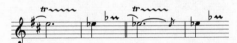

Bow management with the trill suffers surprising textual neglect. Those who do mention this aspect concern themselves largely with the adjustment of bow speed to the length of the trill, in order to avoid a bow change in the middle of a long trill.[130] Joachim and Moser, however, suggest some practical help in coping with Beethoven's long trills: 'If a shake on account of its length cannot well be played in one bow-stroke, the illusion of the long breath may be maintained by changing the bow quite unnoticeably on the *weak* or *unaccented* beat of the bar.'[131]

Some editors write out turns fully in the text (e.g. Wilhelmj (1896), Sauret), illustrate their interpretations as 'footnotes' (e.g. Hubay, Jacobsen and, to a limited extent, Szigeti), or use a 'mix' of both methods (e.g. Rostal), while others leave the execution of such ornaments entirely to the performer's discretion. Bachmann permits the performer little freedom in 1/131, specifying that the 'groups' should be played 'exactly in time' as in Ex. 7.35a.[132] Most other editors mirror his interpretation,

---

130 For example, Franz Joseph Froehlich, *Vollständige theoretisch-praktische Musikschule für alle beym Orchester gebräuchliche wichtigere Instrumente* (Cologne and Bonn 1810–11), IV, sec. 6, pp. 43–4.

131 Joachim and Moser, *Violinschule*, III, p. 182.

132 Bachmann, *An Encyclopedia*, p. 226.

apart from his addition of a sharp to the c^2 of the first turn. Among other unusual interpretations of Beethoven's designated turns should be cited Wilhelmj's (1896) of 1/342 and Hubay's slightly more drawn-out, *espressivo* rendering of 3/143 (Exs. 7.35b and c). Finally, some editions, notably Wilhelmj's[133] and that published in Vienna in 1844, fail to take account of all Beethoven's 'graces'; by contrast, Wilhelmj's edition of 1896 adds to Beethoven's text at 1/469, introducing some obvious rhythmic misprints in the process (Ex. 7.35d).

Ex. 7.35a   Beethoven: Violin Concerto Op. 61, first movement, bar 131 (Bachmann)

Ex. 7.35b   Beethoven: Violin Concerto Op. 61, first movement, bar 342 (Wilhelmj)

Ex. 7.35c   Beethoven: Violin Concerto Op. 61, third movement, bars 143–4 (Hubay)

Ex. 7.35d   Beethoven: Violin Concerto Op. 61, first movement, bars 469–70 (Wilhelmj, 1896)

Vibrato, more the domain of the performer than the editor, does not warrant detailed discussion here. Nevertheless, it is important to point out that it was used selectively and sparingly as an expressive melodic ornament on long notes and in cantabile passages practically throughout the nineteenth century. Only towards the end of the century did a radically different approach begin to evolve, and it was not until after the first decade or so of the twentieth century that a new attitude to vibrato became established. The new aesthetic involved continuous rather than selective use of the device more as an ingredient of good tone production than as a particular expressive ornament, and the technique of vibrato production began to

133 But not the edition of 1896.

embrace the left arm as well as the fingers and hand. Some attribute this new approach to Ysaÿe and the Franco-Belgian school; others accredit Kreisler with its introduction.[134] Kreisler himself records that 'Wieniawsky intensified the vibrato and brought it to heights never before achieved, so that it became known as the "French vibrato". Vieuxtemps also took it up, and after him Eugene Ysaÿe, who became its greatest exponent, and I.'[135] Flesch summarises the situation thus:

We must not forget that even in 1880 the great violinists did not yet make use of a proper vibrato but employed a kind of *Bebung*, i.e. a finger vibrato in which the pitch was sub-jected to only quite imperceptible oscillations. To vibrate on relatively unexpressive notes, not to speak of runs, was regarded as unseemly and inartistic. Basically, quicker passages had to be distinguished by a certain dryness from longer and more expressive notes. Ysaÿe was the first to make use of a broader vibrato and already attempted to give life to passing notes, while Kreisler drew the extreme consequences from this revaluation of vibrato activity; he not only resorted to a still broader and more intensive vibrato, but even tried to ennoble faster passages by means of a vibrato which, admittedly, was more latent than manifest [literally 'more thought than actually executed'].[136]

Redervill claims: '[Kreisler's] vibrato and trill seem to be nearly double the speed of most other artists . . . this great artist gives life to his tone by using the rapid vibrato continuously.'[137]

There was inevitably a transitional period at the beginning of the current cen-tury when supporters of the old aesthetic rejected the new. This explains the defensive attitudes of Joachim, Auer, Wessely and others who looked upon vibrato primarily as an expressive effect.[138] Auer, for example writes:

'– those who are convinced that an eternal vibrato is the secret of soulful playing, of piquancy in performance – are pitifully misguided in their belief . . . No, the vibrato is an effect, an embellishment; it can lend a touch of divine pathos to the climax of a phrase or the course of a passage, but only if the player has cultivated a delicate sense of proportion in the use of it.'[139]

However, Wessely's views about vibrato (1913), though essentially of the old school, show some signs of compromise, advocating use of the device in moderation: 'The "vibrato" must correspond to the various shades of the phrase in which it is being

---

134 See Brown, 'Bowing Styles', p. 111; Flesch, *The Art of Violin Playing*, I, p. 40; Keller and Flesch, eds., *The Memoirs of Carl Flesch*, p. 120. *Der beseelte Violinton* by Siegfried Eberhardt, ed. G. Küthmann (Dresden 1910), trans. as *Violin Vibrato* (New York 1911), was the first treatise to deal extensively with this new aesthetic and its technique.

135 L. P. Lochner, *Fritz Kreisler* (London 1951), p. 19.

136 Keller and Flesch, eds., *The Memoirs of Carl Flesch*, p. 120.

137 E. R. Redervill, as quoted in Lochner, *Fritz Kreisler*, p. 273.

138 See Auer, *Violin Playing*, pp. 47–51; Lochner, *Fritz Kreisler*, p. 19; Joachim and Moser, *Violinschule*, II, p. 96.

139 Auer, *Violin Playing*, pp. 48–9.

used and thus, like the painter's brush, be capable of delineating the many hues of colour which the violinist feels to be the emotion and reflection of his innermost soul.'[140] Certainly by the 1920s teaching manuals were increasingly advocating the use of a continuous vibrato.

Since Beethoven wrote no cadenzas for his Violin Concerto, countless violinists, composers and editors have composed their own, few limiting their contributions to the technical means and musical style of Beethoven's times.[141] Fittingly perhaps, Joachim's cadenzas for the work have proved the most enduring (despite Spohr's criticism (1855) that they are 'superfluously long, very difficult and ungrateful'),[142] but Kreisler's, written at the age of nineteen,[143] have been almost their equal in popularity. Beethoven did, however, compose cadenzas for his piano version of the concerto. Max Rostal and Wolfgang Schneiderhan are among those who have transcribed these for violin.

Beethoven's Violin Concerto has been dubbed 'the touchstone marking the maturity of the performing artist'.[144] That it has survived, blossomed and maintained its stature as a concerted work of the first rank throughout the currency of the numerous and diverse performing trends, techniques and styles outlined in this study testifies to its position as 'the concerto of concertos'[145] within the violin repertory. To provide comprehensive coverage of the finer details of these styles as demonstrated in the various texts and editions of the work is out of the question within the confines of this essay, even though performing conventions have become more standardised during the last fifty years or so (particularly with regard to matters of rhythm and the use of vibrato and portamento). However, it is hoped that the most significant issues of nineteenth- and early-twentieth-century performance have received sufficient discussion for readers to be stimulated to further constructive and penetrating thought about many of the myriad aspects of historical performance practice. Szigeti urges students of Beethoven's work to be 'humble before the magnitude of the achievement of the Master and the challenge its reproduction represents for us'.[146] The student who is faced with this challenge today would do well to ponder on the infinitely greater challenge it offered the likes of Clement, Joachim and their immediate successors when it was still uncharted territory.

140 Hans Wessely, *A Practical Guide to Violin Playing* (London 1913), pp. 90–1. Interestingly, he prescribes 'dolce and sempre vibrato' for the passage commencing at 1/331.
141 Alfred Schnittke's efforts, with their somewhat facile avant-garde effects, are an extreme case in point.
142 Boris Schwarz, *Great Masters of the Violin* (London 1983), p. 246n.
143 Kreisler's cadenzas were not published until 1928.
144 Andreas Moser, *Geschichte des Violinspiels* (Berlin 1923), as cited in the score edited by W. Altmann (London, Eulenberg 1942), p. III.
145 Szigeti, Preface to his edition; Keller and Flesch, eds., *The Memoirs of Carl Flesch*, p. 152.
146 Szigeti, Preface to his edition, p. 5.

8

TRADITIONAL HABITS OF PERFORMANCE IN EARLY-TWENTIETH-CENTURY RECORDINGS OF BEETHOVEN

ROBERT PHILIP

It is an uncontroversial statement that musicians and audiences in the late twentieth century are better informed about the performance practice of Beethoven's day than they were in the first half of this century. We are now used to Beethoven played on instruments with gut strings, fortepianos, hard drum-sticks, old flutes, oboes and bassoons, narrow-bore trumpets, and the consequences for balance and sonority. We have grown accustomed to new ideas on tempo in Beethoven, based on re-examination of his metronome markings. We have, it seems, gained an immense amount of knowledge about Beethoven performance. But have we also lost something? Do recordings from the early decades of this century, from the days before modern scholarship, have anything to teach us?

Recordings made in the early years of this century are, from our perspective, half-way back to Beethoven in time. Traditions of musical performance are evolving continuously, and, despite the advances of modern scholarship, it is therefore reasonable to suppose that there might be features preserved in early-twentieth-century recordings which are closer to the practice of Beethoven's day than our own. It is worth, in particular, examining those aspects of early-twentieth-century playing which now seem most old-fashioned, and which are therefore most removed from a late-twentieth-century style. Perhaps they contain traces of the distant past.[1]

VIBRATO

It is now generally accepted that string and wind players of Beethoven's day used vibrato much more sparingly than players of the late twentieth century. What is less widely known is that this old attitude to vibrato survived into the early twentieth century. The modern, more or less continuous, string vibrato only became widespread by about the 1920s, particularly through the influence of Kreisler. Kreisler's 1926 recording of Beethoven's Violin Concerto sounds very modern for its time, with its continuous vibrato. Huberman's 1936 performance is more old-fashioned

---

1 For a more general examination of early recordings and their implications, see Robert Philip, *Early Recordings and Musical Style: Changing Tastes in Instrumental Performance 1900–1950* (Cambridge 1992).

despite its later date, in that his vibrato is much more variable, tending to lapse in fairly quick-moving passages, or in transitional parts of phrases. The oldest generation of string quartets to record Beethoven – the Flonzaley, Capet and Rosé Quartets, and the 'old' Budapest Quartet (led by Hauser) – all show this variable use of vibrato. To modern ears it helps create the impression of a somewhat bald style of phrasing, particularly in fast-moving passages, which a player of the late twentieth century (even a period-instrument player) would think rather 'unmusical'.

Similarly, woodwind vibrato was much less widespread in the early decades of the century than it is now. The French school, founded by the flautist Paul Taffanel and the oboist Georges Gillet, was already using vibrato by the turn of the century, and its influence was strong in America and, from the 1930s, in Britain. Woodwind playing in the Austro-German tradition used little or no vibrato before the Second World War. The oboe cadenza in the first movement of Beethoven's Fifth Symphony is played in this old style by oboists of the Berlin Philharmonic Orchestra (conducted by Nikisch, 1913), the Berlin State Opera Orchestra (conducted by Strauss, 1928) and the Vienna Philharmonic Orchestra (conducted by Schalk, c. 1931).

FLEXIBLE TEMPO

Recordings demonstrate that, in Beethoven as in later music, it was the practice in the early twentieth century to vary the tempo considerably within a movement. Table 8.1 shows the fluctuations in tempo in five recordings of the 'Kreutzer' Sonata (exposition of the first movement). Of the five violinists, only Busch controls the tempo as closely as most modern performers, though his tempo for the Presto is much faster than usual, then or now. Kreisler and Huberman are particularly flexible. Kreisler plays the opening four bars very freely, and his pianist, Rupp, enters at bar 5 at a much slower tempo. Huberman begins very slowly, and his pianist, Friedman, increases the pace at bar 5. In the Presto, Kreisler/Rupp and Huberman/Friedman reach their maximum tempo just before the second subject, and then relax to a much slower tempo, as do Thibaud/Cortot and Szigeti/Arrau. All five performances emphasise the firm dotted rhythm of the new theme at bar 144 by a drop in tempo, followed by a recovery to the end of the exposition (Busch/Serkin again fluctuate less than the others). In all cases, these changes of tempo suggest not a lack of control, but a deliberate strategy for underlining the changing character of the music.

The same is true of the tempo fluctuations in the first movement of the 'Spring' Sonata, shown in Table 8.2. The contrast between the flowing, lyrical opening theme and the rhythmically assertive second subject (bar 38) presents a problem to the modern performer, who is brought up to believe that a tempo must be found which will more or less suit them both. Many modern performances give the

Table 8.1. Violin Sonata in A major Op. 47 ('Kreutzer'). Tempos in first
movement exposition

		Thibaud Cortot 1929	Huberman Friedman 1930	Kreisler Rupp 1936	Busch Serkin 1941	Szigeti Arrau 1944
Adagio sostenuto						
Bar 1	♩ =	30	32	c. 52	30	26
Bar 5	♩ =	34	46	44	34	30
Bar 9	♩ =	38	34	50	36	32
Bar 13	♩ =	36	40	56	36	40
Presto						
Bar 19	♩ =	170	152	136	176	160
Bar 28	♩ =	164	152	144	176	160
Bar 45	♩ =	156	160	148	168	166
Bar 73	♩ =	156	164	152	168	160
Bar 91 (dolce)	♩ =	110	112	124	152	c. 116
Bar 107	♩ =	110	108	116	152	120
Bar 117 (tempo I)	♩ =	154	160	148	168	160
Bar 144	♩ =	136	148	136	160	144
Bar 176	♩ =	152	160	144	160	160

impression that a choice has been made between a relaxed tempo which suits the
opening but then sounds lumpy at bar 38, or a tempo which works at bar 38 but
which sounds uncomfortably brisk at the opening. Performers earlier in the century
were free to choose a substantially different tempo for each theme.

In modern performance, a limited relaxation of tempo is still considered acceptable, but acceleration is particularly discouraged. Hurrying is now regarded as an
elementary fault which should be stamped out during training, rather than, as in
earlier times, a natural expression of musical tension which can be exploited for the
shaping of a movement. One of the consequences of this is that, when relaxation
does occur in modern performance, recovery to the original tempo is often less
immediate, and more reluctant, than in old performances; and because fast tempos
are generally less fast than they used to be, the recovery to tempo is less extreme.
There are striking examples in recordings of Beethoven. In the opening orchestral
exposition of the Violin Concerto, the second subject (oboe at bar 43) is taken at a
similar tempo in most recordings, of whatever date, generally within the range ♩ =
108–116. But the tutti passages before and after it are treated quite differently at

Table 8.2. Violin Sonata in F major Op. 24 ('Spring'). Tempos in first movement

		Busch Serkin 1933	Kreisler Rupp 1935	Szigeti Schnabel c. 1941	Szigeti Arrau 1944	Heifetz Bay 1947
Allegro						
Bar 1	♩ =	140	132	136	108	144
Bar 38	♩ =	152	156	152	132	160

different dates. In most modern recordings they are at almost the same tempo as the second subject, but in pre-war recordings they are much faster, reaching ♩ = 124 to 140 at the tutti at bar 73. In the old performances, the changing tensions of the music are marked by a pattern of alternating relaxation and recovery which continues throughout the movement. The relaxations of the solo passages are compensated for by the tuttis, in which the pre-war conductor presses ahead vigorously, without inhibition. In modern performances, the tempo set by the soloist is often very relaxed, but there is little compensating energy in the tuttis. In graphic terms, there are plenty of troughs (and often one big trough in the central G minor passage), but a lack of compensating peaks. Similar, though less extreme, comparisons between the old and the modern approach can be made in the first movement of the Fourth Piano Concerto, where the habit of accelerating in energetic passages and relaxing in calmer passages is very widespread in pre-war recordings.

RHYTHMIC DETAIL

As well as clearly defined changes of tempo, early-twentieth-century performances also had a more flexible and, to modern taste, more casual attitude to rhythmic detail. One manifestation of this is a tendency to over-dot dotted rhythms. There are countless examples to be heard in recordings of Beethoven, notably in pre-war recordings of the first movement of the 'Eroica' Symphony, the second movement of the Fourth Symphony, and the third movement of the F minor String Quartet Op. 95. The finale of the 'Moonlight' Sonata gives an illustration of a type of rhythmic flexibility which was common in the early twentieth century. Pianists vary greatly in their interpretation of the rhythm which first appears in bar 22 (Ex. 8.1). Lamond (1922) plays the rhythm more or less as written each time it occurs. Paderewski (1937) plays the quaver (the first note of the phrase) virtually as a semiquaver, except at the final appearance of the rhythm (bars 168–74). Friedman (1926) does the opposite, playing the quaver long and slightly early, though

Ex. 8.1   Beethoven: Piano Sonata in C♯ minor Op. 27 No. 2 ('Moonlight'), third movement, bar 22

progressively less so at later appearances of the rhythm. Schnabel (1934) plays the rhythm more or less as written when it first appears, but later sometimes shortens the quaver almost to a semiquaver, like Paderewski.

The shortening of short notes extended beyond the treatment of dotted rhythms. Groups of semiquavers in fast movements were often played rather fast and lightly. This is one of the features of Schnabel's playing which now seems particularly characteristic of him. But it was a general habit among instrumentalists early in the century. The recordings of Beethoven by the Busch Quartet are full of such unemphatic short notes. There were clearly no 'rules' about this sort of rhythmic flexibility in the early twentieth century. Like flexibility of tempo, it was part of the basic musical rhetoric of the time.

TEMPO RUBATO

Another aspect of this rhetoric is a type of *tempo rubato* which was common in the early twentieth century but which has since almost entirely fallen out of use (except in jazz and popular music). It involves the dislocation of a melody from its accompaniment, by playing some notes early or late. This, unlike the free treatment of dotted rhythms, was a practice widely acknowledged by writers in the early twentieth century, and its nineteenth-century pedigree was well known. A typical description of this type of rubato is given by the piano teacher Charles Pearce (1920):

Wherever – for the sake of expression – time is 'robbed' from some note (or notes) and given to some other note (or notes) the strict time of the entire passage should not be so departed from as to destroy the general sense or feeling of rhythm.

Any independent accompaniment to a melody played with *tempo rubato* should always be played in strict time. Especially should *all* notes come together on the downbeat of each measure, exactly as they are printed in the music.

. . . *Tempo rubato* is a *modern device* to be used in the music of no composer before the time of Weber.[2]

This description, when compared with the actual practice of the time, is revealed as a mixture of true observation and wishful thinking. Despite the insistence of several writers that *tempo rubato* is appropriate only in 'modern' music, it is heard very frequently in early-twentieth-century recordings of Beethoven. It is certainly

2   Charles W. Pearce, *The Art of the Piano-Teacher* (London 1920), paras. 660–1.

characteristic of this type of rubato that it produces flexibility in the melody independent of the rhythm of the accompaniment. But, contrary to what Pearce suggests, the strong beats are precisely the places where dislocation is most likely to occur. Paderewski used this type of rubato almost all the time; Hofmann disapproved of it, but used it subtly and occasionally, for example to emphasise the dissonances at bars 16 and 18 of the first movement of the 'Moonlight' Sonata. Lamond uses it throughout the second movement of the 'Moonlight' Sonata, creating an almost strummed, guitar-like quality. In the slow movement of the 'Pathétique' Sonata, Lamond uses rubato only sparingly in the opening statement of the theme, but in the second section, from bar 17 onwards, he uses a great deal of dislocation, which has the effect of emphasising the sudden distancing of the melody from the accompaniment (Ex. 8.2). This type of rubato, which was very widely used in the early years of the century, was falling out of fashion by the 1930s. Schnabel and Fischer use it only subtly, and the growing insistence on rhythmic precision has led later generations of pianists to avoid it.

Ex. 8.2   Beethoven: Piano Sonata in C minor Op. 13 ('Pathétique'), second movement, bars 17–21 as played by Lamond. \ indicates late note.

PORTAMENTO

Another habit which has been discouraged, or at least refined, in the late twentieth century is the use of portamento by string players. As used in early-twentieth-century recordings, it has something in common with old-fashioned *tempo rubato*, in that it tends to create rhythmic irregularity and the momentary separation of one line from another. In Beethoven, this is particularly noticeable in recordings of the older generation of string quartets, notably the Lener, Flonzaley, Capet, Busch and Budapest (led by Hauser) Quartets. In the old style of playing, in which portamento is of more routine occurrence than in modern playing, a melodic progression in any of the four lines of a string quartet is suddenly placed in relief if portamento is used. Early recordings of the opening Adagio of the C♯ minor Quartet Op. 131 provide a good example. Both the Capet Quartet (*c.* 1927) and the Busch Quartet (1936) play occasional portamentos in all parts which, though they sound old-fashioned (particularly the rather slow portamentos of the Capet Quartet), also have the effect of emphasising and clarifying the contrapuntal texture. The effect is most striking at bars 20–6 of the Capet performance, where each player in turn plays a prominent portamento over the rising third. To modern ears, the Busch Quartet seems a little more selective. In the same passage, only the last of the rising thirds has a portamento (to the high d♯^{3} in bar 26).

The prominence, frequency and placing of portamento has changed very greatly during the twentieth century. Most early-twentieth-century recordings of Beethoven contain a substantial amount of prominent portamento compared with later recordings. Soloists vary substantially in their use of portamento. Often it still sounds beautiful, once one becomes accustomed to it, but early recordings contain much sliding which now sounds random and routine. Early-twentieth-century editions of, for example, the slow movements of the 'Spring' and 'Kreutzer' Sonatas often incorporate shifts in places where a stretch or a change of string would nowadays be preferred. In the theme of the slow movement of the 'Kreutzer' Sonata, Arnold Rosé (1917) fingers bars 13–14 with two single-finger slides in quick succession (Ex. 8.3). He repeats this fingering at each appearance of this phrase (bars 32–3 and 51–2). In recordings of this movement, Thibaud, Huberman, Kreisler, Busch and Szigeti all play a portamento at the descending third each time it occurs, Thibaud most slowly and prominently, Busch most discreetly, but none plays a noticeable portamento from b♭^{2} to a^2 in bar 14.

Ex. 8.3   Beethoven: Violin Sonata in A Op. 47 ('Kreutzer'), second movement, bars 13–15, as fingered by Rosé

In orchestral playing, string players in the early twentieth century each used their own fingerings (as they still do to a large extent), and this often led to very frequent portamento, its prominence depending on how many players were shifting at a particular point. The effect is sometimes impossibly lugubrious to the modern ear, particularly in British playing of the 1920s. This is true of the opening theme of the slow movement of Beethoven's Symphony No. 4, as played by the Hallé Orchestra under Harty (*c.* 1927) with frequent, prominent, slow sliding. In the same passage, the BBC Symphony Orchestra under Toscanini (1939) is, by comparison, very discreet, illustrating the great change in British orchestral style during the 1930s. In the first movement of Beethoven's Fifth Symphony, the second subject is played with prominent portamentos, up and down a fourth, by the Berlin State Opera Orchestra under Strauss (1928), the Royal Philharmonic Orchestra under Weingartner (1927), and the London Philharmonic Orchestra under Koussevitzky (1934). Later recordings have more discreet slides – such as the NBC Symphony Orchestra under Toscanini (1939) and the Hallé Orchestra under Barbirolli (1947).

These habits of early-twentieth-century performance are becoming increasingly familiar as early recordings reappear transferred to compact discs, but they have so far had little impact on scholars or performers interested in period style. The general reaction to early-twentieth-century recordings seems to be to assume that, although they may have relevance to the study of Elgar, Strauss or Rachmaninov, they have nothing to teach us about the practice of earlier periods, such as that of Beethoven. There is a clear distinction in the modern mind between the 'period', even 'authentic', Beethoven of Norrington, Hogwood and Tan, and the 'old-fashioned' Beethoven of Busch, Schnabel or Harty. But to assume that the early twentieth century has nothing to offer the practitioners of period Beethoven implies two further assumptions: first, that early-twentieth-century style was of recent development, and contained no elements derived from long tradition, and secondly, that our late-twentieth-century taste, armed with modern scholarship, gives us better judgement about the practices of Beethoven's day than musicians of the early twentieth century could aspire to. But these assumptions are surely based on wishful thinking. Richard Taruskin identified one area in which modern taste misleads us, when reviewing Roger Norrington's recording of Beethoven's Ninth Symphony. Taruskin argues convincingly that the idea of constant tempo in extended movements is an invention of the late twentieth century:

[For Beethoven] metronome markings were good 'only for the first measures, as feeling has its own tempo'. No one, to my knowledge, ever maintained a position to the contrary before the twentieth century, when . . . composers began demanding an 'objective', depersonalised performance style for their own music, and performers allowed this rigid 'neo-classical' mode of execution to rub off on what by then had solidified into the 'classical' repertory minus the neo.[3]

It is possible to broaden Taruskin's point to a more general claim that much of the basic performance practice of the late twentieth century, which we take entirely for granted, is of very recent development. If this is true, then in order to get back to earlier traditions of performance, back to Beethoven, we would do well to take as our starting point the period before these modern practices developed – that is, the period of early recordings.

3 Richard Taruskin, 'Resisting the Ninth', *Nineteenth-Century Music*, 12/3 (1989), p. 254.

There is no shortage of documents from the nineteenth century to support this point of view. There is evidence from Beethoven himself, and on through Weber and Spohr to Liszt and Brahms, that flexible tempo was an essential part of performance throughout the nineteenth century. A tradition of *tempo rubato* in which the melody is rhythmically free of the accompaniment can be shown to have extended from at least as early as Leopold Mozart in the 1750s through W. A. Mozart to Spohr, Liszt, Chopin, and on to the early twentieth century. Countless writers on violin and cello playing and singing make it clear that portamento was an important ingredient of legato performance throughout the nineteenth century. And many nineteenth-century writers on string and wind instruments describe vibrato as little more than an occasional ornament (when they allow it at all), and certainly not as a continuous colouring.

The basic evidence for all this is inescapable. It leads to the conclusion that much of the style of the early twentieth century, which now sounds old-fashioned, represents the end of a long tradition of performance extending back to Beethoven and beyond. This is not to say that, to play as in Beethoven's time, all we have to do is to play as in the early twentieth century. Nevertheless, there is clear evidence that, in fundamental ways, musicians of the early twentieth century were closer to the traditions of Beethoven's day than we are now.

Of all the topics discussed in this chapter – flexible tempo, rhythm, rubato, portamento and vibrato – only one has so far impinged on period performance of Beethoven, and that is restraint in vibrato. The reasons for this have nothing to do with the early twentieth century. It is simply that performers on period instruments became accustomed to playing with little vibrato in music of much earlier periods, and the habit was easily (and historically appropriately) adapted to Beethoven. Modern audiences have grown used to the sound of wind and string instruments played with little vibrato; it has become acceptable, and it therefore presents no problem. But will performers of Beethoven ever start embracing old-fashioned flexibility, rubato, and portamento? To modern taste, early-twentieth-century recordings, in which these habits are still current, can sound uncontrolled, chaotic and sloppy. It is for this reason, rather than because of historical arguments, that modern performers have been so reluctant to experiment with these old conventions.

So far, period performers have got away with the unspoken assumption that late-twentieth-century neatness and cleanness are somehow 'authentic' in Beethoven, or at least that they are what he would have wanted, even if he was unfortunate enough not to have them in the early nineteenth century. This is not far removed from the old and discredited argument that Bach would have preferred the modern piano to the harpsichord. The combined evidence of nineteenth-century documents and early-twentieth-century recordings must surely mean that this assumption cannot hold for much longer. The flexibility, informality, and expressive irregularities of the early twentieth century were not just an aberration, which we have now grown out of, but the last manifestation of a long tradition of performance. No doubt that tradition was in a state of constant change, as performance always is, and we can never know quite how it was in Beethoven's day. But any performer who seriously hopes to recreate the performance practice of the early nineteenth century must re-establish contact with that tradition. The recordings of the early twentieth century provide a vital key to it.

9

A COMPARATIVE SURVEY OF RESCORINGS IN BEETHOVEN'S SYMPHONIES

DAVID PICKETT

Beethoven wrote his First Symphony in 1799–1800 and completed the Ninth in 1824. During the quarter century which intervened he contributed much to the craft of instrumentation, notably by his emancipation of the timpani, his free use of stopped notes on the horn, and his upward extension of register in the case of both wind and string instruments. These developments continued after his death; by 1848, when Wagner wrote *Lohengrin*, a much transformed orchestra was available to the composer. With the exception of the introduction of the tuba, this was not a difference of kind, as occurred when the violin displaced the viol, or the fortepiano the harpsichord, but one mainly of quantity, in terms of an extension of available pitches, which offered the composer an enlarged palette of timbres.

Three other features contributed to the development of instrumentation in the nineteenth century: the emergence of the conductor; the design of the classical concert hall represented by the Leipzig Gewandhaus, Vienna's Grosser Musikvereinsaal and the Concertgebouw in Amsterdam; and the concurrent increase in the size of orchestras. By the turn of the twentieth century, string sections of the dimensions 17–17–11–10–10, together with doubled wind, were common in Vienna and elsewhere.[1]

EARLY PERFORMANCES

The reports which we have of early performances of Beethoven's symphonies do not make for comfortable reading. Insufficient rehearsal, incompetent players in inadequate number, unworthy conductors – all contributed to obscure the works' true significance. In England, where the symphonies were first presented by the Philharmonic Society (the first seven in performances without a conductor), the recitatives at the beginning of the Finale of the Ninth Symphony were played as late as 1841 by Domenico Dragonetti as a double-bass solo; and Moscheles, the conductor and friend of the composer, had rearranged the vocal parts and supported

---

1 See Ernst Hilmar, 'Mahlers Beethoven-Interpretation', in Rudolf Stefan, ed., *Mahler-Interpretation* (Mainz 1985), pp. 29–44.

them with the organ.[2] We read of the same Dragonetti, in 1845, at the age of 81, leading a section of thirteen double-basses in these recitatives at the Beethoven Festival in Bonn.[3] Early performances of the 'Pastoral' Symphony were given by the Philharmonic Society with cuts in the second movement 'to make it go down'.[4] Even in Hallé, Daniel Gottlob Türk, the director of the musical society in 1809, always omitted the introduction to the Finale of the First Symphony because 'he felt sure it would make the audience laugh'.[5]

France, or at least Paris, seems to have been lucky to have profited from the interest and talent of François-Antoine Habeneck. According to Wagner, who heard a rehearsal during the 1839–40 season, Habeneck spent two years preparing the Ninth Symphony with the Conservatoire Orchestra before giving it for the first time in Paris in 1831. The performance, which took place on 27 March, was also noteworthy for the fact that other works intervened between the Scherzo and Adagio.[6] Berlioz recalled that it was also customary in Paris at that time to play the Allegretto of the Seventh Symphony in place of the Larghetto of the Second Symphony.[7] Wagner was also firmly of the opinion that the symphonies received unsympathetic performances at the hands of Mendelssohn in Leipzig, going so far as to devote a substantial portion of his 1869 essay *Über das Dirigieren* to correcting some of the misinterpretations he ascribed to Mendelssohn.[8]

The stories of the establishment of bad performing traditions of the symphonies are in fact legion, and are only paralleled by the tale of woe which is the history of the publication of the scores. We know that at the first rehearsal of the 'Eroica' Ferdinand Ries narrowly missed getting his ears boxed for pointing out the famous 'wrong entry' of the second horn in bar 394 of the first movement, that François-Joseph Fétis read the part as if for horn in B$\flat$,[9] and that Sir Michael Costa changed the second violin part from a$\flat^1$ to g^1.[10] Indeed, the first printed score enshrines this bowdlerism.[11] The distinction between the staccato dot and the wedge was lost soon after the first editions and to this day, only the Fifth and Sixth Symphonies have been treated to a thorough *Urtext* edition.

---

2 See George Grove, *Beethoven and His Nine Symphonies*, 3rd edn (London 1898), p. 383.

3 See John Mewburn Levien, *Beethoven and the Royal Philharmonic Society* (London 1927), p. 28.

4 See Grove, *Beethoven and His Nine Symphonies*, p. 225.

5 *ibid.*, p. 13.

6 See Igor Markevitch, *Edition encyclopédique des neuf symphonies de Beethoven* (Luynes 1985), nine scores and nine volumes of commentary. Neuvième Symphonie – Synopsis, p. 8.

7 See Grove, *Beethoven and His Nine Symphonies*, pp. 36–7.

8 Richard Wagner, 'On Conducting', in *Three Wagner Essays*, trans. Robert L. Jacobs (London 1979), pp. 49–93.

9 See Grove, *Beethoven and His Nine Symphonies*, p. 66.

10 See David Wooldridge, *Conductor's World* (London 1970), p. 81.

RICHARD WAGNER (1813–83)

This, then, was the situation before Wagner began to conduct the symphonies and to deduce from internal evidence how they should be performed. He himself took great interest in the Ninth Symphony. In 1830 he copied out the full score, and shortly afterwards made a piano reduction. He also conducted the work on three occasions in Dresden and once in London, culminating in the celebrated performance which inaugurated the laying of the foundation stone of the Bayreuth Festspielhaus on 22 May 1872.[12] In March of the following year, Wagner completed his seminal essay, *Zum Vortrag der neunten Symphonie Beethovens*,[13] based on his experience of conducting this and the other symphonies. This essay, which has long been available in English translation, needs to be read in conjunction with the essay on conducting. In the latter, Wagner made clear that he considered 'a correct understanding of the *melos*' to be at the heart of what we should call interpretation, and it is this concept, and the clarity of performance that it demands, which motivated him to make quite drastic proposals for the modification of Beethoven's instrumentation – not all of which he actually tried out.

According to an extant seating plan, Wagner envisaged strings for his 1872 performance in the proportion 18–16–12–10–? and all the other parts doubled with the exception of the percussion instruments and the bassoons, of which latter there were to be no less than eight.[14] Together with two bass tubas, this makes a grand total of a hundred instruments, not considering the double-basses, which were unaccountably omitted from the plan.

Since Wagner's essays are easily accessible, it will suffice here to point out that his instrumental modifications are directed exclusively towards restoring a balance to Beethoven's orchestra and fall into three basic categories:

(1) the modification of brass parts where he felt the limited scale of the natural instruments had forced Beethoven to compromise. The fact that only one written $D(d^2)$ was available on the natural instruments frequently obliged Beethoven to prescribe an awkward jump of more than an octave, making life very difficult for the second horn or trumpet players. Wagner also added notes to complete a texture where he considered that Beethoven would have used the brass instruments more extensively, had he been able.

(2) upward extension of flute and violin parts where the contour of the melody had been badly distorted by Beethoven forcing the notes to 'break back' into the lower octave.

11 Published by Chianchettini et Sperati (London pre-1820), reprinted by Detroit Reprints in Music (USA 1975).

12 The orchestra comprised excellent players from all over Germany, including Arthur Nikisch in the violin section. At Wagner's request, Hans Richter was the timpanist.

13 Richard Wagner, 'On Performing Beethoven's Ninth Symphony', in *Three Wagner Essays*, pp. 95–127.

14 See Richard Wagner, *Sämtliche Werke*, XX/1 (Mainz 1989), p. xxxv.

(3) extensive remodelling of two passages of woodwind writing in the Ninth
Symphony into relief melody, which Wagner alleges to be obscured by
Beethoven's instrumentation. Interestingly, Wagner credits Liszt with the discovery of the true melodic content in his two-handed piano transcription of
the work of 1864 and uses this, and not his own too-literal transcription, as the
basis for the reconstruction of the passage.

Wagner's essay, although attacked by Grove and others in its day, is a model of
restraint in comparison with the retouchings of later conductors. He contents himself
with pointing out some of the undeniable pitfalls of Beethoven's instrumentation
when performed with a large orchestra and directs the reader to follow his own
conscience in making whatever changes seem advisable to allow Beethoven's music
to communicate itself to the audience. Wagner himself was well aware of the controversial nature of his suggestions, referring to 'our academic conductors, who will
doubtless condemn these proposals of mine as violations of a holy script'.[15]

THE WAGNER TRADITION

After Wagner we can trace a succession of conductors in the German school who,
in their performances of Beethoven's symphonic canon, adhered to the principles
laid down in his essay. In the first generation is Hans von Bülow, a contemporary
of and collaborator with Wagner, whose direct influence can be discerned in the
interpretative styles of conductors as diverse as Gustav Mahler, Richard Strauss and
Felix Weingartner. This second generation made extensive changes to instrumentation. The third generation, represented here by Willem Mengelberg, Bruno
Walter, Otto Klemperer and Wilhelm Furtwängler, approached the works in differing ways, taking fully into account the tradition begun by Wagner and continued
by Bülow, Weingartner and Mahler. All operated on a principle of *Werktreue*
which seeks to penetrate behind the actual notes of the work and allows the interpreter full rein to change instrumentation or notes in cases where these are deemed
to be the result of a compromise or a miscalculation of the composer. All recognised
that this is a dangerous path to tread, and deliberated hard before making changes to
the works. Some of the practices of these conductors will be examined individually;
but first it is valuable to see what their reactions were to the specific instrumental
changes proposed by Wagner for the Ninth Symphony.

15 Wagner, *Sämtliche Werke*, XX/1, p. liv: '[es sei denn, daß es uns nur darauf ankomme, zu ihrer
    Aufführung etwa so den Takt zu schlagen, wie diess gemeinhin von] unseren wohlbestallten akademis-
    chen Konzertdirigenten geschieht, von deren Seite ich mich aber trotzdem darauf gefasst mache,
    wegen meiner so eben mitgetheilten Vorschläge als eitler Frevler an der Heiligkeit des Buchstabens
    behandelt zu werden.'

WAGNER'S DIRECT INFLUENCE

Wagner's proposed alterations to the woodwind scoring of bars 138–45 and 407–14 of the first movement were adopted in principle by Weingartner, Mahler and Mengelberg, all three differing in detail from Wagner and from each other. They were, however, rejected by Toscanini, Furtwängler, Walter and Klemperer. His proposals to reconstruct the violin line in bars 276–81 of the Scherzo were followed by Mahler, Furtwängler, Mengelberg, Walter, Toscanini and Karajan – only Klemperer rejecting them. Among these conductors, Mahler, Weingartner, Walter and Toscanini also raised the violins an octave in bars 416–18 of the first movement, the others clearly feeling that the onset of the *fortissimo* which follows was sufficient justification for Beethoven's disposition. Wagner, noting how difficult it is for the important thematic material in the woodwind to be heard against the powerful string octaves of bars 93–108 and 330–45 of the Scherzo, recommends reinforcing the woodwind with the horns, who are able to contribute little in Beethoven's original. There have been different responses to this: Mahler, Weingartner and Strauss all accepted this advice in principle, while incorporating their own minor variants; in the recordings of Mengelberg and Toscanini one can hear little else but horns; while Furtwängler managed to blend the horns skilfully into the texture. Walter and Klemperer used Beethoven's original scoring, but reduced the power of the strings, allowing them to assert themselves only at the beginning of each phrase. In Karajan's 1962 recording, the strings are allowed their head and it is only the ear of faith which hears the woodwind with any clarity.

A different situation obtains in respect of the additions which Wagner proposes to the trumpet fanfares at the beginning of the Finale. In Furtwängler's recordings, the trumpets are completely dominated by the horns and woodwind, though it is clear that he made some modifications, at least in the case of the second fanfare. Mengelberg, Weingartner, Walter and Toscanini all variously changed the notes to bring the trumpets in line with the woodwind. In Walter's recordings the trumpets are not so overbearing as to obscure the other wind, and indeed, like Furtwängler, he made more of a feature of the horn parts. Klemperer and Karajan both retained Beethoven's original.

HANS VON BÜLOW (1830–94)

Hans von Bülow was a most remarkable man. Both Liszt and Wagner valued his musicianship highly. His musical career brought him success in three areas. As a concert pianist he gave the first performance of Tchaikovsky's First Piano Concerto; as a pedagogue he held prestigious teaching posts in both Berlin and Munich; and as a conductor he prepared and conducted the premieres of Wagner's *Tristan* and *Die Meistersinger* and Liszt's 'Faust' Symphony – all without score. Bülow seems by all accounts to have been a waspish individual and in later years was accused by some of having advanced rather arbitrary interpretations in the concert hall. But opinions on this last point are contradictory: Walter and Mahler, who both came under his spell independently, were unable to find serious fault with him as a conductor, while Weingartner devotes a substantial portion of his essay on conducting to severe criticism of Bülow and his imitators.[16]

In 1880, Bülow was appointed conductor of the ducal court in Meiningen where he spent the first eighty days of his incumbency in studying only Beethoven with an orchestra which had at the time but eight violins. This orchestra, which toured Germany, Austria and Russia in 1881, was universally admired for its quality of ensemble, though it was admitted that the individual players were not all of the calibre of those in other orchestras. When he performed the Ninth Symphony in Meiningen, Bülow had no doubled wind, but was able to employ strengthened string sections of 12–10–8–6–6.[17]

Many of the 'traditional' reinstrumentations may be traced back to Bülow. Some of them have been ascribed to him by his contemporaries. Weingartner tells us that Bülow was responsible for the completion of the trumpet part in bars 655–62 of the first movement of the 'Eroica', one of the most common modifications, which until recently was universally accepted.[18] Mahler and Weingartner both adopted this, though Strauss preferred to employ the three horns an octave lower. It can be heard tastefully executed in recordings by Klemperer, Mengelberg, Walter, Furtwängler, Karajan (in both his 1962 and 1977 recordings), Giulini and Barbirolli; and with trumpets blasting away as if to bring down the walls of Jericho in the recordings of Szell and Toscanini. Recordings which retain Beethoven's original include those by Erich Kleiber and Hermann Scherchen, with the latter achieving a quite comic effect when the trumpets are obliged to abandon the melody.

Throughout the 'Eroica', Beethoven is careful to take the first trumpet no higher than the tenth harmonic (reading g^2), presumably considering the concert $b\flat^2$ to be too unreliable. Weingartner felt no need to justify his simple instruction to use the top $b\flat^2$ in bar 316 of the Finale, and his advice accorded with Mahler's usage and that of all conductors on recordings sampled here: Mengelberg, Furtwängler, Walter, Klemperer, Toscanini, Szell, Karajan, Giulini and Barbirolli. Even Scherchen and Kleiber could not resist the temptation, and so widespread was this change that it seems highly likely that it must also have been Bülow's practice.

From Carl Krebs we learn that Bülow instructed half of the cellos and basses to play *non legato* with accents (*gestoßen*) in bars 114–20 of the second movement of the Fifth Symphony; and according to Laser he played the two *piano* string chords

16 Felix Weingartner, *Über das Dirigieren* (Berlin 1896).
17 See Christian Mühlfeld, *Die Herzogliche Hofkapelle in Meiningen* (Meiningen 1910), p. 28.
18 See also Carl Krebs, *Meister des Taktstocks* (Berlin 1919), p. 150.

in the last four bars of the movement pizzicato for greater contrast.[19] Another of Bülow's arbitrary changes mentioned by Weingartner was the pizzicato he placed in bar 132 of the same movement.

Strauss, who had good reason to be sympathetic to Bülow, having been greatly encouraged by him early in his career, was clearly very familiar with his interpretations of the symphonies. While mentioning several passages where Bülow's interpretations gave him pleasure, Strauss does not hesitate to point out also the questionable elements. Among other things, he draws attention to Bülow's reading of the *fortissimo* in bar 228 of the first movement of the Fifth Symphony as beginning on the second note, and his reinforcement of the oboes by trumpets in bars 34–41 of the first movement of the Seventh Symphony.[20] This reinforcement is heard in the recordings of Kleiber and Walter (NYPO recording only), where it serves to make clear the canon between the woodwind and the violins. Weingartner reveals that he himself, worried by the dominance of the trumpets in this passage if they are allowed to play the original *fortissimo*, had them play in unison with the violins and contented himself with doubling the woodwinds.

Whereas Weingartner declines to accuse Bülow of being the perpetrator, Strauss describes quite clearly the latter's use of timpani to strengthen the bass line in bar 190 of the first movement of the Eighth Symphony – a procedure which Toscanini once tried in rehearsal.[21] When it seemed to him appropriate, Bülow was not beyond changing Beethoven's notes, as in bar 470 of the Scherzo of the Ninth Symphony where he substituted b for c^1 in the second bassoon part, presumably to make the following *subito piano* coincide with Beethoven's unexpected C major harmony.[22]

The most extensive discussion of a Bülow interpretation, that of the Ninth Symphony, is given by Walter Damrosch in his essay published in 1927.[23] In addition to Wagner's recommendations, Damrosch, who studied with Bülow briefly in 1887, notes the following textual changes:

First movement

bars 304, 308 and 310 Last two demisemiquaver Ds omitted in the timpani to 'intensify the rhythm of the theme and increase its terrible significance'.

bars 405–6 First violins play an octave higher until the first note of bar 406 and second violins follow suit in bar 406, to continue the upward motion of the melodic contour.

bars 481–94 Woodwind doubled, and clarinets added to the bassoons in bar 489.

19 Quoted in Krebs, *Meister des Taktstocks*, p. 150.
20 This change is not, however, to be found in the score referred to below.
21 See Wooldridge, *Conductor's World*, p. 79.
22 See Felix Weingartner, *On the Performance of Beethoven's Symphonies*, trans. Jesse Crosland (New York 1969), p. 209.
23 Walter Damrosch, 'Hans von Bülow and the Ninth Symphony', *Music Quarterly*, 13 (1927), pp. 280–93.

bars 545–6 Timpani adds three semiquaver Ds at the end of bar 545, and a quaver A at the beginning of bar 546.

Fourth movement

bar 431 et seq Additions to the third and fourth horn parts enable them to reinforce the second violins and cellos more consistently. 'Throughout the fugue the strings are thus amplified.'

bars 541–2 Timpani have A, *p crescendo*.

bars 655–61 First trombone and first and second trumpets reinforce the altos throughout.

bar 720 et seq Altos replaced by tenors. 'Bülow produces an electric effect because the penetrating quality of the higher notes of the tenors bring[s] out the theme with a verve and enthusiasm impossible for the altos in that register.'

bars 938–40 Trumpets reinforce woodwind.

Although this is a highly selective list – and there are several passages where one keenly wishes Damrosch had given Bülow's solution to a genuine problem – it is clear that many of Bülow's changes were made to make the detail of the work more impressive and not in answer to an urgent need to bring order where chaos reigned.

It is a source of great regret that few of Bülow's conducting scores have survived to the present day, since they would be useful for the purpose of authenticating the specific claims made by his followers and detractors. The former Königliche Bibliothek in Berlin contains scores from Bülow's estate, among them one of the Seventh Symphony with his markings.[24] There are several changes of dynamic, some of which disfigure the original, notably the *subito piano* a note earlier than Beethoven indicated it in bar 2 and a corresponding *ff* in bar 90 of the third movement. There are the added trumpet notes in bars 125 and 127 of the first movement, which Weingartner also gives, without any reference to Bülow. Fermatas are placed over the first and last chords of the second movement, to the end of which is appended the underlined note 'N.B. immer pizzicato', indicating that Erich Kleiber was not the first conductor to interpret Beethoven in this way. These and other entries are consistent with the reports of Bülow given above, though they do not verify any of the more controversial aspects described.

GUSTAV MAHLER (1860–1911)

The spirit and many of the reported details of Bülow's interpretations are also to be found in the extant conducting materials of Gustav Mahler. Most of what has been written about Mahler's instrumental *Retuschen*[25] has been restricted to a consideration

24 This score, identified by the signature KB 410/6 and bearing on a pasted-in label the words 'aus dem Nachlaß Hans von Bülows', is in the Staatsbibliothek zu Berlin (Unter den Linden).

25 *Retuschen* is the word traditionally used by scholars in the context of Mahler's reinstrumentations and I have used it liberally here in preference to the dubious word *retouches*.

of the Schumann symphonies, but it should be noted that Mahler conducted the Beethoven symphonies on far more occasions than he did those by Schumann. He conducted the Ninth Symphony in Prague in 1886, and subsequently in Hamburg, Vienna and New York.

Many of Mahler's scores of the Beethoven symphonies are available for study, and in the case of the Fifth, Seventh and Ninth Symphonies there exist versions dating from two different period of his career. Furthermore, Mahler's orchestral parts exist for the Third, Fifth and Seventh Symphonies. The evidence of these scores and parts allows us to assign dates when Mahler practised certain rescorings, and from some of the parts we can tell at which concerts they were used. For instance, as far as the Ninth Symphony is concerned, the score which Mahler used in Vienna and New York is still extant, as is one which he used in Hamburg. Mahler's Hamburg score is fully reworked using an orchestra with winds of 4–3–3–3/6–4–3–1, and it also contains indications for the disposition of the off-stage band which he used in the *Alla Marcia* section of the Finale. The score which Mahler used in Vienna and in New York is marked up for an even larger orchestra: 6–4–4–5/8–4–3–1, with a string complement in New York of 16–14–12–10–8.[26]

A study of Mahler's library reveals a highly creative approach to the problems of interpreting Beethoven with a large orchestra in a reverberant hall and, at least in New York, with an inadequate ensemble. One can see that his ideas were constantly in a state of flux and that, just as in his own works, he was constantly revising them. Throughout his scores and parts one finds evidence that his approach was not static, but continually changing in response to the orchestra and the acoustics he was working with. One can allow that Mahler was over-zealous at times, but one cannot accuse him of a slavish and over-pious acceptance of a text which in all conscience he could not work from, and one has to admire the energy with which he pursued his ideal: for that is what it was, not a means of drawing attention to himself – something of which a conductor like Stokowski could on occasion be justly accused. Mahler must have spent hours marking up his scores and, at least until around 1897, his orchestral parts also; and as a reward for his truly Herculean labour he was constantly reviled in the Viennese and New York press.

His own manifesto, written in rather stilted German with the help of his friend Siegfried Lipiner, was prepared to combat the public criticism which he encountered in Vienna in 1900, and is worth reproducing in full:

As a result of certain assertions by a section of the public, some people may form the opinion that in today's performance the conductor has arbitrarily changed details of Beethoven's symphonies, especially of the Ninth. It therefore seems imperative not to suppress a clarifying note on this point.

26 In the absence of orchestral materials I do not consider it conclusive that Mahler did more than contemplate the employment of the tuba in his later version of this work.

Through the worsening of his hearing to the point of complete deafness, Beethoven had lost the indispensable close contact with reality, with the physical sounding world, just in that period of his creation in which the mightiest intensification of his conceptions urged him on to the discovery of new means of expression and to an until-then undreamt of drastic force-fulness in the treatment of the orchestra. Just as well known as this fact is the other: that the constitution of the brass instruments of that time utterly excluded certain pitch progressions necessary to the formation of the melody. This very deficiency has brought about with time a perfecting of those instruments; and henceforth it appears frankly offensive not to utilise them fully in the most perfect possible execution of Beethoven's works.

Richard Wagner, who in word and deed was passionately at pains throughout his whole life to rescue the execution of Beethoven's works from what had gradually become an unbearable negligence, has in his essay 'On the Performance of Beethoven's Ninth Symphony' directed one to that way of executing this symphony which corresponds as much as possible with the intentions of its creator, and to which all more modern conductors have con-formed. Out of his own acquired and confirmed conviction and experience of the work, the conductor of today's concert has also done this, without fundamentally going beyond the boundaries suggested by Wagner.

Naturally, there can be absolutely no talk of a re-instrumentation, alteration, or even of an 'improve-ment' of Beethoven's work. The long-practised multiplication of the number of string instruments has – and that likewise already long since – had the consequence of an increase also in the wind instruments, which should serve exclusively the reinforcement of the sound, *but which in no way should be assigned to receive a new orchestral role.* In this, as in every point concerning the interpretation of the work in the whole as in the details, it can be proved with score in hand (the more cogently by examination in greater detail), that far from arbitrariness and preconceived design, but also misled by no 'tradition', it has everywhere been the sole object of the conductor to sympathise with Beethoven's will down to the apparently most trifling detail, and in the execution also not to sacrifice or to allow to be submerged in a confused bustle of sound the least of the master's wishes.[27]

27   Kurt Blaukopf, *Mahler, sein Leben, sein Werk und seine Welt in Zeitgenössischen Bildern und Texten* (Vienna 1976), p. 224:

Da in Folge gewisser öffentlich gefallener Aeusserungen bei einem Theil des Publikums die Meinung entstehen könnte, also wären seitens des Dirigenten der heutigen Aufführung an den Werken Beethoven's, und insbesondere an der Neunten Symphonie, willkürliche Umgestaltungen in irgend welchen Einzelnheiten vorgenommen worden, so scheint es geboten, mit einer aufklärenden Bemerkung über diesen Punkt nicht zurückzuhalten.

Beethoven hatte durch sein in völlige Taubheit ausgeartetes Gehörleiden den unerlässlichen innigen Contakt mit der Realität, mit der physisch tönenden Welt gerade in jener Epoche seines Schaffens verloren, in welcher ihn die gewaltigste Steigerung seiner Conceptionen zur Auffindung neuer Ausdrucksmittel und zu einer bis dahin ungeahnten Drastik in der Behandlung des Orchesters hindrängte. Ebenso bekannt wie diese Thatsache, ist die andere, dass die Beschaffenheit der dama-ligen Blechinstrumente gewisse zur Bildung der Melodie nöthige Tonfolgen schlechterdings ausschloss. Gerade dieser Mangel hat mit der Zeit eine Vervollkommung jener Instrumente herbeige-führt, welche nunmehr nicht zu möglichst vollendeter Ausführung der Werke Beethoven's auszunützen, geradezu als Frevel erschiene.

Whether one talks about 're-instrumentation' or about 're-touching', there is no doubt that Mahler's study and preparation of his scores and parts for the Beethoven symphonies was as thorough as that of any conductor before or since. In the Seventh Symphony for instance, in addition to the normal rehearsal letters which are found in printed materials, he inserted 146 extra orientation numbers to enable him to rehearse efficiently and in great detail. By 1909, his cello and timpani parts of the Finale of the same symphony had so many changes in them that they had to be written out in manuscript in order to be legible.

Mahler's *Retuschen* are so numerous that hardly a page of score is left without some change. This has the advantage that a uniformity of approach covers up the transition between Beethoven's original and a too obviously anachronistic patch applied to save a desperate situation. Many of the changes are so subtle, and/or so skilfully made that only the performers would be aware of them. Indeed, the more one studies his scores, the more it becomes clear that most of the contemporaneous complaints about Mahler's *Retuschen* stemmed from information leaked to the press by disaffected players.

Naturally, the more controversial of Mahler's *Retuschen* have received most attention in critical literature, and indeed some of them sound quite bizarre to modern ears – for example, the reinforcement by stopped horns of the clarinets in bars 38–41 and the violas in bars 90–3 of the Scherzo of the Fifth Symphony, the extensive rewriting of the string parts which completely obscures Beethoven's complex but clear orchestral structure in bars 349–404 of the Finale of the Seventh Symphony, and the interchange of the trumpet and horn parts in bars 89–96 of the first

(27 contd.) Richard Wagner, der sein ganzes Leben hindurch in Wort und That leidenschaftlich bemüht war, den Vortrag Beethoven'scher Werke einer nachgerade unerträglich gewordenen Verwahrlosung zu entreissen, hat in seinem Aufsatze 'Zum Vortrag der Neunten Symphonie Beethoven's' (Ges. Schriften, Bd. 9) jenen Weg zu einer den Intentionen ihres Schöpfers möglichst entsprechenden Ausführung dieser Symphonie gewiesen, auf dem ihm alle neueren Dirigenten gefolgt sind. Auch der Leiter des heutigen Concertes hat dies in vollster, aus eigenem Durchleben des Werkes gewonnener und gefestigter Ueberzeugung gethan, ohne im Wesentlichen über die von Wagner angedeuteten Grenzen hinauszugehen.

Von einer Uminstrumentirung, Aenderung, oder gar 'Verbesserung' des Beethoven'schen Werkes kann natürlich absolut nicht die Rede sein. Die längst geübte Vervielfachung der Streichinstrumente hat – und zwar ebenfalls schon seit Langem – auch eine Vermehrung der Bläser zur Folge gehabt, die ausschliesslich der Klangverstärkung dienen sollen, *keineswegs aber eine neue orchestrale Rolle zugetheilt erhielten.* In diesem, wie in jedem Punkte, der die Interpretation des Werkes im Ganzen wie im Einzelen betrifft, kann an der Hand der Partitur (und zwar je mehr in's Detail eingehend, desto zwingender) der Nachweis geführt werden, dass es dem Dirigenten überall nur darum zu thun war, fern von Willkür und Absichtlichkeit, aber auch von keiner 'Tradition' beirrt, den Willen Beethoven's bis in's scheinbar Geringfügigste nachzufühlen und in der Ausführung auch nicht das Kleinste von dem, was der Meister gewollt hat, zu opfern, oder in einem verwirrenden Tongewühle untergehen zu lassen.

movement of the same symphony.[28] Mahler also makes many changes in the brass which, if not played too loud, do serve to allow these instruments to participate fully in the texture at points where Beethoven was obliged either to omit them or to give them repeated notes which fitted the limited scale of the instrument. Instances where the horns have been rescored by Mahler in this way include bars 26–7 and 237–8 of the Finale of the Seventh Symphony, and bars 440–53 of the first movement of the Fifth Symphony.

The most significant addition to brass parts by Mahler appears in bars 188–200 of the Finale of the Ninth Symphony where he employs eight horns and two trumpets to make audible the melody which, in its original setting, Weingartner accurately says 'is entrusted entirely to the first woodwind instruments and disappears as completely for the hearer as if the earth had swallowed it up'.[29] Mahler's brass additions are supported by careful proportioning of the wind parts, which are in places doubled.

Also characteristic of Mahler's *Retuschen* are changes in the octave disposition of the woodwind, particularly the clarinets, careful use of doubling wind players, and in extreme cases the reinforcement of the flutes by an E♭ clarinet. Mahler often redistributes and doubles the string parts, most commonly by doubling the first violins by the seconds and assigning Beethoven's original second violin part to some of the violas. A good example of this is found in bars 278–99 of the first movement of the Seventh Symphony. In other passages he reduces the number of strings for the purpose of achieving a more intimate sound.

Although many more of Mahler's changes are inaudible, they do help to facilitate the performance. In the first movement of the Ninth Symphony, for instance, Mahler omits the last note of the second violins from bar 159; the third, fourth and fifth notes of the first violins in bar 426; and substitutes his third horn pair for the first horn pair in bars 467–8. In all cases, these omissions allow the players to prepare for larger responsibilities just ahead. Sometimes Mahler is too clever, as when a concern to give more support to the choir in the double fugue of the Ninth Symphony causes him to fill in most of the 'holes' left in the brass parts by Beethoven, creating thereby the problem that there is nowhere for the players to breathe!

Mahler's *Retuschen* were copied verbatim by several conductors. Schoenberg and Webern both gave performances of Beethoven's Ninth using Mahler's own materials; Vaslav Talich is known to have used the score and set of parts of his Beethoven Seventh *Retuschen* which are in the library of the Czech Philharmonic Orchestra; Mahler himself lent several of his scores to Willem Mengelberg and, according to Peter Heyworth, Klemperer at one time possessed a score of Beethoven's Sixth Symphony with Mahler's *Retuschen*.

28 For fuller details of this and other *Retuschen* of Mahler, see David Pickett, 'Gustav Mahler as an Interpreter' (PhD Diss. University of Surrey 1988).
29 See Weingartner, *On the Performance of Beethoven's Symphonies*, p. 225.

FELIX WEINGARTNER (1863–1942)

The evidence regarding Mahler's apparent interest in publishing his versions of the Beethoven symphonies is conflicting; but on balance he appears to have seen them as being mainly for his own consumption. However, Felix Weingartner wrote a book about the performance of Beethoven symphonies in 1906 which was revised in 1916 and 1928 and which is still available in its English version.[30] In the Preface to the first edition of his book, Weingartner begins with some general principles wherein he reiterates the problem of the limited scale of the brass instruments, and then states:

I tried first of all to animate the execution by means of careful notation, where this appeared necessary, and endeavoured to render obscure passages clearer by this means, without altering the instrumentation. By careful notation I made the more important parts more prominent and put the less important parts more in the background; not with the idea of producing arbitrary shades of expression, but simply to preserve the unbroken melodic progress of the symphony, a clear understanding of which is the only safeguard against obscurity in execution. In many cases where I had originally thought an instrumental alteration to be indispensable, I found to my joy that a carefully executed notation not only amply met my own requirements, but also corresponded much more to Beethoven's intention than the alteration contemplated.

Passages do occur, however, where notation alone would not suffice, and in such cases I was obliged to have recourse to instrumental interference. This book, in which every one of these cases is examined and justified in detail, is sufficient proof of the careful consideration with which I proceeded in the matter.

Elsewhere Weingartner reiterates that the advice which he gives is based on years of experience with the works in performance. In discussing bars 232–5 of the first movement of the Ninth Symphony he states: 'After a great many performances I became convinced that the second violins, even when numerous, could not give the theme here with the incisiveness which it requires. I therefore resolved to bring in the oboes doubled [to reinforce them]'.[31] Igor Markevitch tells us that Scherchen attributed this change to Bülow.[32]

There is much useful advice in this book, though in many cases the dynamic nuances referred to in the Preface are only relevant to Weingartner's own performance practice, since they do not all deal with the rectification of faulty balance, but serve as additional expressive marks. He is not afraid to point out what he considers to be a mistake of Beethoven's, e.g. the placing of the *subito forte* in bar 246 of the Finale of the First Symphony.

30 The current English version follows the German edition of 1928, and for a full understanding of Weingartner's changing views the earlier editions are therefore indispensable.

31 See Weingartner, *On the Performance of Beethoven's Symphonies*, p. 186.

32 Markevitch, *Edition encyclopédique*, Neuvième Symphonie – Analyse et gloses, p. 47.

218   David Pickett

Weingartner doubles wind parts in most of the symphonies. Like Mahler, he takes great care to specify where the doubling is to begin and end, hinting that the general custom of the time was merely to instruct the auxiliary wind players to double everything in *forte* passages. He accepts without question the addition of horns to bars 303–5 of the first movement of the Fifth Symphony and, as with the high trumpet B♭(b♭^{2}) in the last movement of the 'Eroica' discussed above, one suspects that Bülow may have initiated this practice which was followed by Mahler, Strauss, Walter, Mengelberg, Toscanini, Furtwängler, Karajan and Erich Kleiber. There are, however, subtle distinctions of balance between these conductors, as to whether the horns dominate or support the bassoons. In bars 132–6 (505–9)[33] of the Finale, Weingartner adds horns to the clarinets, sharing this usage with Mahler, Mengelberg, Walter, Furtwängler and Karajan.

Like Mahler, Weingartner changed Beethoven's instrumentation according to prevailing circumstances. In bars 106–12 (479–85) of the Finale of the Fifth Symphony, Weingartner recommends strengthening the bass line by the addition of the third trombone, but adds: 'If, however, owing to the acoustic properties of the hall, the arrangement of the players or the special excellence of the orchestra, the basses were sufficiently audible without the help of the trombone, of course I did not add it.' Between the different editions of his book, Weingartner changed his mind on several important details. One is the addition of horns and trumpets in bars 254–9 of the first movement of the 'Eroica', which he proposed in 1906 and later rejected.

In the Ninth Symphony, Weingartner recommends doubling the wind instruments, including trumpets though not trombones. Having considered them fully, he accepts many of Wagner's emendations, regarding the changes in the above-mentioned woodwind parts in the first movement as 'absolutely essential for the clarity of the passage'. In the second subject of the Scherzo he suggests an improvement to Wagner's horn parts. From Stanford, Weingartner learnt that the manuscript copy of the Ninth Symphony owned by the Philharmonic Society contains in bar 116 of the Finale the injunction in Beethoven's hand '2do Fag col B[asso]'. He took the trouble to make enquiries in Berlin about the original manuscript; but in 1906 was not entirely convinced of the validity of this instrumentation, recommending only that it be tried out. Later, having done so, he changed his mind and reported in a revised edition of his book that 'this correction produces a beautiful effect'.

Noting the problem of balance in bars 193–8 of the Finale, Weingartner counsels against using the brass instruments for its solution, instead proposing that three players be assigned to each of the first woodwind parts. Like Mahler he also allows the filling in of the gaps in brass parts in the choral double fugue, and he recommends staggered breathing for the sopranos in the sustained a^2 later in that section.

33 Here as elsewhere in this chapter the figures in parentheses denote a bar count which includes the Scherzo.

Although Weingartner's conclusions may not always be approved by all interpreters of Beethoven, he does apply logical reasoning to the interpretative problems posed by these works. What results is a well-thought-out attempt to pass on the fruits of his experience by a conductor who, in his time, was greatly admired for his undemonstrative and tasteful approach to the classics of the concert hall. One cannot escape the conclusion that his book should still be required reading for the young conductor, whatever his own interpretative decisions may be.

RICHARD STRAUSS (1864–1949)

A protégé of Bülow – he was his assistant in Meiningen – Strauss was an experienced conductor, both in the concert hall and in the opera house. During the 1936–7 season, at the age of seventy-three, he conducted a cycle of Beethoven symphonies in Munich, and at the same time entered his comments on their interpretation into a set of Eulenburg miniature scores which had been bound with blank sheets interleaved. These comments have been published, both in German and in English translation, and among them, in addition to some interesting observations on Bülow's practice noted above, Strauss recommends a few changes to Beethoven's orchestration.[34]

He prefaces his remarks on the Ninth Symphony by stating: 'Everything essential concerning this symphony [has been written] by Rich[ard] Wagner. Regarding Wagner's orchestral retouchings I should personally like to advise against the trumpet changes at the beginning of the last movement. The original is more characteristic and sounds less 'modern'! Gustav Mahler's proposed coarsenings are to be totally rejected, even if well intentioned!'[35]

Like Mahler and Weingartner, he has a slightly different version of the horn parts in the second subject of the Scherzo from that proposed by Wagner. Like Mahler he allows the first and second horns to double the third and to follow the viola up to the c^2 in bars 135–40 of the second movement of the 'Eroica'. Five bars before the end of the 'Eroica', Strauss reinforces the clarinets with the oboes and, although this advice may be rejected on the grounds that Beethoven could himself have done this, it is a fact that without them the scale passage is normally close to being inaudible.

34 Richard Strauss, 'Anmerkungen zur Aufführung von Beethovens Symphonien', ed. Franz Trenner, *Neue Zeitschrift für Musik*, 25 (1964) pp. 250–60. See also Richard Strauss, 'Notes on the Interpretation of Beethoven's Symphonies', ed. Franz Trenner, trans. Leo Wurmser, *Recorded Sound*, 24 (1966), pp. 110–17; 25 (1967), pp. 135–9.

35 Strauss, 'Anmerkungen' p. 259: 'Alles Wesentliche über diese Symphonie ist von Rich. Wagner. Bezüglich der Wagnerschen Orchesterretouchen möchte ich persönlich von den Trompetenveränderungen des Anfangs des letzten Satzes abraten. Original ist charakteristischer und klingt weniger "modern"! Ganz zu verwerfen sind die von Gustav Mahler (wenn auch in guter Absicht!) vorgenommenen Vergröberungen!'

Strauss's recommendations are not without curiosities, among these the reinforcement of the woodwinds by horns and trumpets in the last three bars of the
second movement of the Fifth Symphony, and the reinforcement of the contrabas-
soon by a virtuoso part for the third trombone in an attempt to bring out the canon
beginning in bar 391 (764) of the Finale of the same symphony.

WILLEM MENGELBERG (1871–1951)

From 1895 until 1941, Willem Mengelberg was conductor of the Concertgebouw
Orchestra in Amsterdam. He invited Mahler as a guest conductor on several occasions and also borrowed scores of works by Beethoven, Schumann and Mozart to
study his *Retuschen*.[36] It comes as no surprise, therefore, to discover that Mengelberg
employed Mahler's *Retuschen* in Beethoven's Fifth Symphony. His familiarity with
Mahler's precedents can be clearly heard on a concert recording made in 1940. In
the first movement, the tell-tale signs are bars 439–53, and in bars 90–3 of the
Scherzo one is able to hear Mahler's stopped horn parts. But Mengelberg does not
follow Mahler's example blindly; unlike Mahler, he does not employ the stopped
horns in bars 38–41 of the Scherzo. He has other sources for his ideas, following
Weingartner in using the third trombone to reinforce the bass line in bars 106–12
(479–85) of the Finale and Strauss in deploying the same instrument from bar 391
(764). In the trio of the third movement we hear Mengelberg adding an extra
kettle drum to fill in the rests perforce left by Beethoven.

In the 'Pastoral' Symphony, Mengelberg imports two changes which are not
motivated by considerations of balance, and which are apparently his own invention.
These are the mutes used by the trumpets in bars 60–1 (324–5)[37] of the storm and
the substitution of pizzicato for arco in the first violin part of bars 125–31 (544–50)
of the Finale. Mengelberg thus allows the violins to interact in a natural way with
the violas who are in canon with them, and to respond to the part of the second
violins in previous bars.[38]

In bars 34–41 of the first movement of the Seventh Symphony, Mengelberg
disagrees with Weingartner and reinforces the first violins with the trumpets. From
their audibility it is, however, also clear that the woodwind are doubled. Mengelberg's
most audacious rescoring comes in bars 189–98 of the Finale of the Ninth Symphony,
where he abandons the first violin part and gives them that of the first oboe (the
first flute from the middle of bar 196), in order that the prime melody of the passage may dominate the texture.

36 See Eduard Reeser, *Gustav Mahler und Holland* (Vienna 1980), pp. 43–4, 48 and 59.

37 Here, as elsewhere in this chapter, the figures in parentheses denote a bar count which includes the
    Scherzo and storm.

38 It sounds to my ears as though only half the first violins are playing pizzicato and the rest arco, and I am
    unable to account for Mengelberg's apparent indecisiveness here.

In many ways, the recordings of Mengelberg's Beethoven performances remind us of a style which had been long since abandoned in 1940, but we should not let that blind us to their real merits, not the least of which are the care and pains which he took over orchestral balance.

ARTURO TOSCANINI (1867–1957)

It is often forgotten that Toscanini was an exact contemporary of Strauss, Weingartner, Mahler and Mengelberg; his career began as long ago as 1886 and continued for nearly seventy years. A careful study of Toscanini's recordings reveals that his oft-quoted phrase, *come scritto*, does not always refer to the actual notes which the composer wrote; he made changes to the scoring of the music of both Debussy and Brahms when it seemed appropriate to him. It has been argued convincingly that Toscanini was not steeped in the traditions of the German repertoire; but although his tempos were often faster than those of his German contemporaries he was well aware of and usually applied the *Retuschen* of Germanic conductors. He studied and used Mahler's score of Schumann's 'Rhenish' Symphony, and for the Beethoven symphonies he mostly refers to Weingartner's book. Toscanini continued to use the same *Retuschen* right up to the end of his career, and we often hear him on a recording made in his old age still applying a solution which Weingartner had earlier abandoned, or employing a change which Mahler also used.[39] For instance, in the second movement of the 'Eroica' Symphony, Toscanini uses all the horns from the beginning of bar 135, as did Weingartner, but then continues the line up to the c^2 in bar 140, as practised by Mahler and Strauss. In the first movement, like Mahler (and Weingartner at one time), he adds trumpets and horns in bars 254–9. Also like Mahler, he employs his extra horn pair to fill in harmonies in bars 205–6 and 211–12 of the first movement of the Seventh Symphony.

Toscanini's main personal contribution seems to have been his penchant for adding notes to the timpani parts where Beethoven was unable to employ them. This can be noticed in the storm of the 'Pastoral' Symphony, bars 25–8 (289–92), 53–4 (317–8) and 78 (342); and in bars 155–7 of the Trio of the Fifth Symphony's Scherzo, although differently from Mengelberg; and quite independently of any other interpreter in bars 117–18 (490–1) of the Finale.

BRUNO WALTER (1876–1962)

Bruno Walter was not a formal pupil of Mahler, although he is sometimes assumed to have been. He did, however, have the opportunity of observing Mahler's work

39 Though undocumented, it is quite possible that Toscanini heard Mahler's Beethoven performances with the Philharmonic Orchestra, when they were both working in New York.

in the opera house and to a lesser extent in the concert hall when they worked together in Hamburg between 1894 and 1896 and in Vienna from 1901 until 1907. Walter also attended Bülow's concerts when he was a teenager in Berlin and recounts being present on an occasion when Bülow conducted the Ninth Symphony twice in the same evening.[40] From a practical point of view, however, it was to his experience of Mahler's *Retuschen* that Walter turned when he himself conducted.[41]

In Walter's formative years Wagner was still a controversial figure whose music and writings were absorbed by young musicians. Walter was no exception to this, though he did rethink his attitude to Wagner's rescorings during his career. Some of the rehearsals for Walter's last recordings of the Beethoven symphonies have been issued on disc, and Walter can be heard telling the orchestra that 'in former years' in the Scherzo of the Ninth Symphony he used the horns as Wagner directed for the second theme, but that he no longer does so.[42] Nevertheless, in that series of recordings, made without doubled wind and with a string complement in the Ninth Symphony of 12–10–8–6–4,[43] one can hear other changes of instrumentation which he continued to practise to the end, most of which derive from Mahler although they are often implemented differently:

(1) Third Symphony, first movement, bars 113–16 and 143–6: horns reinforce bassoons.
(2) Fifth Symphony, first movement, bars 439–53: horns reinforce bassoons.
(3) Sixth Symphony, first movement, bar 37: first horn takes the written A omitted by Beethoven.
(4) Sixth Symphony, Finale, bars 227 (646): trumpets reinforce the first clarinet and first bassoon.[44]
(5) Seventh Symphony, Finale, bars 26–7 and 237–8: the first horn reinforces the first oboe an octave lower.

In one important place, Walter declines to use the comprehensive means which Mahler employed. This is in bars 189–98 of the Finale of the Ninth Symphony, where Walter is content to rewrite the notes assigned to the horns, but only where Beethoven used the instrument, i.e. up to bar 194. This is a partial solution which only delays the disappearance of the main line for a few bars.

40 See Bruno Walter, *Theme and Variations*, trans. James A. Galston (London 1947), p. 50. Damrosch copied this programme in New York.
41 One of the most conspicuous of the rescorings common to performances conducted by both Mahler and Walter was the addition of horns to the entry of the theme in bars 389–400 of the Finale of the 'Jupiter' Symphony.
42 Nor did he do so with the New York Philharmonic Orchestra in 1949.
43 See Artur Holde, *Bruno Walter* (Berlin 1960), photo on pp. 51–2.
44 In his recording with the Philadelphia Orchestra, he used Beethoven's original trumpet parts.

Walter's attitude to rescorings was summed up in his book on performance where, among other remarks on this subject, he states:

As long as it is done solely in the spirit of the work, and strictly for no other purpose, retouching may surely be counted among the legitimate means of interpretation. It goes without saying that the conductor has to refrain from interfering with the score as long as this is at all feasible; but if he cannot, by means of the given instrumentation, achieve clarity of dynamics or meaning, he may and should induce it by means of a (preferably small and unnoticeable) retouch; after all, faithfulness to the letter of the work should never obscure its spirit.[45]

OTTO KLEMPERER (1885–1973)

Like Walter and Mengelberg, Otto Klemperer was not a formal pupil of Mahler, though he can definitely be said to have learnt from him. Klemperer heard Mahler conduct his highly retouched version of the Seventh Symphony in Prague in May 1908 and much later stated: 'People are always telling me, "Oh, I heard the Seventh Symphony conducted by so-and-so and it was wonderful." I say, "You must not tell me such things. I have heard the same symphony conducted by Mahler and I know." '[46] Klemperer declared that:

All this talk that one shouldn't change a single note in a score is nonsense. *Werktreue*, that is, faithfulness to the work, is a very different matter from merely using the pure text, isn't it? In my opinion, Wagner's retouchings of Beethoven's Ninth sometimes go *too* far, especially in the scherzo where the second theme is scored for woodwind only and he added horns. Through them the whole movement takes on a sensuous character it doesn't really have. And Mahler went further. I've seen his score of the Ninth, though I've never performed it . . . Some of those in the Seventh Symphony appear to me to be absolutely right. Others, in the Ninth Symphony for instance, are, I believe, wrong . . . I don't do as much as Mahler did, and then only where I find it absolutely necessary . . . where there is a melody or melodic theme in the first violins which I want to bring out, I also give it to the second violins, and the second violin parts I give to some of the violas, so that it is still there. In the Eighth Symphony, in the first movement, there is a passage on the cellos and the basses, where all the other instruments have only harmony, and I add four horns, and that sounds very well. Then in the funeral march of the Eroica, I begin with eight violins and use all sixteen only later.[47]

Klemperer often changed his mind about his interpretations, even over the question of repeats, but he consistently gave more of Beethoven's music in its original

45 Bruno Walter, *Of Music and Music-Making*, trans. Paul Hamburger (London 1961), p. 136.
46 Peter Heyworth, *Conversations with Klemperer*, rev. edn (London 1985), p. 121.
47 Heyworth, *Conversations with Klemperer*, pp. 34–5, supplemented by the German version where there is a line missing in the English edition.

scoring than did most of his contemporaries. Thus, as described above, in the Ninth Symphony he rejected Wagner's suggestions completely, and added no new colours to bars 189–98 of the Finale. He also drew back from employing the horns in the first movement of the Fifth Symphony to reinforce the bassoons. Apart from the desperate makeshift which he relates above, with which he experimented in the first movement of the Eighth Symphony,[48] and his redistribution of string parts, Klemperer restricted himself in his performances of the Beethoven symphonies to an indulgence only in the additional trumpet parts of the 'Eroica' Symphony described above.

WILHELM FURTWÄNGLER (1886–1954)

Only marginally less abstemious than Klemperer was Furtwängler. Although often charged by his detractors with other crimes in the performance of Beethoven, from the evidence of his recordings he cannot be found guilty of tampering with the original scoring of the works on many occasions. As detailed above, he did employ the horns to reinforce the bassoons in the first movement of the Fifth Symphony and also in bars 132–6 (505–9) of the Finale, and made the changes to the trumpet part characteristic of most conductors of his generation in the two places in the first and last movements of the 'Eroica'. Despite his general admiration for Wagner, he declined to change the woodwind parts in the first movement of the Ninth Symphony and only partially implemented Wagner's changes to the fanfares which open the Finale, though he incorporated his recommended changes in the Scherzo. His approach to the disappearing theme in bars 189–98 of the finale was the same as Walter's: he made limited changes to the horn parts but only up to bar 194.

IGOR MARKEVITCH (1912–83)

On first consideration, Igor Markevitch might appear irrelevant to the present study, since he is better recognised as a superior interpreter of Tchaikovsky and Stravinsky than as a Beethoven conductor; but it is not generally known that he had many opportunities to observe Mengelberg in rehearsal in his youth. In the course of the last twelve or so years of his life he devoted much time to preparing his *Encyclopaedic Edition of the Beethoven Symphonies*. This edition was published between 1982 and 1985 both in France and Germany (DDR), with slight differences between the two versions,[49] and has made an important contribution to our knowledge of performance practice in the symphonies.

The musical text is based on the standard Peters edition, unfortunately carrying over some of the traditional variants of that edition, of which Markevitch was

---

48 The horn parts described were used only in concert, and are not on Klemperer's recording.
49 Markevitch, *Edition encyclopédique*. Igor Markevitch, *Die Sinfonien von Beethoven* (3 vols., Leipzig 1983).

probably unaware since he based his work on Breitkopf scores.[50] The most valuable parts of the edition are the commentaries, which fall into several categories: historical synopsis, critical study of the individual symphony, analysis, and a glossary with discussion of performance practice. The glossaries form a truly fascinating document. Building on the work of previous commentators, they are noteworthy for discussing the bowings used by the major German orchestras and conductors of previous generations, including Fritz Busch in Dresden, Furtwängler in Leipzig and Berlin, and Mengelberg in Amsterdam. In discussing changes to the instrumentation, Markevitch ranges far and wide, quoting among others Mahler's scores and Weingartner's book, and also proposing his own solutions.

Markevitch's own solution to a problem already much discussed here, that of bars 189–98 of the Finale of the Ninth Symphony, goes beyond Weingartner's cautious use of the doubling woodwind players. He reports Mengelberg's redeployment of the first violins noted above, and describes his own experiments which culminated in splitting the first violins, one half playing with the woodwinds and the other playing Beethoven's original. Although still a stop-gap, this is certainly no worse than Mahler's additional horn and trumpet parts. On the recording which Markevitch made with the Lamoureux Orchestra one hears his attempt at the original Mengelberg solution, and he refers in his edition to a performance with the Dresden Staatskapelle in 1976 in which he was satisfied by his later change when used in conjunction with that of Weingartner given above. A radio recording made of this performance confirms that the passage emerges tastefully, and that his solution commends itself well.

From Wagner to Markevitch: the path is a long one, traversing a century of careful thought by some of the best musical interpretative minds. The aim of this study has been to delineate some of the decisions made by these interpreters, to glimpse the process by which they influenced each other, and to compare their solutions to certain problems. At first glance it may appear that the subject has merely historical interest; but to conclude thus would be to miss its significance. There is value in what is passed down between the generations, and to ignore the deliberations of men such as these is to waste much that is precious. In the post-atomic age we are inclined to put more faith in Science than Art; but no matter how much of a scientific approach we bring to it, musical interpretation is, in the final analysis, a subjective process, and will remain so. Guido Adler hit the nail on the head when he wrote about Mahler's *Retuschen*:

The intention is commendable, but the means are to be sanctioned only in so far as they match the intention of the reproducer without permitting any pretension to universal validity to arise – for the alterations of Mahler no more than for those of Wagner still

50 For example, the second horn at the end of the second movement of the Fourth Symphony.

employed by many conductors of our time. Since the original of Beethoven continues to be inviolably preserved, no lasting detriment can result from this. Whether interpretation can and should go so far is a question in itself. The imperfections in the fulfilment of that ideal which hovers before the composer, and which he wishes to realise in the work of art, are lasting attendant manifestations of the qualities of the work. Whether on the whole the latter gains true completion through such alterations cannot be verified. For the general public, which hardly notices such additions, this question is of less moment. The matter is one of conscience, which one can deny neither Wagner nor Mahler. The historian will have to stand up for the unalloyed preservation of the authentic text; yet he can still recognise the good intention of the clarification without granting it any universal validity.[51]

Table 9.1 *Recordings referred to above*

Symphony	Orchestra	Date	Record number
Barbirolli			
No. 3	BBC Symphony	1968	SXLP30209
Furtwängler			
No. 3	Vienna Philharmonic	1944	TV4343
	Vienna Philharmonic	1952	ALP1060
No. 5	Vienna Philharmonic	1954	ALP1195
No. 9	Berlin Philharmonic	1942	CD653
	Bayreuth Festival	1951	CDH 7 69801–2
Giulini			
No. 3	Los Angeles Philharmonic	1979	2531 123
Karajan			
Nos. 1–9	Berlin Philharmonic	1961–2	429 036–2
No. 3	Berlin Philharmonic	1976	2543 027
Erich Kleiber			
No. 3	Vienna Philharmonic	*c.* 1951	ECS535
No. 5	Concertgebouw	1952	417 637–2
No. 7	Concertgebouw	1952	417 637–2
Klemperer			
No. 3	Philharmonia	1955	33CX1346
	Philharmonia	1959	SAX2364
No. 5	Philharmonia	1955	33CX1051
No. 7	Philharmonia	1955	33CX1379
	Philharmonia	1960	SAX2415
No. 8	Philharmonia	1957	SAX2318
No. 9	Philharmonia	1957	SAX2276/7
Markevitch			
No. 9	Lamoureux	1961	6580 006

51   Edward R. Reilly, *Gustav Mahler and Guido Adler* (Cambridge 1982), pp. 31–2.

Mengelberg

No. 3	Concertgebouw	1940	416 201–2
No. 5	Concertgebouw	1937	243 725–2
No. 6	Concertgebouw	1938	243 728–2
No. 7	Concertgebouw	1940	416 204–2
No. 8	Concertgebouw	1938	243 725–2
No. 9	Concertgebouw	1940	416 205–2

Scherchen

No. 3	Vienna State Opera	1958	MCAD2 9802A

Szell

No. 3	Cleveland	*c.* 1960	MBK45639

Toscanini

No. 3	NBC Symphony	1953	AT121
No. 5	NBC Symphony	1952	AT128
No. 6	NBC Symphony	1952	VCM2/1
No. 7	New York Philharmonic	1936	VIC1502
	NBC Symphony	1951	VCM2/2
No. 9	NBC Symphony	1952	VCM2/3 & 2/4

Walter

Nos. 1–9	Columbia Symphony	1958	MK42009–14
	rehearsal of No. 9, second movement	1958	D99893L
No. 3	New York Philharmonic	1949	GBL5617
No. 5	New York Philharmonic	1950	GBL5615
No. 6	Philadelphia	1946	GBL5618
No. 7	New York Philharmonic	1951	GBL5619
No. 9	New York Philharmonic	1949/53	GBL5620

10

BEETHOVEN'S PIANO MUSIC: CONTEMPORARY PERFORMANCE ISSUES

MARTIN HUGHES

Nowhere is the development of an instrument better chronicled than in the piano works of Beethoven. His enthusiastic greeting of each new development with an appropriate expansion of technical and musical language leads one to suspect that he would have admired the concert piano of today. Ironically, however, it is the very advances in technique of pianos and pianists that have distanced us from Beethoven's revolutionary achievements.

What, then, are the challenges that confront today's performer of Beethoven – the contemporary performance issues? There are three factors – the instrumental problems posed by the development of the piano since Beethoven's day; the challenge of rediscovering a language which has been distorted by time, tradition and the use of the modern instrument; and, last but not least, precise interpretative issues that have emerged with the availability of *Urtext* editions.

Needless to say, the most important challenge remains the one that faced Beethoven's contemporaries, albeit in a different light – the language itself. Although today's view of Beethoven has been obscured by the influence of the Romanticism that followed, his music would have presented very real problems for the performer even in his own day, especially in the context of his great Viennese predecessor Mozart.[1] That these difficulties have been compounded by historical perspective and the contemporary instrument may seem surprising, but it is precisely historical experience on the one hand, and the increased possibilities of the instrument on the other, that have made the intensity of focus required for the satisfactory interpretation of Beethoven all the more demanding and elusive. Performing the solo piano music of a composer as texturally complex as Beethoven has always been one

---

1 Today, most pianists' knowledge of Beethoven's immediate predecessors is indeed limited to Haydn and Mozart, with possibly a slight knowledge of Clementi. This goes some way towards explaining the apparent total originality of Beethoven's language from the outset. However, a study of C. P. E. Bach, Cramer and, in particular, Dussek, would reveal that this was not so. We need look no further than the First Sonata Op. 2 No. 1 in F minor, to find distinct references to C. P. E. Bach's sonata in the same key, while Dussek's Sonata in C minor Op. 35 No. 3 certainly influenced Beethoven's early works in the same key.

of the problems of performing the solo works; and while the modern piano offers a wider range of orchestral colour, the rise in the status of the performer since the time of Beethoven has probably also resulted in greater intrusion upon the text than he would have thought possible.

How can we restore the original power of the text? An early step has to be an appreciation of the parameters of Beethoven's tempos. The relationship, or rather the lack of it, between the time signature and the tempo marking at the start of Beethoven's movements is now well established. The link between the two is at best inconsistent, and often irrelevant. The Prestissimo Finale of Op. 10 No. 1 and the Presto first movement of Op. 10 No. 3 are examples – neither can be strictly applied to the minim, as indicated. Here, as often elsewhere, they are an indication of the spirit of the piece, the impression of haste, rather than a mathematical calculation of a precise tempo area. Performers of Beethoven on the fortepiano have done much to re-establish the supremacy of clarity and coherence over speed in faster movements, and the number of pianists ignoring the *ma non troppo* of the final movement of Op. 57 in favour of a virtuoso presto is at last diminishing.[2] Indeed, real extremes of tempo are rarely heard from string quartets or orchestras even in the late works, and pianists would do well to examine their scores in these terms. However, it is not generally the prestissimos that present the gravest threat; it is in the slow movements that the sustaining power of the new instrument has allowed pianists to adopt slow tempos far beyond the possibilities of the lung or the bow, to usurp line, eschew narrative in favour of melodrama, while the simple dignity of the music is overlaid with an exaggeration of phrase and tone that, far from revealing the music, actually obscures its meaning with the indulgences of the performer. Additionally, the cult of the interminable slow movement stemmed from a belief in the sixties that slow meant profound, a phenomenon fostered as much by the improvement in the gramophone record and the concert hall acoustic as by any artistic view.

Dense scoring has often been put forward as a reason for adopting very slow tempos; the rare examples where this does apply will be examined later in the chapter. In general, however, Beethoven's scoring is transparent, especially in the later works, and if the orchestral colouring of the Adagio of Op. 31 No. 2 or the great Largos of Op. 7 and Op. 10 No. 3 result in an occasional thickening of texture, then the considerations of line and phrase remain. Op. 109 and Op. 111 are two of the late works that have particularly suffered from the adoption of excessively slow tempos. The scoring throughout these last works is perfectly spaced to extract full expressive value from melodic and harmonic movement without the need for an overlay of expressive weightiness. The opening of the twenty bars of Adagio that follow the March of Op. 101 are a supreme example – a simple narrative dignified

2   But how often do we still hear pianists slowing the tempo for the semiquavers in the final presto of the 'Appassionata'?

by the presence of octave movement in the bass while the right-hand chord spacing enhances every movement of the melody. The most surprising element of this introduction is its informality, which contributes to the sense of openness, timelessness, space and calm. Beethoven's *ma non troppo* marking here complements the *Eine Saite* in rejecting a cumbersome approach.

The 'Diabelli' Variations is another work that attracts extremes of tempo. As the work that presents the greatest challenge in tempo selection, it consequently undergoes the greatest transformation in different hands. In particular, variations 14 and 20 frequently appear interminable, and while variations 29 and 31 might easily fall into this category, the former benefits from being propelled by obvious melodic interest and a *non troppo* marking, and the latter's elaborations can withstand almost any degree of Largo. In variation 14 the presence of crotchets in the left hand (as opposed to continuous double-dotted quavers and demisemiquavers) gives the music a definite pace despite the overlaying imitation in the right hand, and whatever tempo is adopted, this feeling of 'pulse', and the tension created by immobility followed by sudden movement must not be lost. Again, the density of the left-hand scoring can easily be exaggerated on the modern piano, though this same density of scoring is predictably used as a means of crescendo later in the variation.

Variation 20 is the most controversial as far as tempo is concerned. Were this a piece by Bach the high values would be looked upon simply as a characteristic of chorale writing. In a sense, of course, it is, which perhaps explains Beethoven's exceptional adoption of the minim in a $\frac{3}{2}$ time signature. (He makes his excuses with a $\frac{6}{4}$ in brackets.) However, the difference lies in the fact that the whole variation is syncopated. This must be conveyed to the listener, again through a tempo that conveys a calm $\frac{3}{2}$, and a touch that contrasts the calm first beat with a slightly sudden second chord of each bar. The tension of the line is again paramount as Beethoven guides us through the further harmonic reaches of this variation.

When commenting on Beethoven's performance of the Allegretto second movement of Op. 14 No. 1, Schindler made the comment that Beethoven played it 'more like an allegro furioso'.[3] Tempo in $\frac{3}{4}$ movements in the sonatas has always been a matter of some debate, but a comparison of five sonata movements in $\frac{3}{4}$ clarifies the situation considerably and goes some way towards explaining Schindler's report.

Op. 2 No. 1, Op. 10 No. 3, Op. 14 No. 1, Op. 28 and Op. 54 all contain $\frac{3}{4}$ movements variously marked Allegretto, Allegro, Menuetto allegretto and In tempo d'un menuetto. As with the $\frac{3}{4}$ 'Scherzos', for instance the Op. 2 No. 3 Scherzo Allegro, the overriding factor is the additional indication of Scherzo or in these cases Menuetto. Beethoven's idea of a Menuetto is clearly defined by the first

3 Anton Felix Schindler, *Biographie von Ludwig Beethoven* (Münster 1860), trans. Donald W. MacArdle as *Beethoven As I Knew Him* (London 1966), p. 39.

movement of Op. 54, whose complexities allow only a very staid tempo. Slightly quicker is the Op. 2 No. 1 Menuetto allegretto, frequently played too fast, followed by the third movement of Op. 10 No. 3, with the marking Menuetto allegro. The removal of the word Menuetto in Op. 14 No. 1, or for instance in Op. 10 No. 2 or indeed anywhere else, immediately implies the introduction of one in a bar, partially explaining Schindler's remarks, and we conclude that the first movement of the 'Pastoral' Sonata Op. 28 must go faster still. Here, however, as in Op. 14 No. 1, the tempo indication no longer relates to beat or pulse, but merely gives an indication of flow within one in a bar.

Our present-day piano is a product of the latter half of the nineteenth century. Anyone who has played one of the surviving concert Steinways of the 1880s will recognise essentially the same instrument as we have today, though demands for brighter tone have resulted in minor changes to the hammer felt. During that same period, however, there have been considerable changes in musical taste and scholarship from the glorification of the performer to a search for authenticity in performance. In the case of Beethoven's piano music, these developments can be traced through the contrasting editions of two giants of German intellectualism, von Bülow and Schnabel. While the arrival of *Urtext* editions has clarified many questions surrounding Beethoven's style, indeed perhaps because of the precision of his written legacy, attention has now been turned to the instrument on which we perform.

The orchestral search for an authentic sound of the 1830s has had a dramatic effect on the interpretation of Beethoven's orchestral works over the past decade. With the creation of specialist orchestras often playing on period instruments, the music of Beethoven has been allowed for the first time to reflect not only forwards, but also backwards to the origins whence it grew. Textures have been cleansed, and sections thinned, resulting in buoyant tempos which are difficult to refute. One of the most important effects of this revolution has been the total abandonment of the very same funereal tempos which were once also the province of the great symphony orchestras.

The transfer of this doctrine to the piano works, however, has been less successful. To start with, the combined sound of period instruments in an ensemble has bite and clarity when compared with a traditional symphony orchestra. Sadly, a solo fortepiano is rather less attractive to the ear than a piano; not even the possibility of modern fabrication can significantly improve on what was a transient instrument of weak design. Its feeble and often uneven tone, its lack of colour and its mechanical unreliability make it unsuitable for concert use, and indeed it owes its revival largely to commercial recording where these issues can be overcome. But that is not to say that it has no contribution to make to musical argument – quite the reverse. In spite of the instrument's technical disadvantages, the clarity of texture and brightness of attack that has won so many converts to the cause of period orchestras are more easily attainable on the fortepiano than on the modern instrument, and its use in outer movements is always illuminating. In chamber music, its dynamic weakness and lack of colour are disguised by other instruments, adding lightness and rhythmic poise, while the sustaining power of the supporting ensemble achieves line and phrase that would otherwise be impossible. Indeed, the very limitations of the fortepiano can transform slow movements in much the same way as do those of the classical orchestra. Should we view the deficiencies of the fortepiano as an obstacle to the definitive interpretation of Beethoven? Could it be said that the instrument of his day was an impediment to his creative output? No, for all its faults, the opposite was true. While Beethoven relished the arrival of every new dimension of instrumental development, he invariably wrote for the instrument in front of him, and if he exploited its range and increased power, he also scored for its clarity, and marked for its pedals. Delighted with the modern piano though he would have been, there can be no doubt that he would have scored and probably composed very differently for the instrument of today.

The burden falls therefore on today's pianist to revise his instrument's capacity in line with what could have been Beethoven's reasonable expectations. As we have already shown, the first victim of this lighter approach is the very slow tempo, unsustainable on the instrument of the day. Pursuant to this is an appreciation of Beethoven's occasional use of dense scoring, and the need for tonal discretion when confronted with the thicker sound of today's piano. The limited sustaining power of Beethoven's piano obliges a flow to the tempo of the slow movement of the D minor Sonata Op. 10 No. 3, allowing the quavers to emerge almost as an improvisation around the D minor chord, so striking after the conclusion of the first movement. The recapitulation is an admirable example of Beethoven's use of thickened scoring to increase expressive (and often dynamic) power, a factor which might have a bearing on choice of tempo. Ferdinand Ries, while pointing out that Beethoven generally kept strictly accurate time and only rarely quickened the tempo somewhat, adds that 'at times he restrained the tempo in his crescendo with a ritardando, which had a beautiful and most striking effect';[4] certainly the increased dynamic power of six instead of three notes per quaver would allow the tempo to expand. Consistently dense scoring of this nature is rare in Beethoven, though the start of the slow movement of the 'Hammerklavier' Sonata Op. 106 provides an extended example, particularly unusual in the later works. The almost Brahmsian chordal writing of the opening passage is tempered, however, by the instruction *una corda, mezza voce, appassionata e con molto sentimento* which immediately calls into question the appropriateness of the slow, expansive interpretations of some pianists. Even without this cautionary marking, we should already have been forewarned

4 Wegeler and Ries, *Remembering Beethoven*, trans. Noonan, p. 94.

by the choice of key and level of pitch – such important pointers in the understanding of Beethoven. Compare the opening bars of the slow movement of the 'Archduke' Trio, composed seven years earlier, where the same density of thematic scoring occurs in a theme in D major, without any hint of *una corda* or *mezza voce*. One is justified here in bringing greater tonal power to bear, but even so the *ma pero con moto* and, more importantly, the *semplice*, relegate fullness of tone to third place behind line and voice-leading. An interesting comparison is afforded here with the marvellous slow movement of the G major Violin Sonata Op. 96, where a similar piece of scoring at almost the same pitch is rendered transparent by the use of semiquavers, which also perform the role of the subtlest *moto perpetuo* supporting the line of the chorale.

Beethoven's use of the repeated triad is typical of the density of writing that is unsuited to the modern piano. As a means of propulsion it has been with us since the first Trio of Op. 1. Throughout the literature it remains an extraordinary form of accompaniment, unique in that it is the only form of rhythmic subdivision that increases movement without improving the line. The left-hand chords at the opening of the first movement of this same Violin Sonata Op. 96 illustrate the problem of voicing and balance for pianists, especially in this context of establishing a flowing exchange with the violinist. Despite this disruptive element, Beethoven's use of this device in slow movements is interesting, stripped as it is of the aggressive character that made it so appropriate in Mozart's A minor Sonata. In the slow movement of Op. 22 its notation in quavers in E♭ suggests a calm warmth quite becoming to the modern piano, while in the arias of Op. 110 the throbbing semiquaver left-hand chords add an element of agitato to an 'accompaniment' that is rich in harmonic intensity and voice leading.[5] The steadily climbing bass is but one feature of a carefully measured accompaniment whose density does not last beyond the first bar, and the possibilities of voicing throughout the passage contrast markedly with this figuration in an earlier work such as Op. 22.

The opening chord of the G major Piano Concerto is a rather different example of the increased beauty of sound of the modern piano being the music's undoing. Given the importance of the juxtaposition between the G major of the soloist and the B major of the strings, one might wonder why Beethoven did not start the movement with the simple five-note chord with which he continues the motif, leaving the scoring consistent as he does with the orchestra. Certainly, there is no indication from the orchestral reply that the chord should be treated separately from the following quavers. The answer must be that he considered, quite rightly, that the smaller chord was too insignificant a sound with which to begin a work

5 It is worth noting the number of thematic suspensions in both movements, though whether this is a reason for, or result of, the style of accompaniment, one can only speculate. This degree of melodic suspension otherwise only occurs in the sonata-rondo finales in the Sonatas Opp. 7 and 22.

with orchestra, and so the extra notes were added for calorific value. But the calm presentation of G major at the start of the work must not become an event in itself, all too easy on the modern piano. The transformation of this chord into an event of such sonic importance will not only sever it from the main body of the phrase, but nullify the logical position of the orchestra's stunning response in B major. Add to that the frequent blurring of the staccato quavers, and the adoption of a faster speed for the orchestral entry, and all connection between piano and orchestra has vanished.

Thankfully there is no doubt about Beethoven's staccato markings of the repeated chords at the opening of the concerto. However, unmarked repeated chords should not always be assumed to be staccato. Op. 96 bars 28 onwards gives an example of the sometime expressive role of this writing, where Beethoven withdraws the staccato markings in line with on-the-string playing from the violinist. One may question why there are no staccato marks for the repeated chords of the Finale of the A major Cello Sonata Op. 69, or even the first movement of the 'Waldstein', when Beethoven goes to such trouble to mark each repeated quaver in the Finale of Op. 10 No. 2. Whereas no one would suggest that the opening of the 'Waldstein' could be played in any way other than in a detached style, the melodic shaping and phrasing of the repeated quavers of Op. 69 have such an obvious line that perhaps Beethoven never intended them to be staccato. There is also the question of tempo; above a certain speed staccato becomes impractical, and although the tempos of the Finales of Op. 10 No. 2 and Op. 69 are not compatible, certainly the staccato markings in the former would have the effect of limiting the tempo. The repeated quaver accompaniment figure in the first movement of Op. 90 points more towards urgency than disruption in a forward-moving expressive role similar to the afore-mentioned passage in the Violin Sonata Op. 96, and the specific staccato markings of bar 53 leave little doubt that the remaining quavers are long.

The opening bars of Op. 90, while presenting no problems with staccato quavers, does broaden the discussion to unmarked crotchets. The presence of the opening quaver chords is lost if the crotchet upbeat of the piano response is not fully held, and since the crotchets bridging bars four and five are marked with a slurred staccato, the principle of playing the first *piano* crotchet legato into bar four seems perfectly valid. The same range of treatment of crotchets occurs as early as Op. 2 No. 1, the opening of which offers another opportunity for a contrast to be made between the staccato and non-staccato crotchet. For Beethoven to mark the repeated c's in bars 93 and 94 with a slurred staccato invites speculation on the role of repeated crotchets throughout the movement, and it seems reasonable to assume that the repeated left-hand chords at the opening should therefore be more tenuto than the repeated c's, perhaps in the manner of the Op. 90 example quoted above. The tenuto crotchet is much more firmly established and more widely used in the next

sonata Op. 2 No. 2, while the final bars of the first movement of Op. 7 are a fascinating example of the use of length in underlying a particular dynamic and texture.

To what extent a performer of Beethoven today should treat the absence of
staccato marks as an indication to play to the full value of a crotchet is debatable, but
the writer has no doubt that such an approach is an important factor in rhythmic
texture. One of Beethoven's favourite notations is the juxtaposition between the
quaver and staccato crotchet, or the semiquaver and staccato quaver, as in Op. 10
No. 3 bars 17 to 20 and Op. 10 No. 2 bars 48 to 51. A more refined version occurs
at the bottom of the first page of the first movement of Op. 106, where in bars 29
and 30 Beethoven removes the staccatos as part of a gradual scaling down of
aggression. That is not to say that there are not inaccuracies and discrepancies, even
in Beethoven.[6] The Allegro molto e vivace second movement of Op. 27 No. 1,
while concerned solely with textured harmonic movement, has an inconsistent lack
of staccato markings in the Trio section at bar 44 onwards. Despite Beethoven's
predilection for increasing note-length with crescendo, it seems unlikely that the
staccato pattern should not match up with the answering section at bar 66 onwards.
Other examples of Beethoven's deliberate use of the full crotchet in contrast to the
staccato are consistent, yet frequently ignored. The recapitulation of the first movement of Op. 79 (bar 123) takes the longer crotchet of the development section,
and throughout the coda considerable play is made of the contrast between the
two, though this is rarely heard. Another movement where the length of both the
crotchet and the quaver is an important ingredient is the Scherzo of the 'Archduke'
Trio Op. 97. There seems little doubt that Beethoven here intended not only to alternate the character of the theme between staccato and non-staccato, but also, logically
enough, to contrast theme and accompaniment and indeed crotchet, quaver and
minim wherever possible. That these markings are ignored is one thing; what is more
serious is that their observance so much improves the feeling of line and flow that
the tempo is likely to be altered. Since this in turn will affect choice of dynamic level
and the perceived proportions of the movement, attention to note-length emerges
as an important step in the interpretation of Beethoven. If further proof were required
we need only turn to the varied treatment of the third-beat crotchets in the Trio
section (bars 168–79, 204–15, 265–76), all aspects of which require a tempo that
permits the player to characterise each of these notes exactly as Beethoven asks.

Any discussion on the contemporary problems of Beethoven interpretation must at
some point touch on Beethoven's pedal markings. *Una corda* presents no problems;
while we can no longer reduce the hammer attack to one string, we are at least left
in no doubt about Beethoven's intentions in employing the device. The far greater

6 Sometimes, though not often, Beethoven relies on the performer's common sense to recognise a general indication when he sees one, such as at the beginning of the slow movement of Op. 22, where
   there is no reason to suppose that the left-hand articulation should change in bar 2.

artistic scope of the sustaining pedal, however, presents greater challenges. The comparative rarity of Beethoven's indications leads one to assume that he would only include pedal markings in contexts where its use might reasonably be discounted, and indeed much of his long harmonic pedalling comes into this category. If the recitative of the first movement of the D minor Sonata Op. 31 No. 2 and the Rondo of the 'Waldstein' Sonata Op. 53 are the two most discussed examples of Beethoven's pedal markings, the Bagatelle Op. 33 No. 7 is an even more extreme example of a pedalling style that nowadays requires a half-pedal or half change to preserve the spirit if not the letter of Beethoven's instruction. It is, however, this confirmation of the overriding harmonic aspect of his music that raises questions about the lack of markings elsewhere, and what his assumptions of pedal use might have been. The fundamentally harmonic nature of the whole of the Sonata Op. 31 No. 2 poses typical problems. Should the *forte* statement at bars 21 and 22, and its answer in bars 22, 23 and 24, benefit from a half-pedal to underline its origin in the D minor chord, and indeed to look ahead to bar 144? This question persists throughout the development, culminating in bars 119 and 120. The discussion over arpeggiated figuration continues throughout the sonata, and while one can assume that bars 51 to 58 in the slow movement may enjoy the cover of pedal, can the *forte* outbursts in the Finale be treated as one chord? Again, the unmarked areas of the 'Waldstein' Sonata provoke more discussion than the marked: is the first movement development pedalled harmonically throughout? Presumably yes, and *forte* throughout also, though the reiteration of the *forte* marking at bar 136 suggests that Beethoven expects some moderation in the upper reaches of the bass line at bars 134 and 135. However, we should note that in the first movement of the G major sonata Op. 79, another strongly harmonic movement, Beethoven restricts his harmonic pedal markings in the development to the *piano* passages, though the *forte* passages are harmonically identical. On further examination, the Rondo movement of the 'Waldstein' Sonata shows a similar tendency; all the piano development is pedalled, yet even the harmonic assertions of bars 360–77 are specifically denied any additional reverberation. Whether this encouragement of the pedal at low dynamic levels was an artistic or a practical consideration, we do not know, but we must assume that, as far as Op. 79 is concerned, the lack of pedal marking and the *leggieramente* indication in the *piano* right-hand arpeggios of the first movement signify that they are, untypically, as melodic as they are harmonic, and should be pedalled sparingly, if at all.

This rejection of an obvious harmonic pattern in favour of a more string-quartet-like texture is quite common in later Beethoven. Although in the E♭ Sonata Op. 81a Beethoven pedals the dominant seventh transition to the last movement on the strength of a grace-note dominant,[7] he makes no mention of pedal in a somewhat

---

7   The pedal markings at bars 37 and 39 bring into question the lack of markings at the start of the movement. If there is an intended difference, it must be that the larger chords and pedal of the later bars are intended to be more static.

similar circumstance in the 'Waldstein' Introduzione, and indeed in the slow movement of Op. 101 he goes to the length of pedalling the joins while ignoring the
harmonic movement, a clear indication if ever there was one (bars 15 and 16).

Attention must also be drawn to the staccato markings that occur in the demisemiquaver arpeggiated figuration of Opp. 109 and 110, at the closing and opening
respectively. While Beethoven's pedal indication is reserved for bar 184 in Op. 109,
the staccato markings underline the harmonic pointing of the section rather than
any concealed theme; one may safely conclude, therefore, that the passage should be
pedalled. However, in common with the *leggieramente* staccatos of Op. 110 at the
opposite end of the dynamic scale, any realisation of such pointing is best realised by
a staccato accent in a half-pedal, a treatment which is equally effective at both
dynamic levels.

Beethoven's juxtaposition of string quartet writing and sustained harmonic and
pianistic figuration must be supported in each case by an appropriate style of pedalling. In the case of pianistic figuration such as arpeggios, generous harmonic pedalling
presents no problems, and indeed will often of itself support the line and emphasise
structure. In contrast, the string quartet writing in the first phrase of Op. 110's second
movement is a typical example of Beethoven's quartet writing style that demands
perfect legato rather than pedal in the interests of line, let alone clarity. However,
more often priorities are mixed, and the desire to exert harmonic direction and
phrasing is often at loggerheads with the desire to preserve the tension and clarity of
quartet playing – bars 43–8 in the first movement of Op. 53, bars 53–6 in Op. 106
are typical examples of mixed genre, while the last movement of Op. 31 No. 1
presents the same problems confined within pianistic terms.

Perhaps the most unlikely example of Beethoven's pedal markings appears in
Op. 101, bars 87–8. Whether the marking is intended as a form of harmonic reinforcement or as an allusory acoustic fantasy is not clear. While, in view of the
extraordinary language of the final sonatas, it is tempting to assume the latter,
nothing of this nature occurs again.

If conclusions are to be drawn about pedalling, they must start from the basis
that a perfect legato is essential for much of the literature, in order to maintain line,
tension, clarity and texture. Only then can the pedal realise its proper role as a phrasing
and structural device. While our modern instrument will be seen to improve on
the fortepiano in exploiting those characteristics of the string quartet achieved by
legato, pedalling techniques have to be adjusted to cope with greatly increased reverberation. The lightest of half-pedalling[8] will shorten reverberation time and thus
allow longer use, and while the adoption of the deficiencies of earlier instruments
may seem strange, it is far preferable to short bursts of full pedal which undermine
legato, cloud the texture and break up the line.

8   i.e. barely depressing the pedal, so that the dampers just brush against the string.

If to the listener the principal characteristic of the modern piano is its fullness of tone, then for the pianist this is matched by the increased weight of its action. Fortunately, this has had little effect on the general performance of Beethoven; however, the glissando octaves prescribed by Beethoven in the 'Waldstein' Sonata remain a problem for the majority of pianists. The technical difficulty is due chiefly to the *pianissimo* dynamic and comparative calm of the passage – after all, the glissando at the end of the development of Beethoven's First Piano Concerto is far more easily accomplished. Not all the problem is technical, however. The unduly technical emphasis placed on the passage in the context of today's instrument has highlighted an experiment that Beethoven was not to repeat, and indeed, beyond the technical ingenuity of placing this experiment within the work, there is little to commend this passage. Whichever solution produces the more discreet result – glissandos or a legato arrangement between the hands – must be viewed as the better answer.

One less prominent area of musical and technical interest is Beethoven's use of paired semiquavers. While paired notes in general have been a steady feature of Beethoven's compositional style – the opening of Op. 31 No. 2 is an obvious example – his obsession with them in the second movement of Op. 78 presents problems for which there seems to be no easy solution. Any phrasing which owes its shape to subtle dynamic alone, such as might be achieved by a quick bow change, has to be precluded, since the brisk tempo of the movement results in the notes running together. The common solution of changing the rhythm from 𝅘𝅥𝅮𝅘𝅥𝅮 to 𝅘𝅥𝅭𝅘𝅥𝅰. seems unsatisfactory, imparting as it does a rhythmic irregularity which is not emulated by the phrasing of any other instrument. Yet what other solution is there? Were the movement presto, the rhythmic deformity would have been the only solution. Yet in Allegro vivace . . . if the correct rhythm can be upheld and yet a break made between each pair then a consistency is achieved with the figuration throughout the literature.

There is also no obvious solution to Beethoven's use of paired semiquavers in the Adagio recitative of Op. 110. Widely regarded as a reference to the *Bebung* (the practice of introducing vibrato to held notes on the clavichord), there has been no equivalent on any hammer instrument since. Concentration on the repeated a^2s (traditionally performed with a barely perceptible repetition) has distracted from the very real rhythmic drama in which they are housed. The reader should turn to Schnabel's edition for a full analysis of these bars, but suffice it to say that both times the *Bebung* is introduced, it compounds an existing syncopation, first in semiquavers, then demisemiquavers, that must be transmitted in performance. As so often in slow passages of Beethoven, tension is the principal ingredient.

It is not possible in a theoretical article of this length to touch on many areas of pianism that contribute to a performance. If attention has been focused on the subject of tempo and articulation, it is to draw attention to two areas where the sonority of the modern instrument can destroy the logic of Beethoven's language. If dynamics are not included in this cautionary category, it is because an understanding of the importance of texture and line in Beethoven will of itself tend to redress any exaggerated *fortissimos* and *pianissimos*, and indeed the often dramatic nature of Beethoven's dynamics can only profit from a lively observance. Only in sforzandos and rinforzandos must the nature of Beethoven's instrument be ever borne in mind; if they are seen in the context of the prevailing dynamic, little can go wrong. If examination of the text finally leads us to conclude that in certain instances Beethoven's instrument was better suited to the texture than our own, then paradoxically we have arrived at a scale of performance that fully permits us to play Beethoven on the instrument of today. If by so doing, we more fully realise the wider orchestration that Beethoven so often implied, then, indeed, we do him justice.

INDEX OF BEETHOVEN'S WORKS

Works are identified in the left-hand column by opus and WoO ('Werk ohne Opuszahl' – 'work without opus number') numbers as listed in G. Kinsky and H. Halm: *Das Werk Beethovens* (Munich and Duisburg 1955).

INDEX OF NAMES